Successful

Wood Book

9.14.78

Successful

Wood Book

How to choose, use, and finish every kind of wood

Rachel Bard

Structures Publishing Company
Farmington, Michigan

Manufactured in the United States of America

Edited by Shirley M. Horowitz

Design by Carey Jean Ferchland

Cover photo courtesy of Weyerhaeuser Company

Current Printing (last digit)
10 9 8 7 6 5 4 3 2 1

Structures Publishing Co.
Box 1002, Farmington, Mich. 48024

Library of Congress Cataloging in Publication Data

Bard, Rachel, 1921–
Successful wood book.

Bibliography: p.
Includes index.
1. Wood-work. 2. Wood. I. Title.
TT200.B37 674 78-15547
ISBN 0-912336-73-0

Contents

Acknowledgements

Many individuals, associations and companies generously provided information and illustrations for this book, for which the author is deeply grateful. But she states emphatically that any errors and omissions are solely her responsibility.

The following were especially helpful: Frank Pipes at American Forest Institute; Bill Parker and Sharon Morales at American Plywood Association; Ted Duke at American Wood Preservers Institute; Garry Gilbert at Kraft Smith Advertising; Pamela Allsebrook at California Redwood Association; Clary Trice at Olympic Stain; Frank Welch at Red Cedar Shingle & Handsplit Shake Bureau; Rockwell International; Karl Lindberg at Southern Forest Products Association; The Stanley Works; St. Regis Paper Co.; the U.S. Forest Service in Washington, and the Northeast Forest Experiment Station; Bob Johnston and Marsha Ketter at Weyerhaeuser; Ray Moholt and Dorothy Gardner at Western Wood products Association; and Jim Snodgrass at Wood Moulding & Millwork Producers.

Extra thanks to Fred Cummings, who read and advised on the chapter on working with wood; to George Cheek of American Forest Institute, for his counsel on Chapters I and II; and particularly to Dave Countryman of American Plywood Association, who bravely read the entire manuscript and offered invaluable suggestions.

Introduction

Trees, like sunshine and rain, have been familiar to humankind for so long that we tend to take their wonders for granted.

People have been using trees for one thing or another ever since man-recorded time began. Wood is certainly our oldest building material: Our first homes were wood, even antedating the cave, if traced back to when our ancestors lived in trees.

Can there be anything worth saying, after all these years, about wood and its myriad uses? Indeed there is. The intriguing thing about this familiar material is that we keep learning more about it; how it grows, how it performs, what it can be turned into, how to use it. Moreover, what is already known about wood is often not available to the layman in a way he can use or grasp easily.

Here, then, is a primer on wood to help you get the most value for the wood you buy. We hope it will help you appreciate wood more, and use it more effectively. We cover where wood products come from, what the major species and products are, which are best for what application, how to buy them and how to make the best use of them. The appended glossary defines the terms you are likely to run across as you buy, build, and deal with wood.

This is not a construction manual or a how-to-build book. Many technical works have been written on all aspects of forest products and their applications. If you wish to go deeper into any of the subjects touched on in this book, consult the "Other Sources of Information" list at the back. It includes names and addresses of associations which keep up to date on forest products and are generous with their information.

Tamarack—Eastern larch and Western larch—the only softwoods that shed their needles. (Courtesy of U.S. Forest Service)

I. The Resource: The Great American Forest

Even today, after more than three centuries of use and abuse, we have a tremendous forest here in America. It stretches across about a third of our land area, and compared with our other resources, is unique in the depth of its appeal and renewability.

This does not mean, however, that we will always have the forest products we need. In fact, current forecasts predict shortages if our demands keep rising at their present rate. Most of us already have had to face up to unpleasant price rises in all kinds of wood-originated items, from 2x4s to paper cups.

CHANGING ATTITUDES

Obviously, it is important to keep our forests productive and growing. Most people concerned with forest management, whether public or private, agree on this. This attitude is a relatively recent development—a far cry from that of the first explorers and settlers in America, who were dismayed and even angered by the prospect of so many trees. Columbus uneasily reported "a dark forest of tall, straight trees stretching to the stars with leaves never shed." And though there is evidence now that New England did not present the unbroken expanse of dense virgin timber we have long believed, it was certainly more forest than most of the colonists were used to; by the 1700s, most of Europe's great virgin woods had been exhausted.

Later and on another coast, Capt. Vancouver's botanist, Archibald Menzies, was astonished to see conifers twice as high as any he had seen in Europe: Douglas fir, Alaska cedar, Sitka spruce, Coast redwood.

The Colonial period

The practical colonists soon overcame their awe and begin thinking about how the forest could be used. John Smith described a country "overgrown with all sorts of excellent good woodes for building houses, boats, barks or shippes."

So they began to burn and cut and build. At first they built houses as alike as possible to those they'd left behind. The English built sturdy one-room frame post-and-beam houses, often of oak. Oak was hand-hewn, with mortise-and-tenon joints and wood dowels. Early immigrants from northern Europe built log cabins. By the Revolution these could be found all along the western frontier.

Then the colonists built barns... fine imposing wood barns, nothing like the small cowsheds of Europe. They fashioned all the necessities of daily life from the wood so richly available: beds and chairs, plates and ladles, carts and sleds.

And they burned wood with abandon, lacking other fuel. They also burned the forest to clear land for farming.

Before long the colonists were able to export. Europe needed naval stores—turpentine, rosin, pitch and tar—to keep her ships seaworthy. Tall straight pine masts were in demand also. So highly prized were the pines of New England by the Royal British Navy that they sent crews through the forest to pick out the best and brand them with the Crown symbol, the Broad Arrow. The Americans resented this violation of their forestlands and their resentment helped touch off the Revolution.

Nation-building

After the Revolution, with axe and saw our ances-

◀ *This Eastern white pine in New Hampshire was selected as a mast for the English navy in Colonial days, but was not cut. (Courtesy U.S. Forest Service)*

"Treen" was the early word for wood household utensils—literally, products of the tree. These are modern examples, but they evidence the same good sense and good materials (Northeastern hardwoods) as their predecessors. (Courtesy Northeastern Lumber Manufacturers)

tors pushed westward. A distinctively American wood-based culture blossomed.

All through the 19th century the trees crashed down, the plains were plowed, frontiers were erased. Logging began on the West Coast. In Wisconsin and Michigan, forests fell a section at a time.

Meanwhile in New England, where it all began, the woods began to creep back over abandoned farmsteads. Nature has tremendous recuperative powers. In the natural course of events a cleared or burned-over area will regenerate itself in just a few decades. This is one reason we still have three-quarters as much American forest as when Columbus landed.

But even nature could not cope with the surging demand for wood products that built up during the 19th century. Mechanization of lumber production and a new capability to mass-produce nails brought a single-family house within reach of most citizens. The spreading network of railways consumed mil-

It took a lot of logs to get logs out of the woods. Trestle for logging railroad, 200 ft. above the ravine floor. (Courtesy University of Washington)

lions of wood ties. Trestles and covered bridges, riverboats and canalboats—all of wood, what else? Wood fences snaked around farms and pastures, using up unbelievable quantities of wood. Wooden wagons and carts carried people and produce over plank roads. As the century progressed, factories mass-produced wood furniture in quantities and designs that would have astonished Chippendale and Sheraton.

Along with this expanding consumption of wood for traditional uses came a huge new demand on the forest: by the fourth quarter of the century, with perfection of processes to make paper out of wood pulp, the age of paper was launched.

It was high time for some one to point out that maybe the wood supply in this country was not limitless. A few Cassandras darkly referred to the bare hills of China and the sands of the Sahara, and predicted it would happen here. The Federal government took a more constructive approach and in 1891 began setting aside vast areas as Forest Reserves.

In 1898, with the naming of Gifford Pinchot as Chief of the Division of Forestry, the government assumed its role as conservator and manager of the nation's publicly owned forest resources.

Theodore Roosevelt, friend of Pinchot and firm supporter of forest conservation, put the new governmental philosophy in words, defining conservation as: "The preservation of the forest by wise use.... Forestry means making the forests useful not only to the settler, the rancher, the miner, the men who live in the neighborhood, but indirectly to the men who may live hundreds of miles off...", and he could have added, who will live hundreds of years in the future.

Creating national forests did not solve all our problems. There was still greater pressure on available wood supplies than natural regeneration and the Forest Service's vigorous reforestation efforts could meet. With the twin explosions of population

Logs going to market in Michigan, 1887. (Courtesy U.S. Forest Service)

Pacific Northwest forest, early 1900s. (Asahel Curtis photo courtesy Washington State Historical Society)

and technology America was finding more and more wonderful ways to use wood—and providing more and more eager consumers. We will discuss these modern forest products in succeeding chapters.

Since we are not about to stop devising useful new wood products, improving the ones we have, and perfecting our techniques for working with wood, it is encouraging that there is emphasis among timber and forest products companies on speeding up the growth cycle, fuller utilization of the whole tree, re-use, and recycling. In forestry as well as in manufacturing, major attention now goes to insuring the renewability of the resource.

THE FOREST TODAY

In the United States we may think of our forest as being six forests; each displays different characteristics due to variations in geography and climate.

On the Pacific Coast the evergreen conifers dominate: Douglas fir, pines, spruce, true firs, cedars, redwood; they mantle the mountainous landscape and are kept green and growing by the moisture from the Pacific. Hardwood species in the West are comparatively few—maple, poplar, alder, live oak, for example—growing in river valleys and on lower slopes.

Approaching the Rockies we find the forest less dense because of less rainfall. The same evergreens, except redwood, prevail; pines are more dominant. And there is more larch (also known as tamarack)—the oddball conifer that sheds its leaves.

The northern forest, which stretches from the northern portions of Minnesota into New England and south along the Appalachian ridge, is rich and varied and commercially important. It embraces stands of pine, spruce, balsam fir and hemlock, as well as hardwood forests, mainly maple, birch and beech; in mixed forests aspen and poplar coexist with conifers. The northern forest includes the fine New England hardwoods.

Hardwoods also characterize the central forest; in fact, more than 90 percent of our hardwood sawtimber comes from the East. Most of it is second-growth, or some multiple thereof. Re-growth timber grows faster than old-growth timber, and the flourishing forests of birch, cherry, beech and oak give no hint of their interesting ancestry. They may be the great-grandchildren of the hardwood trees that sprang up to replace the conifers the early settlers chopped down. The central forest hardwoods also include hickory and tulip poplar, while the main conifers are yellow pine and cedar. This forest extends into the mid-Atlantic states, where the nation's most densely populated areas are clustered.

The southern forest demonstrates another interesting, and maybe unique, example of regeneration. In this case it is not the achievement of nature alone. Much southern land was cleared thoroughly in the years of Colonial settlement and westward expansion. Replanting some 60 years ago revived the nearly exhausted resource. That generation of trees (largely the fast-growing Southern pines) was nurtured with an eye toward maximum growth and commercial value. Soon the abandoned cotton and tobacco fields were green again with pines for pulpwood. Now as this generation is being harvested, a third is taking its place. Already the South supplies more than half the nation's pulpwood and one-third of its softwood plywood and softwood lumber.

Hardwoods too, though slower-growing than the pines, are very prolific in the South, which is one reason this is such an active furniture-making center.

The tropical forest is tiny in relation to the others, lying at the tips of Florida and southeastern Texas. Mangrove, cypress and mahogany are the principal tropical trees.

On-the-spot production of posts from a giant Sequoia in the 1940s. (Courtesy U.S. Forest Service)

Cypress in the tropical forest, Florida. (Courtesy U.S. Forest Service)

All these forests add up to something over 750 million acres, about a third of the country's land area. Of the total forest, one-third is referred to by the Forest Service as noncommercial: nonproductive forests, national parks, wilderness areas, preserves. National parks and wilderness account for about 1 percent of the nation's land area.

That leaves 500 million acres of commercial forest land, including some National Forests, available to produce the wood products we need more of every year.

Who owns all this forest?

Contrary to what many people think, our commercial forests are not owned by a few big timber companies. More than half belongs to individuals, most of whom own 100 acres or less. Some of them tree-farm their holdings; some sell timber-cutting rights to others; some intend to develop the land or sell it at a profit; some prefer just to let the trees sit there.

Next comes government—federal, state and local—which owns 28 percent of commercial forest land. The government is not in the forest-products business, but it sells timber (and the privilege of cutting it) on federal land to those who are. (State gov-

Natural reproduction in action: about 15 years after logging, an excellent stand of white pine and red spruce coming in under a stand of white pine, in Maine. (Courtesy U.S. Forest Service)

ernments do this too.) And the federal government is responsible for managing and maintaining the National Forests in accordance with the multiple-use concept, which means the forests must provide not just timber, but also wildlife habitat, watersheds, mining, grazing and places for people (campgrounds, roads, trails, etc.).

The forest products companies—several thousand of them—own the smallest portion (13 percent) of our commercial forest land. It is in their best interest to make a profit, so it is no surprise that some of the most impressive examples of intensive forest management are seen on forest industry lands. The forest industry is fully aware of the rising demand curve: We are currently using wood at the rate of more than 14.2 billion cu. ft. per year; predictions are that we will need double that by 2020.

The wigwam sawdust burner, nearly nonexistent now, was once a familiar sight in lumber country. Residue that was burned as waste is now used for composite panels, firelogs, and in other useful products. (Courtesy U.S. Forest Service)

WOOD FOR TOMORROW

There are three ways to deal with this potential crunch and it is likely we will need to take all of them: grow more trees faster, use more of every tree, and step up re-cycling, especially of paper products.

Wonderful strides are being made in learning how to speed up tree growing and in actually putting the new knowledge to work. Some timber companies can now grow a commercially harvestable tree in 30 years where it used to take 100. And they expect to do even better. The idea is to apply science to the basic tree-growing cycle: developing superior tree strains, thinning, fertilizing, harvesting, and replanting, like any successful farmer.

Utilization is another dramatic story. Whereas our total annual timber harvest has grown less than 2 percent in the last three-quarters of a century, we are getting far more out of all those trees: about 10 times as much in paper products, for instance. And literally thousands of other products that were not even imagined at the turn of the century. The significant factor has been the striking reduction in the amount of wood wasted—either burnt up at the lumber mill or left in the woods as debris.

One company, for instance, reports a complete reversal of the utilization picture in one of its western producing areas. In 1950, only about 21 percent of the yield from its forestlands there went into lumber while the rest was burned as fuel or wasted. Just 23 years later, 79 percent of the typical log in that area became lumber, plywood, particleboard, or paper products, with only 21 percent burned as fuel to fire the plant's boilers.

Wood waste that will become compressed sawdust firelogs. (Courtesy U.S. Forest Service)

Another hopeful portent: the inventive wood products industry keeps coming up with new ways to take the tree apart and then reassemble it, with a whole new set of properties. Early examples of this were plywood and particleboard. A new and promising development is fiber orientation, where the whole tree (trunk, branches, bark and stump) is broken down into fiber strands which are then put together again in a new arrangement with new strengths.

Recycling of paper products has become accepted by now; the paper industry gets more than one-fifth of its raw material from wastepaper. (And a third of its energy from its own manufacturing wastes.) Residue from lumber and plywood production is another important source of fiber. But it still takes a lot of virgin wood fiber to make paper—another reason the industry keeps looking for new ways to make trees grow faster.

Aspen, a fast-growing tree, is much used for pulpwood, industrial applications, and fuel. (Courtesy U.S. Forest Service)

II. Wood and What It Does

Anyone who uses and values wood has a natural curiosity about where it comes from, how various species differ, what each one is good for—and what happens to all those trees we harvest every year.

WHAT IS WOOD?

Knowing that wood comes from a tree, and being able to take the tree apart and examine it under a microscope, can't fully explain why wood is unique among all the natural and manmade materials on earth. Trees, familiar as they are, are far from being completely understood. How, for example, does a tree defy gravity and lift water hundreds of feet from roots to topmost leaves? We still aren't sure. But we know enough about the growth and composition of the tree to get a glimmering of the "how," "what," and "why" of wood.

All the trunk's growing takes place in a layer of cells, only one cell thick, between the wood in the tree's center and the bark. These growing cells—the cambium layer—create new sapwood on one side, new bark on the other. The sapwood cells eventually die and become heartwood, but are continually renewed by more cell growth from the cambium. Though the thin cambium layer is responsible for the growth of the entire tree, every part serves a vital purpose.

Trees differ in size, form and distribution of the various types of cells. These differences account for variations among species—in mechanical and physical properties such as color, aroma, decay-resistance, density, grain pattern.

Though, nowadays, as we will see, nearly all the tree may be put to good use, we are concerned here with the woody part: sapwood and heartwood (see diagram in color section).

Plus and minus

Here is a brief review of wood's general physical characteristics and outstanding properties.

1. It is relatively light in weight in relation to its strength, making it easier to handle than other materials.
2. It resists corrosion by chemicals, and has excellent insulation qualities for both heat and cold (because of its fibrous structure and entrapped air). It's the only commonly used thermal insulator that also has good structural qualities.
3. It can be cut and worked with simple, familiar hand tools or power tools, and is easy to join with screws, nails, bolts, or other ordinary connectors.
4. It can be joined with adhesives, and research promises even greater improvement in this characteristic.
5. When dry it is a poor conductor of electricity, which helps in firefighting when power lines are dangling.
6. It absorbs energy far better than concrete or steel, so is excellent for floors—less tiring, easier on the feet.
7. Its strength properties include exceptional impact strength, good in earthquake areas; considerable dimensional stability along the grain and good flexural rigidity permits it to retain its properties when bent.
8. It is surprisingly durable. Beams 2,700 years old have been found in a tomb in Turkey. Centuries-old beams are still supporting Japanese temples. Closer to hand, we see Colonial homes in New England looking much as they did 300 years ago.

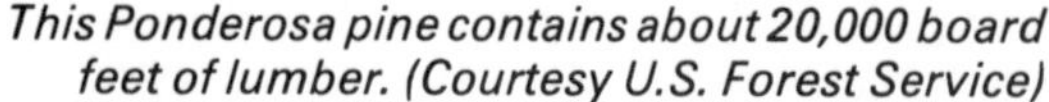

This Ponderosa pine contains about 20,000 board feet of lumber. (Courtesy U.S. Forest Service)

"Young" bristlecone pines (foreground) are probably 100 years old, while those in background may be 1,000 years old. These are among the oldest living things in the world, testimony to wood's stubborn longevity in harshest conditions—Inyo Natl. Forest, California, about 11,000 ft. elev. (Courtesy U.S. Forest Service)

9. Finally, it is beautiful—and the beauty endures. In its natural state, or with a manmade finish, wood appeals to mankind's esthetic sense.

You will have noted that the list includes only advantages. Naturally, wood has its limitations as well. You must work within these limits and avoid forcing it to do something for which it is not suited.

Shrinkage Wood shrinks across the grain when dried from the green condition. As noted above, it is dimensionally stable in the lengthwise direction, and length is usually the most important dimension in woodworking. (This property explains why wood should be dried before manufacture. Plywood avoids this problem by placing alternate veneers with the grain going in directions at right angles to each other, to even out the tension.)

Decay Wood decays if moist, usually because wood-destroying fungi can exist in it. However, completely saturated wood—cell cavities filled with water—does not decay, because fungi can get no oxygen. Wood can be treated to resist decay (see Poles and Pilings).

Combustion Wood is combustible, but can be a far safer material than so-called "noncombustible" construction materials.

Insect Susceptibility Wood may be subject to boring by insects, but treatment can correct this. Also remember that teredos (marine borers) do not attack wood in fresh water.

Variation Wood varies in its properties and behavior in comparison with metals and synthetic materials, and may even vary within the same species. The knowledgeable worker with wood learns to anticipate and compensate.

The special durability of cedar is evidenced by these totem poles at Skedans, Queen Charlotte Islands. These are probably about 200 years old, yet in spite of the extremely wet climate have not deteriorated much. However, their successors are already taking over—bushes and trees that root in their hosts. Typically, Haida carvers felled the huge cedar, trimmed it to length, cut one side away, and hollowed the other side to form a curved shell. Removal of heartwood helped retard splitting. After peeling off the bark they began carving, according to a predetermined formal design. (Courtesy British Columbia government)

HARDWOODS AND SOFTWOODS

The two main subdivisions—hardwoods and softwoods—actually have little correspondence to the mechanical properties of the woods, but refer rather to the kinds of trees they come from.

Lumber men use hardwoods as a trade term to designate wood from flowering broadleaved trees, while softwoods come from cone-bearing or coniferous trees, most of which have evergreen needle-like leaves. The terms are not necessarily related to the density of the wood and how physically "hard" it is. It is true that most hardwoods are harder and heavier than most softwoods. But several hardwoods, e.g., yellow poplar, aspen, Philippine mahogany and balsa, are "softer" than such softwoods as Douglas fir, longleaf pine and yew.

Another rough classification is applied to woods that are prized chiefly for their appearance as opposed to those used largely as structural members; or in fine-furniture terms, as primary and secondary woods. Again, though there is much overlap and many of the most handsome hardwoods are also very strong, their cost may prohibit their use except where they will be on view. They are also usually harder to work.

So we often think of hardwoods as "decorative" and of softwoods as workhorses.

Worldwide, hundreds of species of hardwoods are harvested and marketed. Of the 500 or more separate hardwood species in the U.S., about 30 may be considered of commercial importance.

Fewer species of softwood are harvested, but the volume is much greater. In the United States about 75 percent of our sawtimber on commercial forest land is softwood, with the remaining 25 percent hardwood. (Sawtimber trees are those of a size and quality suitable for harvest and manufacture into structural wood products.)

WHERE IT GOES

How can we Americans gobble up 14.2 billion cu. ft. of wood products every year? That works out to roughly the amount of wood in a 100-ft. tree, for every man, woman and child. Wood is, in fact, the most extensively used raw material we have, surpassing in volume all metals combined.

Most of the wood, of course, goes into construction. Approximately 80 percent of the homes built in America today are wood-frame; the average house represents 1,800 cu.ft. of timber in the form of lumber, plywood, hardboard and other wood-based products. Even brick and concrete buildings need a lot of lumber and plywood. And remodeling and adding on to existing homes takes another big chunk.

There will be more talk about how wood is used in construction in the following chapters. First, let us survey some of its other major uses. It would take an encyclopedia to do them all justice, but here's a rundown of the major ones.

Cabinetry and furniture

In the good old American tradition, we continue to prefer wood for the familiar, useful objects that surround us in our homes and offices. Wood was the handiest material for the early settlers to use for building beds, chairs, cabinets and utensils, just as it was for their homes.

Despite the amazing new materials that keep appearing, wood has sturdily kept its position as domi-

Colonial chair of yellow birch, one of the most abundant hardwoods of the Northeast. (Courtesy Northeastern Lumber Association)

nant material for furniture. For one thing, it is more satisfying to the touch than metal or plastic. It conducts heat slowly, so it is always just comfortably warm. It is light in weight, especially so when employing sandwich paneling with honeycomb or other lightweight core and decorative wood veneer faces (as in chests). Many sections that were solid wood are now veneers (as bottoms and sides of drawers) or plywood (in cabinets). Technology keeps improving adhesives and overlays, and new wood-based composite materials such as compreg (used for solid members or for surfacing) promise the easy-care advantages that television-influenced homeowners long for.

A lot of thin hardwood veneer is still used for packaging—these are cheese boxes. (Courtesy U.S. Forest Service)

Containers

Cooperage The word traditionally refers to barrels and all other wood containers made of staves and heads, securely held together with wood, iron or

Here's how they char the white oak barrels used to age whiskey—with oak from Ozark National Forest, Arkansas. (Courtesy U.S. Forest Service)

When conventional boxes won't do, manufacturers custom-fabricate what's necessary. This huge plywood container is for a jet plane tail assembly. (Courtesy American Plywood Association)

Plywood pallet bins have revolutionized fruit harvesting, almost eliminating the old picking box. (Courtesy American Plywood Association)

steel hoops. Along with barrels, this family of wood products includes kegs, casks, pails, barrels, tanks, vats, even wood pipes and flumes.

Manmade materials have taken over many of the jobs formerly done by products of the cooper's art, such as beer barrels and oil barrels (now almost exclusively metal) and the pork barrel which, since new meat shipping and packaging methods took over, lives on only as a reference to political patronage.

But no one has yet found anything better than an oaken cask for maturing wines, sherries and whiskey; in fact, it is still illegal to age whiskies in this country in anything except new charred white oak barrels.

Wood is widely used for vats and tanks to store chemicals and corrosive materials which would react undesirably with metal. Wooden vats also serve in brine-processing of pickles, olives, etc., and for fermentation of malt beverages and storage of wine. Principal woods used are redwood, Douglas fir (often in the form of plywood) and white oak.

Shipping crates and boxes, too, were once exclusively wood, but may now be made of anything from metal, to plastic, to such wood-derived products as paperboard and containerboard.

But lumber and plywood are still the best all-round materials for most container jobs. Aside from being so available, they are easy to fabricate, have a high strength-weight ratio, resist splitting or puncture, and hold nails well. Big plywood containers travel all over the world nowadays on giant containerships and have a distinct weight advantage over steel.

The plywood-lumber pallet bin is another example of wood products' adaptation to changing times, especially in agriculture, with its high-speed mechanized harvesting. Fruits and vegetables are deposited directly into the big palletized container in which they are to be shipped to the packing or processing plant.

Most of the above are fairly standard wooden containers. But almost every manufacturing company sometimes needs specially designed containers, which can range from huge heavy boxlike crates to package castings, forgings and machinery, or small sturdy cases to transport delicate, easily damaged scientific equipment.

Pallets

While not containers, *pallets* perform some of the same functions—carrying goods or materials from one place to another and/or storing them. They are relatively new in the world of industry, having come into use along with mechanical lifts in the '20s. Palletization has really revolutionized material handling. Handling and storage systems are continually becoming even more sophisticated but the simple wood/plywood pallet is still the best partner. Literally millions of them are in use, and though many are reusable some 50 million new ones enter service annually.

TRANSPORTATION

Transport, like shelter, goes back to the beginnings of man's long involvement with wood. It started with the wood wheel—invented 5,000 years before Christ and still rolling along many of the world's rural roads. The first wheels (on Mesopotamian oxcarts) were solid, but the spoked wheel appeared about 1500 B.C. on fast fighting chariots.

Lumber and plywood pallets are used by the millions to transport and store industry's products and materials. Here, plywood pallets and separator boards carry beer barrels. (Courtesy American Plywood Association)

Nobody knows how many millions of cross-ties are in use on America's railroads, but more than 10 million are used per year for replacements. Good preservative-treated ties like these have an average life expectancy of 33 years. (Courtesy U.S. Forest Service)

Rugged oak cross-ties, before preservative treatment. (Courtesy U.S. Forest Service)

Wood's seaworthiness is evident on any waterfront: fishing boats, dinghies, pilings, piers, floats. Some older ferryboats are wood, though most new ones are steel.

Wheels do not account for much of today's wood products used in transport, but wheeled transport does. Railroads run on wood ties and despite testing of other materials such as steel and concrete, and issuance of thousands of patents, nothing has been devised to match the timber tie. Most ties are oak or other hardwoods, but thanks to the use of preservatives, softwoods can now be used too. Today's ties are said to last five times as long as old untreated hardwoods. Wood's special advantage is its flexibility—it yields to the impacts and supports the tremendous loads of the trains.

Early railroads ran on wooden rails, too, which didn't give way to iron until the 1870s. They also burned wood fuel in horrifying amounts.

As for the motor car, streaking metallically along the highway, it has evolved very rapidly since its beginnings, when it was considered a sort of motorized wooden carriage. Daimler mounted his first engine on a simple wooden cart. Then steel took over the chassis, but for a long time coach building traditions, depending on expert craftsmanship and elegant woods, characterized the motorcar.

Gone now are wood bodywork, running boards, and interiors. Wood is still a status symbol in the automotive world, showing up in steering wheels, interior trim and fascia panels. It has been imitated by wood-grain plastic or metal substitutes, but some traditions endure: The Rolls-Royce dashboard is still walnut.

For the workhorses of transport, it is a different story. In truck and trailer bodies, railroad boxcars, giant piggyback containers, wood and particularly plywood proves more resilient, lightweight and easy to fabricate then metal, and far better at withstanding the shocks and bumps of high-speed movement.

Boats

The wood ship, of course, goes almost as far back as the wheel. From rafts (balsa or papyrus or bamboo), dugouts (pine or cedar or oak), birchbark canoes, to warships—every civilization can point to its triumphs of the woodworker's art in devising waterborne transport.

Today the wooden vessel is a boat, not a ship. Still, despite technological advances and widespread use of metal and fiberglass, wood is still much in evidence in sailboats, fishing boats, life-boats and rowboats. Plywood—exterior or, if you can find it, marine—is an easy-to-use, seaworthy material, especially for the boat enthusiast who builds his own. Oak, teak and mahogany—traditional boat-building woods—are still favored for high-quality work and custom marine applications, but many new tropical hardwoods are taking their place, such as angelique, greenheart, khaya and the lauans (Philippine mahogany).

To round out this brief account of industrial and commercial uses of wood products, we could but won't add literally thousands more, from toothpicks to gliders.

All the above wood products use the material more or less in its natural state. Now for some of its transformations: not wood per se, but not to be ignored in a survey of all the good things that come from the tree.

Mine timbers must not only support enormous loads, but also resist dampness and corrosive seepage. Some, destined for long-term use, are preservative-treated in chemical baths. (Courtesy Northeastern Forest Experiment Station, U.S. Forest Service)

PULP AND PAPER

In the 1950s the Stanford Research Institute projected demand for forest products in the U.S. and forecast an 84 percent increase between 1952 and 1975 in consumption of paper and paperboard. The 1975 estimate was actually surpassed before 1970, when consumption reached 57.7 million tons. Today our average per-capita consumption of paper has reached nearly 600 lbs. per year.

To understand the how and why of this phenomenon, we must first define a few terms and take a quick look at some of the ways pulp and paper are used.

Pulp is the crude fiber that is converted into various products. It may be from various vegetable materials, but is mostly from pulpwood. Most trees that are used for pulpwood are conifers (softwoods), because of their longer fibers. But fast-growing hardwoods are catching up, especially around the Great Lakes, the South and the Northeast.

Roundwood refers to the logs, bolts or other round sections cut from trees, harvested either for wood pulp or lumber. Not to be confused with groundwood, a pulping process where log bolts are held against a grindstone and wood fibers ground off.

A lot of pulp also comes from recycled waste paper and paperboard. The industry gets 20 percent of its raw material from waste paper. This will proba-

Not all the vast amounts of pulpwood devoured by pulp and paper mills come from big commercial forests. Farm woodlots contribute a significant amount. Here, a Mississippi farm woodlot owner skids and stacks pulpwood (loblolly pine) from his plantation. Such woodlots are also the source of sawlogs, fuel, fenceposts, crossties and naval stores (turpentine, rosin, tall oil). (Courtesy U.S. Forest Service)

bly prove an increasingly important source as time goes on. (You can often tell what has been made from recycled material by its gray color, such as cardboard boxes and backs of tablets that are made of recycled newsprint. The color is due to the ink.) Much raw material also comes from residue from manufacture of other wood products such as lumber and plywood—scraps that would otherwise be wasted.

Still more raw material, but in lesser amounts, comes from other vegetable sources: rags (cotton or linen), jute, hemp, straw, cornstalks, and sugar cane or bagasse.

Paper manufacturers keep their eyes open for new pulp sources. Dozens of materials have been considered and tested. These include spiderwebs, horse manure and cattails, but so far no other substance has been able to compete with wood pulp.

Pulp and paper products are broadly categorized as paper and paperboard (the latter sometimes familiarly known as boards). Both are made of matted or felted sheets of fibers. Paper is lighter in weight, thinner and more flexible.

Today, pulpwood for these products accounts for over 30 percent of all industrial wood usage, excepting fuelwood. Most of it becomes packaging. There are some 100,000 different paper products. The general end-uses, and relative consumption, are shown.

Container boards 28%
(includes fiberboard
containers used in shipping;
shelf packages; food wrappers;
milk cartons)

Hardwood pulpwood at a North Carolina mill. Some comes from national forests, some from farmers' woodlots. (Courtesy U.S. Forest Service)

Bending board for folding boxes	16%
Book and fine paper	14%
Coarse and industrial paper (brown paper bags, punch card stock, electrical material, file folders, etc.)	14%
Building paper and board (sheathing papers, roofing felts, asbestos-filled papers, etc.)	9%
Sanitary and tissue paper	7%
Newsprint	5%
Groundwood paper (for directories, catalogs, wallpaper, etc.)	2%
Other	.5%
	100%

WOOD DERIVATIVES

A step beyond pulp and paper in the transformation of the tree are the chemicals and wood derivatives that go into a surprising number of things we use every day. For example:

Rosin, once used to caulk ships' hulls and treat rope, is now used to size paper and as an ingredient in paints, varnishes, plastics and synthetic rubber;

Tannin from oaks and hemlock, and formerly from chestnuts, is well-known as the tanning agent for leather but is also useful as a dispersing agent for water treatment;

A railroad car of pulpwood ready to go to the mill. (Northeastern Forest Experimentation Station, courtesy U.S. Forest Service)

Charcoal production, common in the 19th century, didn't die out with the coming of modern energy sources. Shown here (1940s) in Ohio, workers rack the 4-ft.-long bolts, and a collier climbs to the top of the cordwood pile, covered with a layer of lapwood. Last comes a layer of wet leaves. After firing, it will take 7 to 12 days of constant watching to keep the pile properly fired. (Courtesy U.S. Forest Service)

Lignin, a plentiful byproduct of papermaking, is burned as fuel by the paper industry and also widely used in cement and vanillin, and to give viscosity to oil drilling muds.

There's a big family of wood cellulose-derived products; celluloid was the first and most famous member. Though competition from non-cellulosic fibers has made inroads, wood cellulose is still a very important material. It is used in cellophane, rayon-and-acetate fibers, explosives, and as a food additive to give bulk (but not nutrition) to cattle feed and some of our own foods, such as ice cream.

WOOD FUEL

The least efficient form of wood utilization, burning it as fuel, is still the most prevalent worldwide. In many countries wood is still the major energy source. Even in our industrialized country more wood is used for fuel than for any other purpose except lumber manufacture. It is calculated that during our first 300 years on this continent we burned 12.350 billion cords of wood; until 1900, 95 percent of our fuel energy came from wood.

Most but not all of this went up in smoke from cooking stoves and fireplaces. Locomotives, steamboats and power plants (steam and electric) took their share until coal and oil displaced wood.

Charcoal

Much of the wood harvested was burned to create charcoal, one of man's oldest fuels. It can be produced by primitive or sophisticated methods, but basically involves heating wood in the absence of air. The resulting carbonized wood burns cleanly and radiates great heat. It can serve many purposes besides providing domestic heat.

In the 19th century charcoal was widely used in iron manufacture, in printer's ink and black paint, to clean teeth and relieve an upset stomach, and to purify water. Activated charcoal, which is made more absorbent by being subjected to treatment with steam or carbon dioxide at high temperatures, is still widely used to remove odors, tastes and colors, and in water purification.

The New England hardwood forests were regularly clear-cut to make charcoal for the iron works during Colonial and early independence years. Farmers sold charcoal rights on their woodlots to itinerants who did the dirty job: stacking the wood (maple, beech or oak) around the wood chimney of a pit kiln; covering the wood with twigs, sod or turf; lighting a fire in the central chimney; watching over the smoky mound to keep it from getting too much air (in which case the charcoal would burn to ashes); letting the product cool a few days. The whole process might take several weeks for a big kiln.

Later, charcoal was a valuable byproduct of the destructive distillation of wood for production of methanol, acetic acid and other wood derivatives mentioned above. But as synthetic alternatives became more competitive, the wood distillation industry declined. Now most charcoal is produced as a primary product, not a byproduct. And most of us buy it in a bag at the grocery store to take home for the backyard barbecue.

Firewood

We still use a great deal of wood in its original state as fuel—some 26 million cords a year. As other energy sources grow more costly, and as cold winters coincide with short supplies of gas, oil and electricity, wood sees more use. Stove sales go up, fireplaces are in demand in new homes, and folks with chainsaws apply for permits to cut firewood on public lands.

Wood fuel is theoretically sold by the cord, a pile 8 ft. long by 4 ft. wide by 4 ft. high. But in practice you will probably be sold a "face cord" or "short cord." This is also 8 ft. high and 4 ft. long, but width varies according to the length of the pieces, which may be anywhere from 12 in. to 36 in. Don't pay for a standard cord unless that is what you're actually getting.

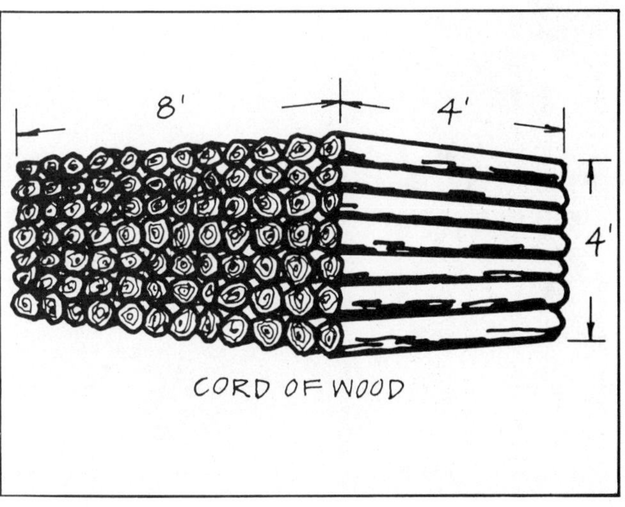

CORD OF WOOD

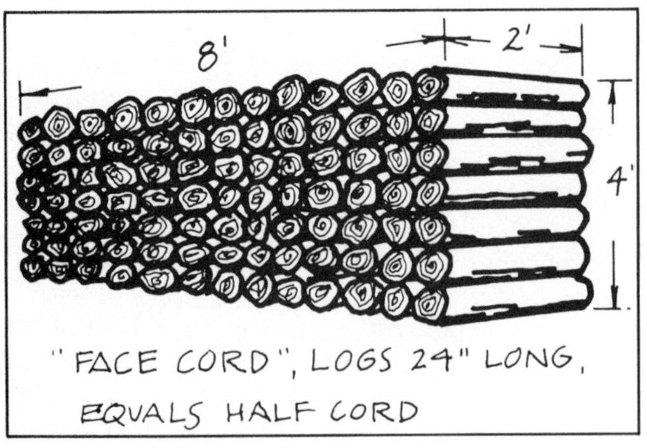

If you are the fortunate owner of your own woodlot, you may be able to supply all your own needs. One may expect to get about one cord per year per acre, without overcutting. If you are going into tree farming intensively (maybe for pulpwood as well as fuel), plant fast-growing species such as aspen, and use good forestry practices. You can get advice from your state foresters, also from the American Forest Institute (listed in appendix).

Suppose you plan to use wood for all your heating, cooking and water heating: You may need anywhere from 2 to 20 cords per year, depending on how well-insulated and weathertight your home is.

Americans have chopped and toted untold millions of cords of wood to keep the home fires burning. (Courtesy U.S. Forest Service)

Type of wood is as important as the quantity. In the first place it should be dry. (Proper drying may take 6 to 10 months.) Hardwoods burn longer than softwoods, but are not as easy to ignite and do not burn with as bright a flame. The table below rates some of the common fuelwoods for their more important qualities. (Information from U.S. Forest Service.)

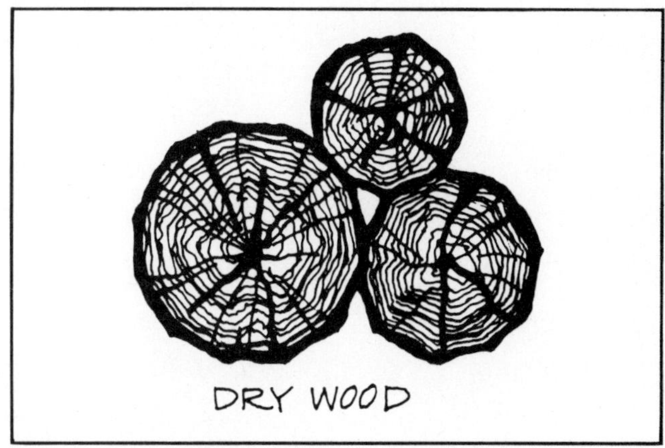

Wood Stoves Wood can be economical compared with fossil fuels. But the woodstove can also be dangerous if improperly installed or used. If possible, have it installed by a licensed heating contractor who

Approximate Weight and Heating Value per Cord (80 Actual Cu. Ft.) of Different Woods, Green and Air-Dry (20 Percent Moisture)

Woods	Weight, lb.		Available heat, million Btu		Equivalent in coal tons	
	Green	Air-Dry	Green	Air-Dry	Green	Air-Dry
Ash	3,840	3,440	16.5	21.0	0.75	0.91
Aspen	3,440	2,160	10.3	12.5	0.47	0.57
Beech, American	4,320	3,760	17.3	21.8	0.79	0.99
Birch, yellow	4,560	3,680	17.3	21.3	0.79	0.97
Douglas-fir	3,200	2,400	13.0	18.0	0.59	0.82
Elm, American	4,320	2,900	14.3	17.2	0.65	0.78
Hickory, shagbark	5,040	4,240	10.7	24.6	0.94	1.12
Maple, red	4,000	3,200	15.0	18.6	0.68	0.85
Maple, sugar	4,480	3,680	18.4	21.3	0.84	0.97
Oak, red	5,120	3,680	17.9	21.3	0.81	0.97
Oak, white	5,040	3,900	19.2	22.7	0.87	1.04
Pine, eastern white	2,880	2,080	12.1	13.3	0.55	0.60
Pine, southern yellow	4,000	2,600	14.2	20.5	0.64	0.93

Ratings for Firewood

Woods	Relative amount of heat	Easy to burn	Easy to split	Does it have heavy smoke?	Does it pop or throw sparks?	General rating and remarks
HARDWOOD TREES						
Ash, red oak, white oak, beech, birch, hickory, hard maple, pecan, dogwood.	High	Yes	Yes	No	No	Excellent.
Soft maple, cherry, walnut	Medium	Yes	Yes	No	No	Good.
Elm, sycamore, gum	Medium	Medium	No	Medium	No	Fair—contains too much water when green.
Aspen, basswood, cottonwood, yellow-poplar	Low	Yes	Yes	Medium	No	Fair—but good for kindling.
SOFTWOOD TREES						
Southern yellow pine, Douglas-fir	High	Yes	Yes	Yes	No	Good but smoky.
Cypress, redwood	Medium	Medium	Yes	Medium	No	Fair.
White cedar, western redcedar, eastern redcedar	Medium	Yes	Yes	Medium	Yes	Good—excellent for kindling.
Eastern white pine, western white pine, sugar pine, ponderosa pine, true firs.	Low	Medium	Yes	Medium	No	Fair—good kindling.
Tamarack, larch	Medium	Yes	Yes	Medium	Yes	Fair.
Spruce	Low	Yes	Yes	Medium	Yes	Poor—but good for kindling.

Source: U.S. Dept. of Agriculture—Forest Service
The table above shows the relative ratings of a variety of dried woods.

is familiar with the state building codes and local ordinances. If not, consult an expert or buy a manual. A few more general tips:*

- make sure of proper clearances from combustible material, such as floors, walls and ceilings;
- install ¼ in. asbestos millboard covered with sheet metal under the stove, with a hearth projecting on all sides;
- have the chimney inspected by a competent mason;
- use proper gauge steel pipes, spacers and connectors;
- burn dry, well-seasoned wood—burning green wood results in dirty chimneys and is a fire hazard;
- dispose of ashes in a metal container outside the home;
- wood stoves should not be connected to a fireplace chimney unless the fireplace has been sealed off or a convertor has been added;
- do not use flammable fuels to ignite wood—use paper or kindling;
- do not use stove to burn trash;
- do not allow fires to burn unattended overnight.

Besides firewood logs, wood-based fuel products include two that will warm not only your home, but the cockles of your conservation-conscious heart: briquettes (compressed wood waste such as sawdust and shavings, often with a binder like coal-tar pitch) and the familiar firelogs made of compressed sawdust.

Some woods contain 100 percent or more moisture (percent of dry weight) when cut. We aim to get this down to 20 percent before burning. The first step is to let the tree lie where it falls, without being cut up. Until the leaves dry up in a few weeks, the tree will continue to lose moisture through them. The tree can then be cut and stacked in regular cord style. For faster drying, it can be penned.

*These and other specifics can be found in *Successful Fireplaces* by R.J. Lytle.

What Is A Tree?

*The **outer bark** is the tree's protection from the outside world. It keeps moisture out during rain, prevents loss of moisture when the air is dry, insulates against cold and heat, and wards off insects. The **inner bark** or "Phloem" is the pipeline through which the food is passed to the rest of the tree. It lives only for a short time then dies and turns to cork, to become part of the outer protective bark. The **cambium cell** layer is the growing part of the trunk. It annually produces new bark and wood in response to hormones that pass down through the phloem with the food from the leaves. **Sapwood** is the tree's pipeline for water moving up to the leaves. Sapwood is new wood; as newer rings of sapwood are laid down, its inner cells lose their vitality and turn to heartwood. **Heartwood** is the central, supporting pillar of the tree. Although dead, it will not decay or lose strength while the outer layers are intact.*
(Courtesy St. Regis Paper Company)

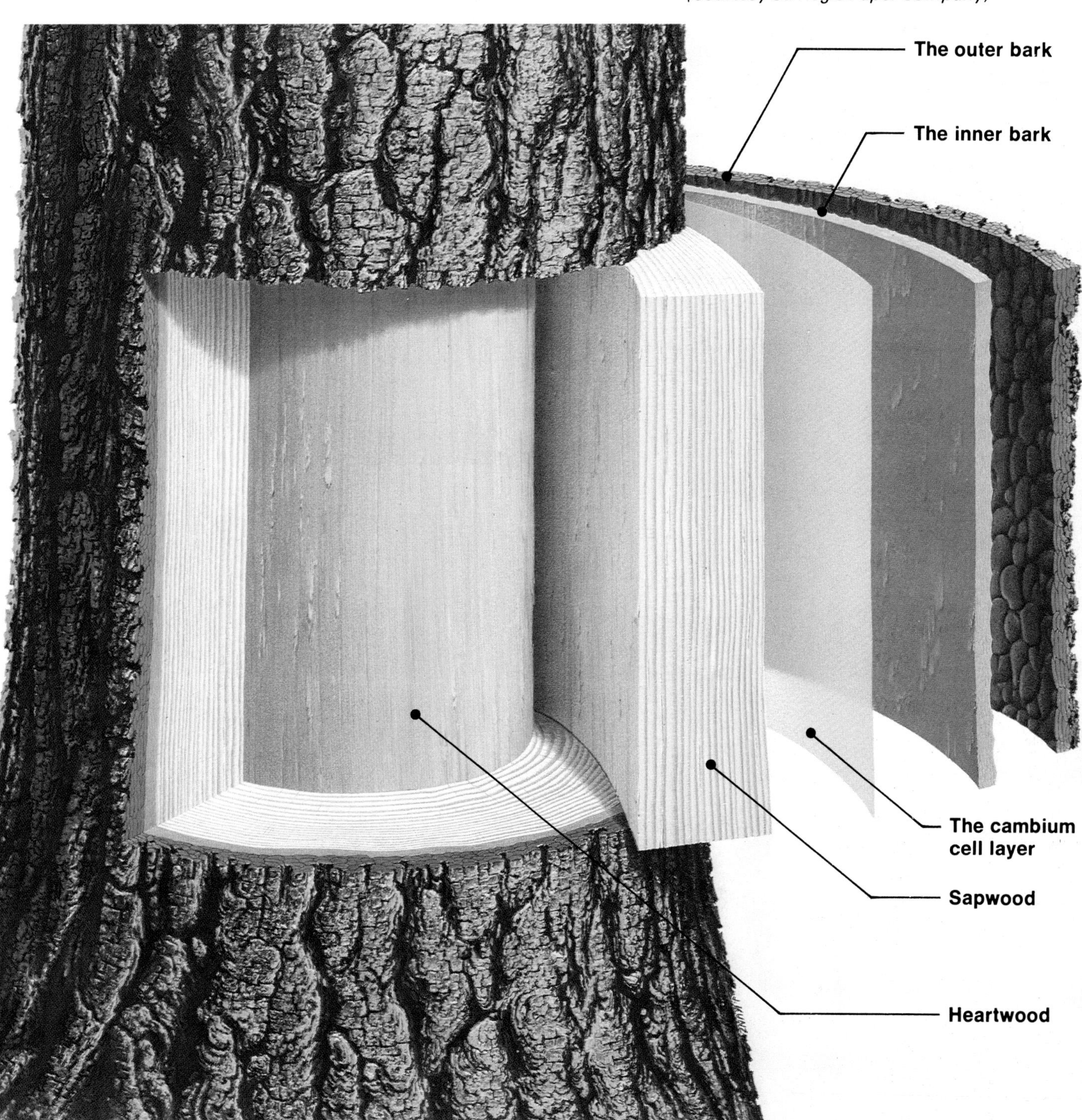

Young seedlings have a better chance with a one-year fertilizing.

Shown is the first step: Douglas fir seedlings in the nursery.

Scientific Tree Farming

Transplanting is done by hand.

Irrigation is another requirement for a hardy crop. ►

The result: a thriving new forest.

Thinning gives the best trees a better chance.

Pine forests and plantations have been cut, replanted, reharvested and regenerated for three-quarters of a century in the South. Southern pine now accounts for a third of our softwood lumber and plywood.

Southern pine is manufactured into timbers, dimension lumber, siding and plywood. Much of it is pressure-preservative treated during its manufacture.

From prehistory
to the present...
Man works
with wood.

Cedar totem poles of the Haida Indians in the Queen Charlotte Islands have survived for centuries. The cedar acquires a soft, unostentatious gray as it weathers naturally

These are 12 of the most important trees in American history. They have built our homes, supplied ties for transcontinental railways, become poles for power, phone and telegraph lines, and provided pulp for paper.

L. to R.: Eastern white pine, Douglas fir, longleaf pine, Western Hemlock.

L. to R.: balsam fir, ponderosa pine, white spruce, white oak.

L. to R.: sweet gum, shagbark hickory, yellow poplar, sugar maple.

Wood is beautiful from its first stages to the final finished product. (Full page photo, courtesy Weyerhaeuser; interior photo, courtesy California Redwood Assn.)

III. Lumber and Plywood

From now on we are concerned with the wood products found in home building, woodworking, remodeling, home repair; that is, construction materials. Even in this narrower category there are thousands of products. How to understand and differentiate them, and decide which are best for your specific purposes, is our next objective.

To give some order to the discussion we will first introduce the two most universally used wood products (lumber and plywood), then run through the major wood uses in construction of framing, walls, roofs, floors and interiors.

LUMBER

Lumber is used to give any structure or object a strong supporting skeleton.

Sawing methods have changed a lot since our forefathers used primitive manual methods like pit-sawing (see sketch), but the basic problem remains the same: how to saw rectangular pieces of wood out of a round log.

The various kinds of products that the log can yield are known by lumbermen as:

Dimension

Dimension lumber, 2 in. up to but not including 5 in. thick and 2 in. or more in width, is used in nearly all types of construction and is graded for strength rather than appearance. Characteristics such as knots, splits and slope of grain are taken into account, since each affects the strength of the piece.

Boards or Commons

Boards are less than 2 in. in nominal thickness, 1 in. or more wide (under 6 in. wide, also known as strips). Used for exterior finish on homes, cabinets or shelving, boards are generally graded for appearance rather than strength. They are classified into

Lumber mill technology has come a long way: (left) ancient man-powered pit sawing; (right) a water-powered saw of the late 1800s. (Courtesy Western Wood Products Association)

grades according to the visible characteristics exhibited by each piece.

Timbers and Beams

These large structural members, 5 in. by 5 in. and larger (also known as stringers, posts, caps, girders, purlins, sills), are used in the supporting framework of home, industrial and farm buildings, and in engineered construction such as bridges, auditoriums and stadiums. Although most grades are designed for strength and serviceability, some grades require both strength and good appearance, such as those used in an open beam ceiling.

Shop

Shop lumber comes in all widths and all thicknesses, and is cut from log sections with numerous areas of clear wood containing usually large, but well-spaced characteristics, such as knots and knotholes. The lumber is transported to a millwork plant where saws remove the undesirable characteristics, leaving clear pieces of high value. These are later manufactured into doors, window frames, molding and other specialty items.

Selects and Finish

Selects and Finish come in all widths and all thicknesses and are usually found nearest the outside surface of a log. They are virtually free of knots and other characteristics that detract from appearance. These are the finest grades of lumber available and are used for interior finishing, cabinet work and uses where appearance is of primary importance.

This sawing method, photographed in 1890, was used by our forefathers 350 years ago. In other parts of the world it persisted into the 1920s. (Courtesy Western Wood Products Association)

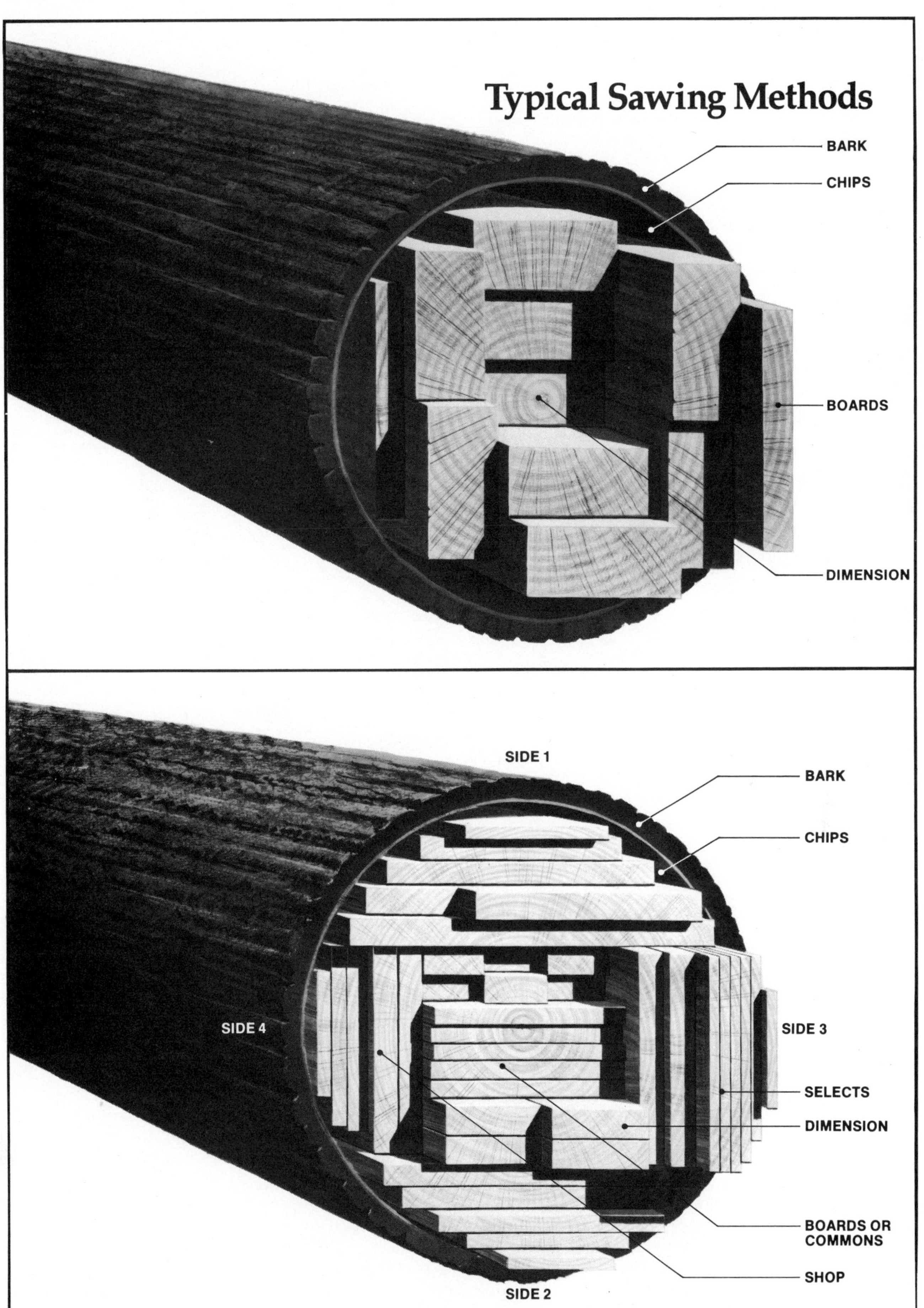

Typical Sawing Methods
BARK
CHIPS
BOARDS
DIMENSION
SIDE 1
BARK
CHIPS
SIDE 4
SIDE 3
SELECTS
DIMENSION
BOARDS OR
COMMONS
SHOP
SIDE 2

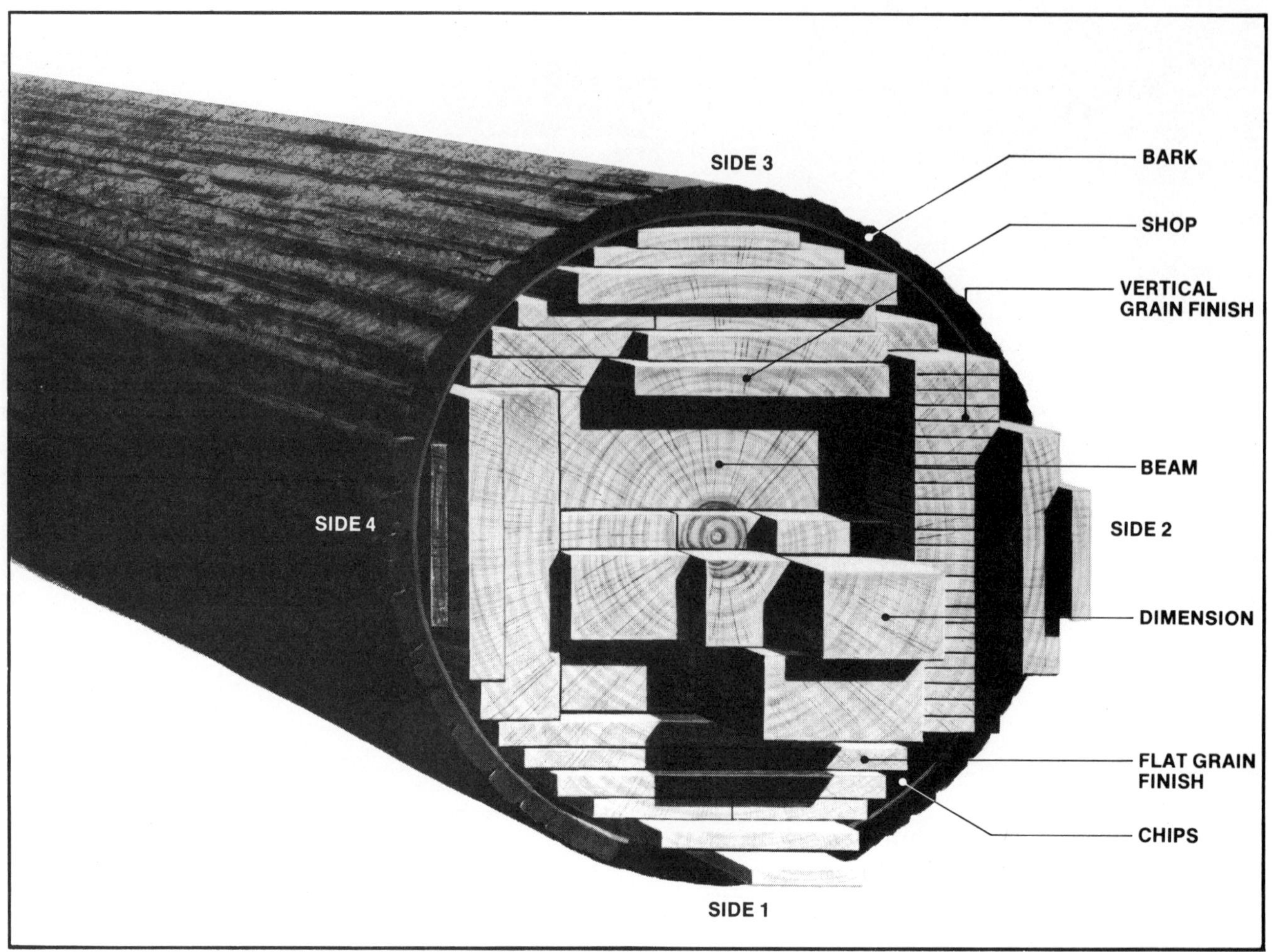

Bark and Chips and Sawdust

Very much a part of the yield of a log, bark is used as cattle litter, garden mulch and in the production of hardboard. Wood chips become raw material for such items as paper, chipboard and particleboard. Even sawdust is utilized in the production of certain kinds of paper and particleboard.

Sizes

There are various ways to saw up a log to get the best mix of products. Which way to go is a decision that used to depend solely on the quick, astute judgment of an experienced headrig sawyer. Now he has help from computers. But he must still decide swiftly and accurately how to slice the log into the best possible assortment of lumber grades, thicknesses and widths. He bases the decision on type and size of log, kind of mill equipment he has available, and the kinds of products currently in most demand.

The typical nonprofessional lumber buyer thinks in terms of uses, not the manufacturer's classifications. But he will buy more wisely if he understands some of the terminology.

When buying lumber for framing, for example, you will be buying dimension lumber as distinguished from boards to be used for sheathing, siding and flooring.

Here's the difference between nominal and actual dressed or finished sizes. Nominal refers to the size of the rough piece of lumber after it is sawed out of the log in the mill. But being very rough, it must be planed, which reduces its size. It will also shrink during seasoning or drying.

Green lumber as it comes from the sawmill still has a lot of moisture in it. The wood will change dimension as it gains or loses moisture, swelling with the former and shrinking with the latter. This may result in warping, checking, splitting or other performance problems. To avoid this the industry has developed techniques to season lumber. Controlled drying removes moisture to the point where it corresponds to that of the atmospheric conditions to which the wood will be exposed. Drying has other advantages: it increases wood's strength and nail-holding power, makes it less susceptible to fungus infection or insect attack, also makes it easier to handle, due to lighter weight.

To be sure of lumber that will not become deformed you should ask for dry or seasoned lumber, which has been kiln-dried under controlled conditions while in the mill. It is somewhat more expensive than green lumber but certainly pays for itself.

In any case, what you buy will be smaller than the original or nominal size of the piece of lumber. For example, a nominal 1x6 is actually ¾ in. by 5-½ in. If you need lumber of an exact dimension, order it from your dealer but be prepared to pay a bit extra. The nominal term does not, usually, refer to length.

Nominal and actual sizes of some of the most-used boards and dimension lumber are shown below.

Nominal size (inches)	Actual Size	
	Dry (seasoned)	Green (unseasoned)
Boards		
1x 4	¾ by 3½	25/32 by 3 9/16
1x 6	¾ by 5½	25/32 by 5⅜
1x 8	¾ by 7¼	25/32 by 7½
1x10	¾ by 9¼	25/32 by 9½
1x12	¾ by 11¼	25/32 by 11½
Dimension lumber		
2x 4	1½ by 3½	1 9/16 by 3 9/16
2x 6	1½ by 5½	1 9/16 by 5⅝
2x 8	1½ by 7¼	1 9/16 by 7½
2x10	1½ by 9¼	1 9/16 by 9½
2x12	1½ by 11¼	1 9/16 by 11½

Measurement of the lumber you buy may be by board foot or linear foot.

The board foot is a unit 1 ft. square by 1 in. thick. To calculate board feet, multiply the length in feet times the nominal thickness times width in inches and divide by 12. For example: if you were buying a 12-ft.-long 2x4, you would calculate as follows: 12 ft. x 2 in. x 4 in. = 96 ÷ 12 = 8 bd. ft.

Some products are sold only by the linear foot, so you have no problem of conversion. These include moldings, furring strips and some kinds of boards and dimension lumber: 1x2s, 1x3s, 2x2s, 2x3s and sometimes 2x4s.

Additional Terminology

The next thing you need to know is the difference between select and common lumber. Select is of high appearance quality, the kind to buy if it will show and if you intend to finish it. Common lumber has defects (knots, checks, splits, shakes) which may detract from its appearance but not necessarily from its performance.

A "check" is a shallow lengthwise separation across the growth ring. A "split" is the same but deeper and more serious from the standpoint of appearance. "Shakes" are separations between the growth rings.

You will also sometimes need to decide between *heartwood* and *sapwood* and to recognize the difference between *flat grain* and *vertical grain.*

As the diagram of the tree trunk in the color section shows, heartwood extends from the pith (center) of the tree to the sapwood. It is usually darker than sapwood and more decay-resistant, especially in such durable species as redwood, Western red cedar and cypress. If color and durability are your main criteria, you may want to pay a little more and get heartwood.

Whether your lumber has vertical or flat grain depends on the way it was sawed from the log. Many who work with wood prefer vertical grain, with its pronounced lined pattern, to flat grain, with its more swirly, irregular grain pattern. Flat grain lumber is also more likely to warp.

A final differentiation is between unmilled and milled lumber. The former is square-cornered and straight-edged as it comes from the saw, with no additional shaping. Dimension lumber is unmilled. But boards for siding or paneling often are milled to give a bevel shape or shiplap or tongue-and-groove edge, for example. Moldings are another kind of milled lumber.

Having mastered all of the above, you still need to know something about how wood products are graded. Most wood associations have established grading standards to which their members (manufacturers of wood products) adhere. Lumber is stamped with the grade-mark which indicates its quality and suitability for various construction uses.

Log scaling—the first step when the log gets to the mill. The scaler verifies species and quality, and estimates how much the log will produce in lumber, chips, sawdust, other usable residues. (Courtesy Western Wood Products Association)

The Western Wood Products Association, largest lumber producers' group in the country, performs this service for manufacturers in the area from the Pacific to the Great Plains. Here are some major species grown in this area and made into construction lumber.

Douglas fir	Western larch
Ponderosa pine	Sugar pine
True firs	Idaho white pine
Western hemlock	Incense cedar
Engelmann spruce	Redwood (graded by Redwood Inspection Service, not W.W.P.A.)
Lodgepole pine	
Western red cedar	

However, when you go to your lumber dealer to buy, you will more likely ask for lumber by the grade that is suitable for the use you have in mind, not by species alone. (Chapter 4 covers grading and classification.)

PLYWOOD

Lumber's uses in and around the home are extremely varied, and so are those of plywood. What is plywood? You might say it is our earliest engineered wood product, made not by sawing up the log, but by unwinding it. The log is rotated against the blade of a giant lathe which slices off the veneer in a continuous sheet. (Sometimes, especially with fine hardwood plywood, the log is not rotary cut but sliced in cross-sections.) The veneer is cut into uniform pieces (usually 4 ft. by 8 ft.). An odd number of these pieces of veneer (or plies) is assembled, with the grain of each at right angles to that of the adjacent piece. The layers are glued together with heat and pressure creating a permanent bond between wood and adhesive. Because of the odd number of layers and the cross-lamination—placement of consecutive layers at right angles—shrinkage is minimized and tension equalized. The resulting panel of plywood is stronger than a hypothetical board of the same dimensions would be.

Another variation is plywood made with an even number of plies, usually four. In such cases the center

Unwinding the log—a pine log is cut into a continuous ribbon of 8-foot-wide veneer by lathe in a Georgia-Pacific plant in Arkansas. (Courtesy American Plywood Association)

Sorting—after veneer is clipped and unrepairable defects are cut out, sheets are dried, then sorted by grade. (Courtesy American Plywood Association)

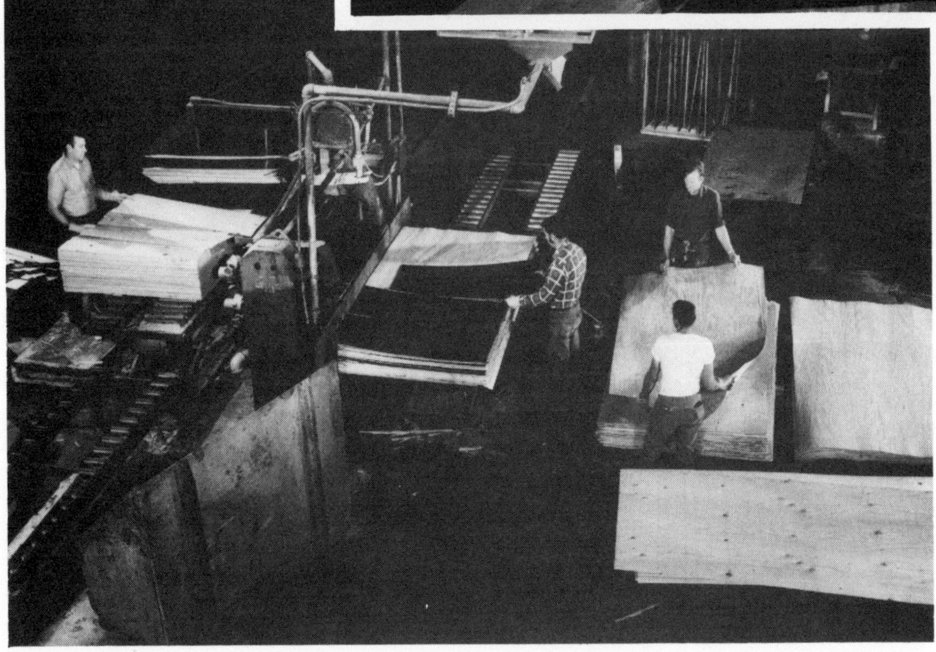

Panel make-up—small defects are patched, then sheets are glued and sandwiched together, with grain of adjacent sheets running in opposite directions. Next step will be bonding in a hot-press. (Courtesy American Plywood Association)

Classification of Species Used in Plywood
(American Plywood Association)

Group 1

- Apitong (a), (b)
- Beech, American
- Birch
  - Sweet
  - Yellow
- Douglas Fir 1 (c)
- Kapur (a)
- Keruing (a), (b)
- Larch, Western
- Maple, Sugar
- Pine
  - Caribbean
  - Ocote
- Pine, Southern
  - Loblolly
  - Longleaf
  - Shortleaf
  - Slash
- Tanoak

Group 2

- Cedar, Port Orford
- Cypress
- Douglas Fir 2 (c)
- Fir
  - California Red
  - Grand
  - Noble
  - Pacific Silver
  - White
- Hemlock, Western
- Lauan
  - Almon
  - Bagtikan
- Mayapis
  - Red Lauan
  - Tangile
  - White Lauan
- Maple, Black
- Mengkulang (a)

Group 2 continued

- Meranti, Red (a), (b)
- Mersawa (a)
- Pine
  - Pond
  - Red
  - Virginia
  - Western White
- Spruce
  - Red
  - Sitka
- Sweetgum
- Tamarack
- Yellow-poplar

Group 3

- Alder, Red
- Birch, Paper
- Cedar, Alaska
- Fir, Subalpine
- Hemlock, Eastern
- Maple, Bigleaf
- Pine
  - Jack
  - Lodgepole
  - Ponderosa
  - Spruce
- Redwood
- Spruce
  - Black
  - Engelmann
  - White

Group 4

- Aspen
  - Bigtooth
  - Quaking
- Cativo
- Cedar
  - Incense
  - Western Red
- Cottonwood
  - Eastern
  - Black (Western Poplar)
- Pine
  - Eastern White
  - Sugar

Group 5

- Basswood
- Fir, Balsam
- Poplar, Balsam

(a) Each of these names represents a trade group of woods consisting of a number of closely related species.

(b) Species from the genus Dipterocarpus are marketed collectively: Apitong if originating in the Phillippines; Keruing if originating in Malaysia or Indonesia.

(c) Douglas fir from trees grown in the States of Washington, Oregon, California, Idaho, Montana, Wyoming, and the Canadian Provinces of Alberta and British Columbia is classed as Douglas fir No. 1. Dougas fir from trees grown in the states of Nevada, Utah, Colorado, Arizona and New Mexico is classed as Douglas fir No. 2.

(d) Red Meranti is limited to species having a specific gravity of 0.41 or more based on green volume and oven dry weight.

pair has grain running in the same direction but at right angles to grain of outer plies.

Plywood may be softwood, hardwood or a combination. Most construction-grade plywood is softwood. Douglas fir was for years the dominant species but many others are now used as well, such as pine, hemlock, spruce and true firs. And cedar and redwood plywood are good choices where appearance is very important, as for siding.

Lately, plywood manufacturers have been learning how to incorporate veneers of tropical hardwoods in structural plywood. First they had to study and analyze the new woods so that, when made into plywood, the panel would be as predictable in its performance as those made of familiar domestic species.

Classifications

Plywood is now manufactured from over 70 different species of wood, of varying strengths. They are divided into five groups, with the strongest in Group I, next strongest in Group II, etc. Every panel graded according to the procedures of the American Plywood Association is given a group number in accordance with the weakest species used in face and back. This group number is part of the information you will find in the stamp on the panel.

As you will see from the footnotes to the Classification Table, one species may vary in its strength properties, depending on where it grows, and these differences are taken into consideration when assigning it to a group. Also, when two or more tropical wood species have similar properties, they are sometimes marketed as one species.

Clockwise, from upper left, the plywood stamp tells you: grade of veneer on panel face; grade on panel back; that it was manufactured according to standards of American Plywood Association; number of the mill; the Product Standard governing manufacture; type of plywood; and Species Group number. (See Classification of Species table, above.)

Other useful facts besides species group to be gleaned from the stamp on plywood include the moisture conditions the plywood has been designed to withstand.

Exterior-type This plywood, manufactured from selected veneers and waterproof glue, is suitable for use outdoors, in boat-building or in damp places.

Interior-type For this plywood, there are different restrictions on the veneer and it may be made with either moisture-resistant or waterproof glue. Most construction-grade plywood has the latter. Interior plywood is used where no moisture will be present or in construction where exposure to the weather will be only temporary.

The gradestamp may also tell you the grade of veneer used on face and back: with A the best-looking, on down to D. In these cases, the two letters that identify face and back veneer become what APA calls the panel grade. In other words, if the panel grade is A-B, you know it is a panel with a good-looking face (A) and a not-quite-so-good back (B); it would be suitable for use where appearance of one side is very important and the other side not quite so important but where both surfaces must be solid. For instance, in many cabinets and built-ins.

Here, in more detail, are definitions of the veneer grades.

A—smooth and paintable. Neatly made repairs permissible. (Repairs may be made during manufacture to remedy minor holes, knots or defects, by patching or gluing in a plug or shim.) Used for natural finish in less demanding applications.

B—solid surface veneer. Repair plugs and tight knots permitted.

C—knotholes to 1 in. permitted; occasional knotholes ½ in. larger permitted providing total width of all knots and knotholes within a specified section does not exceed certain limits. Limited splits (separation of wood fibers) permitted. C is the minimum veneer permitted in Exterior-type plywood.

D—permits knots and knotholes to 2½ in. in width and ½ in. larger under certain specified limits. Limited splits permitted. Used only in Interior-type plywood.

You'll also sometimes see a panel with Grade N veneer; this is a special, very high-appearance veneer grade.

Thus, the gradestamp gives you a clue as to whether the panel is an appearance or a construction grade of plywood. If you see that better-looking veneers, usually A or B, are used, it is probably an ap-

UNDERLAYMENT
GROUP 1 APA
INTERIOR
PS 1-74 000

pearance grade. Other indicators are HDO (High Density Overlay), MDO (Medium Density Overlay) and 303 Siding (used on many textured plywoods used for siding and paneling).

This is not to say that if you buy an appearance grade of plywood it will not have the strength you need for your wood-working projects. The terms "appearance" and "construction" simply imply that in some applications appearance is important while in others it is not.

Normally all grades with N, A or B faces are sanded smooth in manufacture, which saves you the trouble of sanding if you plan to use the plywood for cabinetry or wherever you need a smooth surface.

Construction grades In these grades, veneers on face and back are chosen primarily for strength rather than looks. They include plywood used for basic house construction jobs—sheathing, underlayment, concrete forms. Most such plywood is Interior with Exterior glue, and by far the most common grade is known in the trade as CDX: face veneer is C grade, back veneer is D and it is made with Exterior glue.

Plywood for these uses is unsanded, though some (such as that used for underlayment) may be "touch-sanded"—lightly sanded during manufacture to bring it to proper thickness.

The construction grades also include a family of "engineered" panels which you may not have occasion to buy but which you may be very glad to have in your house. These are stamped Structural I or Structural II and are used where extra strength is needed, as gusset plates or wall and roof sheathing in high wind and earthquake areas.

All Structural plywood and many other construction grades carry a set of numbers, called the Identification Index, which tells you the maximum spacing of floor and roof supports over which the panel may be installed. (There's little need for you to master all this lore about construction grades of plywood unless you will be actually involved in building a house or doing a fairly substantial remodeling job. In that case you might want to ask the APA for explanatory booklets.)

The above refers to softwood plywood, which is made in a variety of grades for both indoor and outdoor use. But it cannot be stressed too much that it must have Exterior-type glue if it is going to be permanently exposed to weather. After spending your good money you do not want to risk seeing your plywood delaminate, just because you bought the wrong kind.

The more costly hardwood plywood is primarily for interior use as paneling, built-ins and furniture. It is generally thinner and has fewer plies than softwood plywood. Although softwood inner plies or a lumber core may be chosen for such uses as tabletops, outer veneers are decorative hardwoods.

IV. Wood for Construction

The various components of the house structure require varying degrees of strength, flexibility, resistance and workability.

FRAMING

Wood products used in the structural skeleton of a house—over the foundations and serving as floor supports, wall and roof framing—include timbers, beams and dimension lumber.

If you build a house on your own you will need a thorough knowledge of these lumber products and how to use them; more knowledge than you can garner from this book. (For starters, see Robert Reschke's *How to Build Your Own Home,* a *Successful Book.*)

But if you are having a home professionally built, or are buying a new house, familiarity with the nomenclature and descriptions of various lumber products will help you to discuss matters intelligently with your architect, builder or real estate dealer. There is nothing like a casual reference to "Select Structural" to make them perk up their ears and realize you cannot be misled.

You do need to know what you are talking about, so snoop around your lumber yard. Converse with your architect and builder friends. And for real expertise, become familiar with the grade-use guides of the various wood associations.

An accompanying chart shows the pertinent grade descriptions for dimension lumber graded by the Western Wood Products Association. Remember that dimension lumber is surfaced lumber, of nominal thickness from 2 to 4 in. The categories and use suggestions below cover most lumber made west of the Mississippi. (Except redwood, discussed later.)

Dimension Lumber, All Species (American Softwood Lumber Standards, PS 20-70 Classifications)

Category	*Grades*	*Uses*
Light Framing (2 in. to 4 in. wide)	Construction, Standard and Better, Standard, Utility	For use where high strength values are not required, such as studs, plates, sills, cripples, blocking, etc.
Studs (2 in. to 6 in. wide, 10 ft. and shorter)	Stud	One of the most popular grades for wall construction, including load-bearing walls. For a stud longer than 10 ft., use Light Framing or Structural Light Framing.
Structural Light Framing (2 in. to 4 in. wide)	Select Structural, No. 1, No. 2, No. 3	For engineering applications where higher strength and stiffness are required, as in trusses, concrete forms, etc. For good appearance plus strength and stiffness, look for Select Structural.
Structural Joists & Planks (5 in. and wider)	Select Structural, No. 1, No. 2, No. 3	For engineering applications requiring lumber wider than Structural Light Framing, such as joists, rafters, and general framing uses.

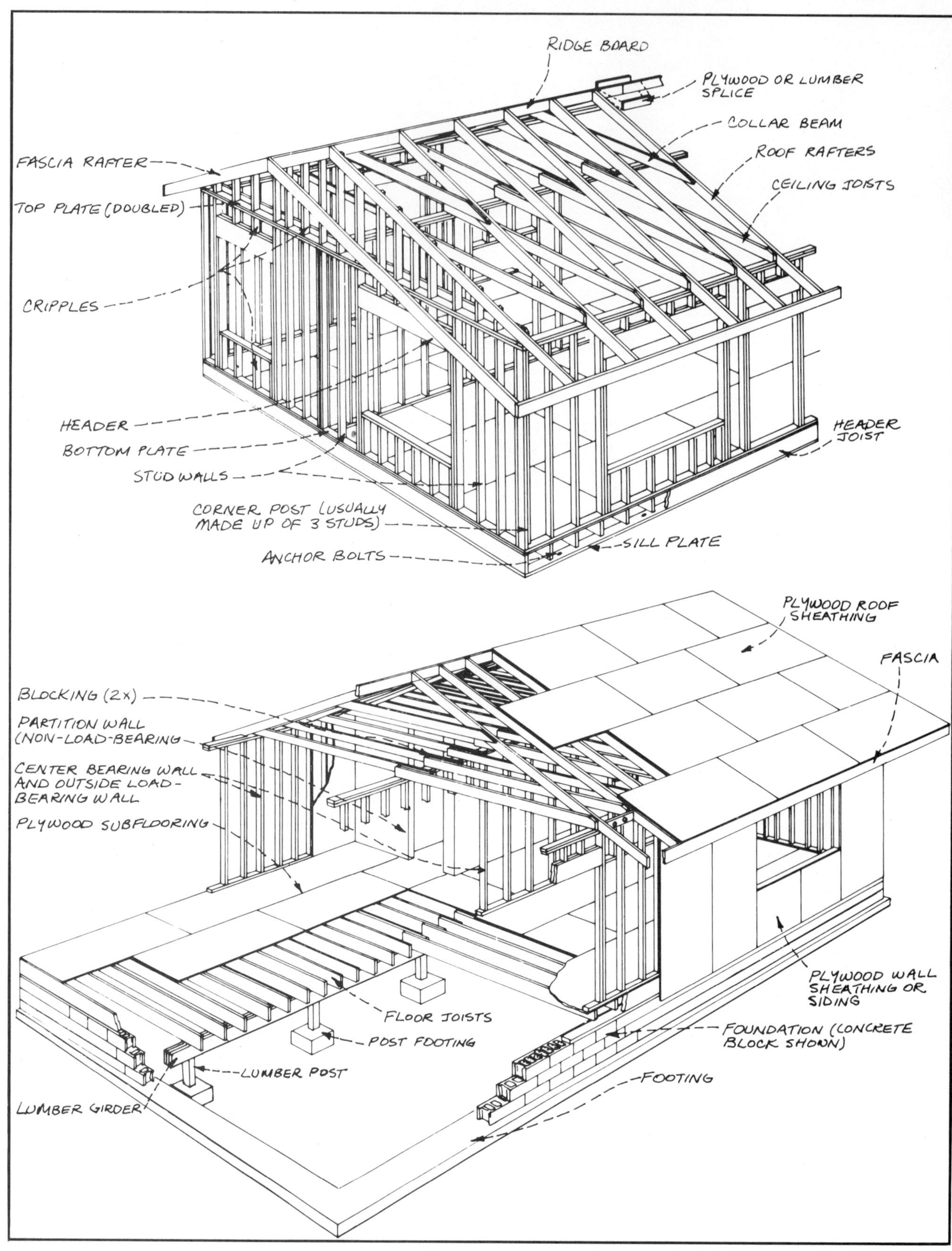

Here are wood's major applications in construction. Above, wall and roof framing. Below, foundations, floor construction, partitions, sheathing, siding. (Art courtesy of American Plywood Association)

Detail of lumber corner framing. (Courtesy of Weyerhaeuser)

You will find the grade included in the information on the gradestamp. The stamp also tells you what species of wood you have—or at least narrows it down.

The western softwood species commonly manufactured into dimension lumber include Western hemlock, Engelmann spruce, larch, Western cedars and all pines and firs. Many of these species are grown, harvested, manufactured and marketed together and have similar performance properties. This makes them interchangeable in use, grading and grade marking.

Thus, Douglas fir and larch are grouped together (DOUG FIR-L); Western hemlock combines with true firs as HEM-FIR. Engelmann spruce, all true firs, hemlocks and pines are grouped as White Woods (WW). And so on.

In the gradestamp shown you learn (reading clockwise from upper left) that the lumber was made by mill no. 12 (every mill that observes WWPA grading standards has a number); that it is Stud grade; that the species is either Engelmann spruce or lodgepole pine. S-DRY means that when manufactured, it was dried to a moisture content not exceeding 19 percent. Finally, the product was graded under WWPA supervision.

The same type of information is on gradestamps of the other association that grades western lumber, the West Coast Lumber Inspection Bureau.

If you are in an area where lumber graded by the Southern Pine Inspection Bureau is more available, be guided by that classification system (see chart on page 54). Southern pine comes from 12 southern states, and includes lumber from four main pine species: longleaf, slash, shortleaf and loblolly.

WALLS

Once a wall is framed, three more things may happen to it, all involving wood products: *sheathing, siding* and *paneling.*

Southern Pine Grade Descriptions for Dimension and Framing Lumber (American Softwood Lumber Standards, PS 20-70 Classifications)

PRODUCT	*GRADE(S)*	*CHARACTER OF GRADE AND TYPICAL USES*
DIMENSION Structural Light Framing, 2 in. to 4 in. thick, 2 in. to 4 in. wide	Select Structural, Dense Select, Structural	High quality, relatively free of characteristics which impair strength or stiffness. Recommended where high strength, stiffness and good appearance are required.
	No. 1, No. 1 Dense	Provide high strength, recommended for general utility and construction. Good appearance.
	No. 2, No. 2 Dense	Although less restricted than No. 1, suitable for all types of construction. Tight knots.
	No. 3, No. 3 Dense	Assigned design values meet wide range of design requirements. Recommended for general construction where appearance not a controlling factor. Many pieces would qualify as No. 2 but for single limiting characteristic. Provides high-quality, low-cost construction.
STUDS 2 in. to 4 in. thick, 2 in. to 6 in. wide, 10 ft. and shorter	Stud	Stringent requirements as to straightness, strength and stiffness adapt this grade to all stud uses, including load-bearing walls. Crook restricted in 2 in. x 4 in.—8 ft. to ¼ in., with wane restricted to ⅓ of thickness.
Structural Joists & Planks, 2 in. to 4 in. thick, 5 in. and wider	Select Structural, Dense Select, Structural	High quality, relatively free of characteristics which impair strength or stiffness. Recommended where high strength, stiffness and good appearance are required.
	No. 1, No. 1 Dense	Provide high strength, recommended for general utility and construction purposes. Good appearance.
	No. 2, No. 2 Dense	Although less restricted than No. 1, suitable for all types of construction. Tight knots.
	No. 3, No. 3 Dense	Assigned stress values meet wide range of design requirements. Recommended for general construction where appearance not a controlling factor. Many pieces would qualify as No. 2 except for single limiting characteristic. Provides high-quality, low-cost construction.
Light Framing, 2 in. to 4 in. thick, 2 in. to 4 in. wide	Construction	Recommended for general framing purposes. Good appearance, strong and serviceable.

continued

PRODUCT	GRADE(S)	CHARACTER OF GRADE AND TYPICAL USES
	Standard	Recommended for same uses as Construction grade, but allows larger defects.
	Utility	Recommended where combination of strength and economy is desired. Excellent for blocking, plates and bracing.
	Economy	Usable lengths suitable for bracing, blocking, bulkheading and other purposes where strength and appearance are not controlling factors.
Appearance Framing, 2 in. to 4 in. thick, 2 in. and wider	Appearance	Designed for exposure. Combines strength characteristics of No. 1 with good-quality appearance.

Siding may or may not be applied over sheathing, depending on the type of siding. The sheathing has two purposes: to strengthen the structure, and to provide backing for attaching siding or roofing. Most sheathing nowadays is a panel material, though you will occasionally still see some shiplap boards for wall sheathing.

For highest strength as well as resistance to wind, seismic and snow loads, plywood sheathing is best. Other types are manufactured fibrous panels with insulating qualities.

Plywood used for wall sheathing is generally C-D or C-C, Interior with Exterior glue.

Siding

Siding is the term used for all products used to cover the outside walls of the structure. (Also called *cladding.*) Though nonwood products may be used for siding, such as aluminum or vinyl, we are concerned here only with boards, plywood, shakes and shingles, hardboard, and fiberboard. Many of these may also appear as paneling, in line with the trend to "bring the outside inside," by using natural-looking wood products on interior walls.

Boards for siding may be chosen from many species. The most desirable are easy to work with, good for painting or staining, and are decay-resistant (as with heartwood). Redwood, cedar and cypress are fine on the first two counts and superb on the third. Eastern white pine, Western white pine and sugar pine are also good. Other frequently used softwoods include Western hemlock, ponderosa pine, Southern pines, and spruce. In the East, where hardwood lumber is more plentiful, it is seldom still used for siding because of its relatively high cost.

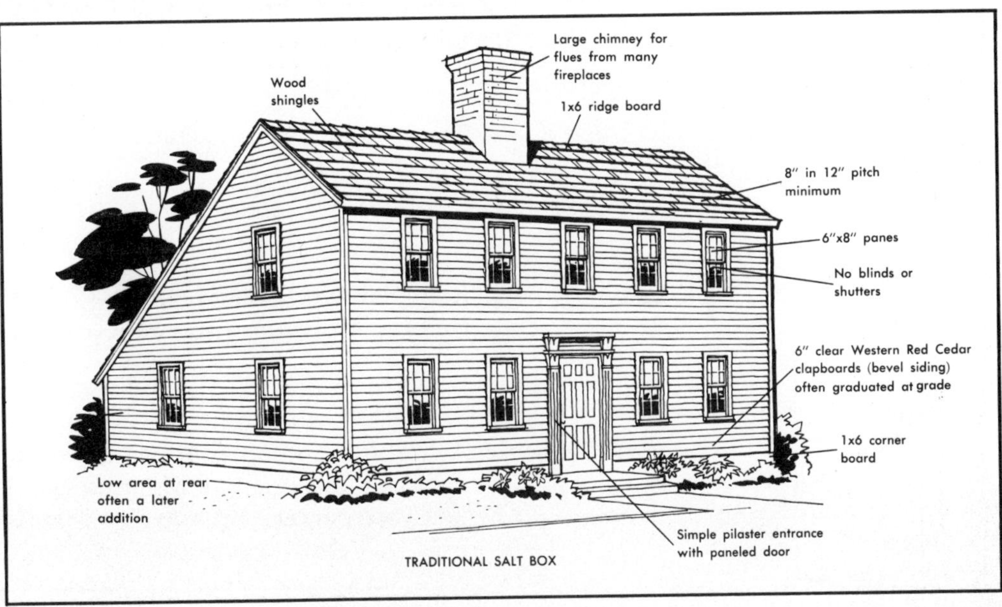

Colonial architecture made extensive use of wood, the most available material. The functional styles still make sense, as shown in this diagram of the color view on p. 76. Steeply pitched roof of the Salt Box was useful to shed snow. Characteristic shape (like that of actual salt boxes of the day) was due to building lean-to additions at the rear when the family grew. (Courtesy Western Red Cedar Lumber Association)

Board siding may be applied vertically, horizontally or even diagonally. Vertical siding is nailed to nailing strips (which should be of nominal 1-in. thickness and 24 in. or less apart), or directly to wall sheathing if it is wood. Vertical siding boards often have battens nailed over the joints. Horizontal siding is generally applied directly to wood framing (over building paper) or to sheathing.

Board siding comes in a variety of shapes and sizes, including bevel, tongue-and-groove, shiplap, and a board that looks like a log. Most of these are descendants of the traditional bevel siding (milled) or clapboard (unmilled) which characterized the early American home. The trend now, though, is to a much wider strip than those 18th-century builders used. Bevel siding today is often 12 in. wide or even more. The advantage is obvious: less labor.

Several of the wood associations have prepared descriptive guides to their sidings products, which are a big help in buying. Here, for example, is a siding use guide from Western Wood Products Association, with application suggestions.

Siding Use Guide (WWPA)

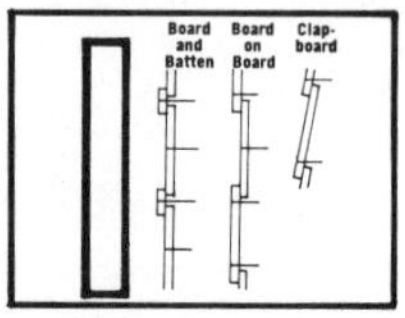

Boards	Available surfaced or rough textured. WWPA recommends 1 in. minimum overlap. Use 10d siding nails as shown.
Channel rustic	Has ½-in. lap and 1-¼-in. channel when installed. May be applied horizontally or vertically. Use 8d siding nails as shown for 6-in. widths. With wider widths, nail twice per bearing.
Drop	Available in 13 different patterns. Some T&G (as shown), others shiplapped. Use 6d finish nails for T&G, 8d siding nails for shiplap.
Bevel	Plain Bevel may be used with smooth face exposed or sawn face exposed for textured look. WWPA recommends 1-in. minimum overlap on plain bevel siding. Use 6d siding nails as shown.
Bungalow	Thicker and wider than Bevel. Plain Bungalow or "Colonial" may be used with smooth or sawn face exposed. Apply as with Bevel, but use 8d siding nails.
Dolly Varden	Thicker than Bevel, has rabbeted edge. Use 8d siding nails.
Log Cabin	Rounded "log" siding board is 1½-in. thick at thickest point. Nail 1½-in. up from lower edge of piece. Use 10d casing nails.
Tongue & Groove	Available in smooth or rough-sawn surface. Use 6d finish nails as shown for 6-in. widths or less. In wider widths, face-nail twice per bearing with 8d siding nails.

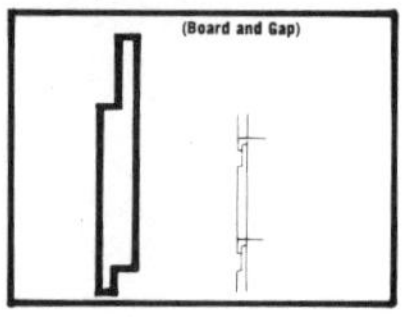

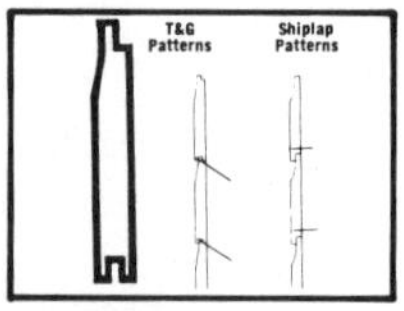

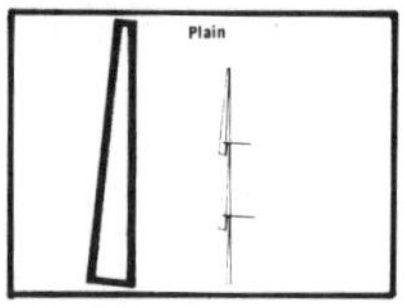

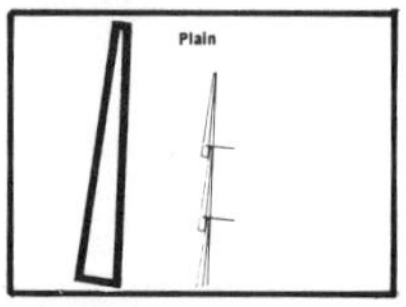

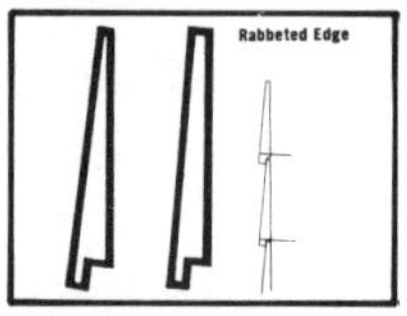

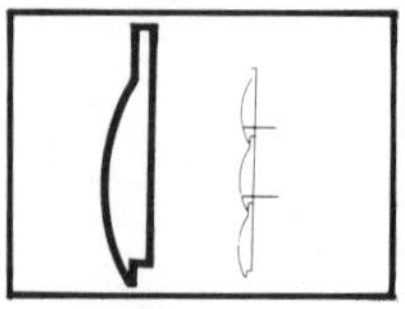

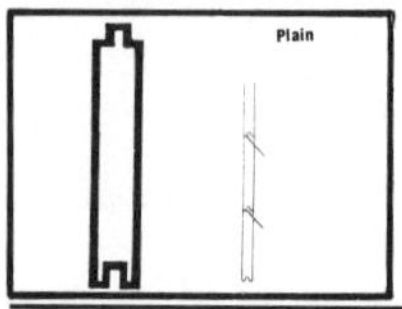

Southern pine siding is also widely available. Product grades used for siding, paneling and sheathing include Finish, Drop Siding, Bevel Siding, Boards and Shiplap. See the grade use guide.

SOUTHERN PINE GRADES FOR SIDING, PANELING AND SHEATHING (SFPA)

Product	*Grades*	*Description and Uses*
Finish	B & Better	Highest recognized grade of finish. Generally clear although limited number of pin knots permitted. Finest quality for natural or stain finishes.
	C	Excellent for painted or natural finish where requirements are less exacting. Reasonably clear but permits limited number of surface checks and small, tight knots.
	C & Better	Intermediate between two above, provides high quality finish.
	D	Economical serviceable grade for natural or painted finish.
Paneling including Fillets (battens)	B & Better C C & Better	Similar to above (Finish), with greater restrictions on stain and wane.
	D	Top-quality knotty pine paneling for natural or stained finish. Knots are smooth and even with surrounding surface.
	No. 2	Somewhat less exacting requirements than for D. Suitable for natural or stained finish.
	No. 3	More imperfections permitted, suitable for economical use.
Partition, Drop Siding, Bevel Siding	B & Better C C & Better D	Same as Finish grades
	No. 1	Same as No. 1 Boards (see below).
	No. 2	Slightly better than No. 2 Boards, high utility value where appearance not a prime factor.
	No. 3	More imperfections than No. 2; suitable for economical use.
Boards S4S (Surfaced on all four sides)	No. 1	High quality, good appearance, generally sound, tight-knotted. Suitable for wide range of uses such as shelving, concrete forms, crating.
Shiplap, S2S (surfaced on two sides), CM (center matched)	No. 2	High quality sheathing.
	No. 3	Serviceable sheathing, can be used without waste.
	No. 4	Below No. 3 pieces permitted, in which usable portions must be at least 2 ft. in length.

The pine sidings in the chart are smooth-surfaced and suitable for painting. For a textured siding that takes stains well, you may want to look at rough-sawn pine siding. Be guided by the following grade descriptions:

C and better Practically clear surface; small tight knots permitted; recommended where finest quality desired.

No.1 Excellent appearance; tight knots; comparable quality available as "D" grade in some areas.

No.2 Sound, firm, permits larger knots; recommended where rustic appearance is desired and serviceability and economy are prime considerations.

Cedar siding Available in either smooth or saw-textured, cedar is legendary for durability, resistance to decay, and its beautiful grain. Western red cedar costs more than pine but has greater dimensional stability. Paint it or stain it or let it adapt to the elements just as the Northwest Coast Indians did with their longhouses and totem poles; in time it turns to a soft silver-gray.

Refer to the grade-use guide, taken from Western Red Cedar Lumber Association, when selecting cedar for siding or paneling.

Redwood siding To many people redwood is the ultimate in readily available sidings. It is not cheap. But it will last about as long as you do and is undeniably one of the handsomest woods.

CEDAR SIDING (SMOOTH OR SAW-TEXTURED)

Grade	*Description*
"Clear VG" (Clear Vertical Grain) Heart Bevel Siding	Intended where highest quality is demanded; exposed width all heartwood, free from imperfections; presents vertical grain appearance.
"A" Bevel Siding	Similar to "Clear" but includes mixed grain along with vertical grain. Permits minor growth characteristics.
"B" Bevel Siding	May be mixed grain (MG) and may contain cutouts in longer pieces. Well suited for painting.
Clear Finish	Available smooth and surfaced 4 sides (S4S), or saw-textured.
Vertical Siding	Mixed grain or vertical grain. V-joint or channel-groove patterns available. For board-and-batten siding, diagonal, trim, paneling, cabinetry.
"Clear Heart"	All heartwood. Takes natural, stain or enamel finishes.
Finish	For interior and exterior trim, cabinetry, paneling, ceilings.
"A" Finish	Similar to "Clear Heart" but includes minor manufacturing irregularities.

Beveled cedar

Beveled redwood

Here are some facts and pointers to refer to in selecting redwood siding.

Grades: The highest is "Clear All Heart," completely clear, permitting only the reddish-brown heartwood. "Clear" is similar but permits some of the lighter-colored sapwood, often specified for visual contrast of the two colors.

Grain: It is normally supplied with a mixture of flat and vertical grain boards unless you specify differently. If you wish all vertical grain (V.G.), so state to your dealer.

Moisture content: For siding, paneling, etc., ask for Certified Kiln Dried redwood.

Surface texture: You'll find redwood siding either smooth, or resawn to give a slightly textured surface. Specify the type you want. (Resawn redwood holds penetrating stains well and weathers nicely.)

Patterns: The basic redwood siding patterns are listed.

(1) Board and batten has wide boards (8 to 12 in.) applied in vertical courses with a half-inch space between. A 2- to 3-in. vertical batten is centered over this space. Variations include board-on-board, with a wider batten strip; reverse board-and-batten, with wide battens over narrower boards; and random width board and batten.

(2) Tongue-and-groove and shiplap V-joint may be applied vertically or horizontally.

(3) Bevel siding may be plain or rabbeted. The former produces a stronger shadow line; rabbeted provides a snugger lap, and lays up faster and with greater coverage.

(4) Channel rustic is a shiplap variation that gives a board-on-board or inverted board-and-batten effect. It is usually applied vertically.

(5) Tongue-and-groove square edge produces a flush joint and a flat wall surface.

Not all horizontal or board siding is solid wood. Hardboard, fiberboard and plywood are also sold in "boards" for bevel siding, 6 to 16 in. wide.

Paneled siding is predominantly plywood. But it is a far cry from the old fir plywood with the flamboyant grain pattern.

Plywood manufacturers have paid lumber manufacturers the sincerest kind of compliment and have perfected ways of making plywood look just like boards. The first such panel was "Texture One-Eleven," with deep grooves cut in the face of an un-

Board-and-batten

Vertical redwood boards

Reverse board-and-batten

Knotty red cedar (Courtesy Western Wood Products Association)

Textured plywood sidings are made in a wide variety of patterns and species. Most of these are also suitable for paneling.

Texture one-eleven (deep square-cut grooves)

Kerfed (rough-sawn surface with shallow square-cut grooves)

Board-and-batten

Plain rough-sawn

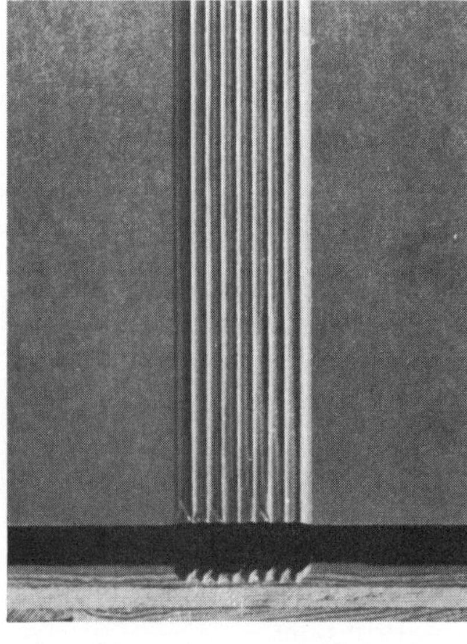

Medium density overlaid (plywood with a resin-fiber overlay), reverse board-and-batten pattern

MDO channel groove, with rough-sawn texture embossed in surface of overlay. (Courtesy American Plywood Association)

sanded panel. Presumably, the name refers to the pattern of vertical parallel lines, as in 111. It is still probably the most widely used plywood siding.

Manufacturers make many other variations of plywood siding by machining different surface textures and cutting grooves that are deep or shallow, square or kerfed (V-shaped), spaced from 2 to 16 in. apart. The wide-grooved pattern that resembles reverse board-and-batten is one of the most popular. The most often seen surface texture is rough-sawn, where the roughened surface is created by scoring the panel with a saw after manufacture.

Still another kind of plywood suitable for siding is medium density overlaid (MDO). During manufacture, a resin-fiber overlay is permanently bonded to the panel. It may be perfectly smooth, or have a rough-sawn texture embossed into the overlay, or have V-grooving.

These products are labeled "303 Sidings" on the American Plywood Association grade-trademark you will find on the panel, but most manufacturers have their own trade names and specialty products.

The advantage of the grooves and shiplap edges is that no special vertical joint treatment is needed since the pattern is uninterrupted at panel edges. But horizontal joints remain a problem in any wall more than 8 ft. high. Many designers deal with the problem by accentuating the joint rather than trying to conceal it. They may lap the upper panel of plywood over the lower, or use flashing along the joint, or various kinds of battens or trim boards. Or you may solve the problem by buying a longer panel; many plywood sidings come in a 9 or 10-ft. length, as well as the usual 8.

The advantage of a roughened surface on plywood siding is the freedom you have in selecting a finish—stain or paint.

Plywood sidings are available in a number of species, of which the most usual are fir, pine, cedar and redwood.

Manufactured panel siding

Up to now we have been concerned with wood products that are not altered significantly from when they were part of a tree. True, plywood is in one sense a remanufactured product in that the thin veneers, when assembled and glued become a panel with a whole new set of properties. But the wood is still recognizable as wood, and this is one of plywood's more appealing attributes.

This next group of wood-based building products exists with no resemblance at all to the tree. Made by reducing wood to small fractions, then putting it back together to make something else, these are manufactured in panel form and in some cases as boards also.

Hardboard is made of wood fibers or clumps of fibers, consolidated ("interfelted") under heat and pressure to form a dense, tough, highly compressed material. It has a smooth grainless surface. In strength and stiffness, the panel is the same in all directions; it compares favorably with natural wood's across-the-grain strength, but is not as stiff and strong as wood's along-the-grain strength. And, like natural wood, it tends to shrink and swell with changes in moisture content.

Hardboard is manufactured in panel or board form, the latter used for lap siding. It is made with a variety of surface treatments, including: smooth and preprimed, ready to paint; prefinished in various colors; with the texture of wood embossed into the surface; and prestained in wood colors. You may also find hardboard panel siding with a stucco-like finish, sometimes used for the half-timbered Tudor look. Panels come in patterns like channel-groove, V-groove, and reverse board-and-batten. Another variation is a strip of hardboard siding that looks like a course of shingles, sold in 16-ft. lengths. Finally, the familiar pegboard is perforated hardboard.

If you are thinking of using hardboard outside, be sure it is tempered—treated during manufacture with oils and resins to make it harder and more moisture-resistant. However, the treatment makes the board more brittle and less shock-resistant.

Lap hardboard siding widths range from 6 in. to 12 in.; lengths from 12 ft. to 16 ft. Panel sidings are generally available 4 ft. wide and in lengths of 7 ft., 8 ft., 9 ft. or 16 ft. They are made in thicknesses to 7/16 in. Hardboard for interior use is generally thinner (3/16 in. or ¼ in.).

Particleboard Also referred to as chipboard and flakeboard, this is a useful panel material for underlayment for finish flooring. But it is also occasionally used for siding and frequently as paneling, with veneer or plastic overlays.

This product is created from particles of wood rather than fibers: mostly wood residues such as planer shavings, plywood mill waste, slabs, edgings, trimmings, sawdust, and pulp-type chips. The particles are bonded with resin binders under heat and pressure to make a panel that is uniformly smooth, but in which the wood particles are visible. Particleboard has fair stability and warp resistance. It is not waterproof, though a highly moisture-resistant type is manufactured. When it is used outdoors

Many people make their own shakes, with traditional mallet and froe. Here, a Missouri woodlot owner splits oak boards. (Courtesy U.S. Forest Service)

Sometimes it takes two. In Georgia, chestnut that has been killed by blight is used by forest residents to make shingles. (Courtesy U.S. Forest Service)

Obviously not machine-made, these handsplit cedar shakes roof a garden storage shed. (Photo by author)

great care should be taken to protect it with proper painting. Be sure it is phenolic-bonded.

Other uses include cabinets, furniture, core stock for doors, counter tops, closet doors and stair treads (under carpeting).

Particleboard thicknesses correspond pretty much to those of plywood, from 3/16 in. to 1¼ in. Standard panel size is 4x8 ft., but most dealers will cut to size if you want smaller pieces.

Insulation board The manufacturing process is the same as for hardboard, but does not require heat and pressure and so is less dense. We may be stretching a point in calling it a wood product, since it is sometimes made with other types of cellulosic fibers besides wood. Like other insulating materials, it is effective through the entrapment of air in thousands of tiny pockets.

Insulation board may be asphalt-impregnated to make it resistant to moisture, and as such is a widely used sheathing material for walls and is also used as rigid insulation over a structural deck and under a built-up roof. It is lighter weight than other sheathings.

Besides sheathing, insulation board is used for interior walls, acoustic ceiling tile and interior partitions. There are a variety of textures and surfaces for these decorative uses.

SHINGLES AND SHAKES

There is almost a mystique about wood shingles and shakes, especially cleaving your own with froe and mallet. Now is a good time to introduce them, since they are used on walls as well as on roofs, and make a good transition from siding to roofing.

Shingles and shakes are similar in looks but are made differently. Each is simply a thin piece of wood, usually with parallel sides and thicker at one end than the other. Laid in overlapping rows or *courses* as roof or wall covering, they shed water as a bird's feathers do.

Shingles are sawn and shakes are hand-split with a froe (heavy-bladed axe-like tool) and mallet. Shingles have a relatively smooth surface, while shakes have at least one rough surface, due to the natural split of the wood along the grain.

Most shingles and shakes are Western red cedar and are made according to the standards of the Red Cedar Shingle and Handsplit Shake Bureau. In times gone by, oak and cypress and redwood were also widely used.

Cedar works well for several reasons. It is a good insulator because of its unique cellular construction—with millions of tiny air-filled cells per cubic inch. It needs no finishing. And a cedar shingle or shake roof, properly installed and maintained, lasts for decades.

With preservative treatment they last even longer. Some are now also given fire-retardant treatment.

When you buy these products, the terms listed here (used by the Red Cedar Shingle and Handsplit Shake Bureau) will help.

Certigrade Shingles

No. 1 Blue Label Premium grade for roofs and sidewalls; 100 percent heartwood, clear and edge-grain.

No. 2 Red Label Not less than 10 in. clear on 16-in. shingles, 11 in. clear on 18-in. shingles and 16 in. clear on 24-in. shingles. Flat grain and limited sapwood are permitted.

No. 3 Black Label Utility grade for economy application and secondary buildings. Not less than 6 in. clear on 16-in. and 18-in. shingles, 10 in. clear on 24-in. shingles.

No. 4 Undercoursing A utility grade for undercoursing on double-coursed sidewalls or for interior accent walls.

No. 1 or No. 2 Rebutted-rejointed Same as above for No. 1 and No. 2 grades but machine trimmed for exactly parallel edges with butts sawn at precise right angles. For sidewall applications where tightly fitting joints are desired. Also available with smooth sanded face.

Certigroove Grooved Red Cedar Sidewall Shakes

No. 1 Blue Label Machine-grooved shakes, manufactured from shingles and with striated faces and parallel edges. Used exclusively double-coursed on sidewalls.

Certi-split Red Cedar Handsplit Shakes

No. 1 Handsplit and Resawn These have split faces and sawn backs. Cedar logs are first cut into desired lengths. Blanks, or boards of proper thickness, are split and then run diagonally through a bandsaw to produce two tapered shakes from each blank.

No. 1 Tapersplit Produced largely by hand, using a sharp-bladed steel froe and a wooden mallet. Natural shingle-like taper is achieved by reversing the block, end-for-end, with each split.

No. 1 Straight-split Produced in same manner but since shakes are split from the same end of the block, they have the same thickness throughout.

Usage

Cedar shingles or shakes are most people's first choice for the roof of a new house. Unfortunately, as cedar becomes more scarce and the price goes up, many of us have to retreat from that first choice. But don't reject these handsome, durable roofing and siding products until you do a careful long-term cost study. They do last longer than most other roofs, and the true cost of a roof should be calculated on a cost-per-year basis.

In new construction, shingles and shakes may go over open or solid sheathing. Plywood (closed) sheathing works very well as a base.

In reroofing or residing, they may be applied over existing wood materials or even over asphalt shingles. The advantage of "over-roofing" is the extra insulation and storm protection of the double roof, and it saves the mess and bother of taking off the old roof.

Shingles and shakes are sold in bundles, four or five bundles per square, respectively. A square will cover 100 sq. ft. of roof area when applied at the standard recommended weather exposure.

If you are doing the job yourself you will benefit from how-to instructions (see suggested readings listed in the back of book). The actual application of shingles and shakes is fairly easy, but attention must be given to corners, valleys and flashings. Nails should be rust-resistant: zinc-coated or aluminum.

To really save labor in applying shingles or shakes, you may want to investigate presheathed panels: cedar shakes or shingles are glued to a plywood core, which has an undercourse of shingle backing. The three-ply, 8-ft.-long panel may be nailed directly to framing, or to plywood or fiberboard sheathing. A similar product, in 4-ft. panels and two-ply instead of three, is handy for small jobs or remodeling and should be installed over sheathing. These are available in several widths.

Either of these panelized shingle products may also be used for interior paneling—nailed directly to the existing wall covering in most cases.

What about the outlook for cedar shakes and shingles as the availability of cedar trees diminishes? This is a very slow-growing species (250 to 300 years to reach maturity). The industry, aware of the shrinkage of the resource and the likelihood that the public will continue to want products of this quality, is experimenting with other species that can fill the gap.

SHEATHING AND DECKING

Other than shingles and shakes, the major use of wood products in roof construction is as sheathing or decking. This is the material applied over the rafters as a nailing base or substrate for the finish roofing. And this is a very large use indeed. Most sheathing is plywood, which is fastest to put in place and also helps strengthen the structure. Just about any sort of finish roof can go over plywood—not only cedar shingles or shakes, but also asphalt shingles, asbestos shingles or (for flat roofs) built-up roofing.

Plywood for roof decking is usually CDX—Interior plywood with Exterior glue—which is suitable because the plywood will not be exposed to weather and appearance is not a factor.

FLOORS

Floor construction also takes a lot of wood. A floor may be built of plywood, boards, particleboard or a combination—depending on the system and your tastes.

The traditional floor was two layers: a subfloor of inch-thick boards laid over floor joists, then covered by hardwood flooring. Today the support framework is still usually wood joists (though some floors are laid over concrete). Joists are generally 2-in.-thick lumber of varying width depending on load, span, spacing and the lumber species and grade. But the material on top of the joists has changed.

With the proliferation of finish floor coverings other than wood, such as composition tile, vinyl tile,

Almost all roof sheathing nowadays is plywood, which is suitable for use under any kind of shingle or roofing material. (Courtesy American Plywood Association)

Traditional floor construction: strip flooring (this is tongue-and-groove West Coast hemlock) over board subfloor. (Courtesy Weyerhaeuser)

Plywood subflooring is widely used, partly because it takes much less time to install than individual boards. (Courtesy American Plywood Association)

Cuts in the plywood for pipes, ducts and wiring must be carefully planned. (Courtesy American Plywood Association)

linoleum, rubber, ceramic tile—and the uniquely American preoccupation with wall-to-wall carpet—the polished hardwood floor has lost its number one position.

However, it is still preferred by many. If this is your choice here are your options.

Your first choice is between hardwood and softwood, because the wood floor may be either. A few softwoods, such as pine and fir, have been and still are used for finish flooring. But for this purpose hardwood lives up to its name and is harder, more durable and takes a better finish. The early American classics are still much in demand: oak, maple, birch, beech.

Wood flooring may be in one of these forms:

(1) Long thin strips, either square-edged for butt jointing, or tongue-and-groove.

(2) Planks similar to strip flooring but wider, usually from 3 to 9 in. wide. They often imitate the old

flooring that was fastened with wooden pegs, and have holes drilled and filled at ends.

(3) Rectangular blocks; they may be simply squares, or as intricately arranged and shaped as parquetry, with its regular, repeating patterns.

The *subfloor*, whether it goes under finish wood flooring or resilient flooring, has to be strong and stiff. And if it is used without a top underlayment, it must also be very smooth. There are several ways to achieve all this.

One system involves a subfloor of 1-in. boards (for strength) with a layer of *underlayment* (for smoothness) on top. Boards may be square-edged shiplap or end-matched tongue-and-groove. The underlayment is usually plywood or particleboard.

A much simpler method of floor construction uses plywood according to the widely accepted single-layer floor system. The plywood must be thick enough and strong enough to serve as combined subfloor and underlayment. The first such two-purpose plywood was ingeniously named 2.4.1 by the industry: a 1-⅛-in.-thick plywood with a smooth face. Other combined subfloor-underlayment systems have been introduced since, using thinner plywood (¾-in. or ⅝-in.), under the umbrella name "Sturd-I-Floor." Should you find yourself constructing a floor, look on the gradestamp for the recommended spacing of floor joists when buying the plywood. It may be 16 in., 20 in., 24 in. or (for 2.4.1, the thickest plywood) 48 in. Though you pay a little more for the thicker plywood, you are not buying as much lumber for joists. And if you are contracting to have the work done you will certainly save on labor costs, since fewer pieces are handled. Also, of course, the smooth and unbroken underlayment surface, with fewer cracks and nails, means there will be no "telegraphing" through to your finish flooring, as so often happens with board underlayment.

Since this system requires plywood to be glued as well as nailed to the joists, it results in a very strong floor and one that rarely squeaks.

An example of coordinating interior decor with exterior—cedar shingles for siding and paneling. (Courtesy Red Cedar Shingle & Handsplit Shake Bureau)

V. Using Wood Inside and Out

INTERIOR WALLS

We have already mentioned the sidings that are also suitable for paneling interior walls: cedar shingles or shakes, textured plywood and regular siding boards (pine, fir, hemlock, cedar or redwood).

Shingles & Shakes

Shingles and shakes on interior walls are a rather new idea, but a logical one in view of the widespread taste for an informal, outdoorsy atmosphere throughout the home. In most cases it might be a bit overpowering to shingle all four walls of a room, but a shingled accent wall, partition or even a ceiling can be an interesting and attractive feature that adds warmth and cosiness. Many people use shingles or shakes to cover sauna walls. There is no special grade for interior use; just follow the same guidelines as for exteriors.

Siding Boards

When choosing wood siding boards for interior use, you will probably select square-edge, shiplap or tongue-and-groove boards; seldom bevel siding, because of the very strong pattern. If your decor is formal, consider clear, smooth boards that are suitable for painting. For a more informal or rustic look, investigate saw-textured boards, or those with natural wood characteristics—knots, checks.

Paneling

As for panel products for walls, the manufactured ones—hardboard and particleboard—are least expensive. They come in hundreds of variations suitable for interior use, including simulated wood-veneer finishes and many other patterns and textures with no resemblance to wood at all. Gingham checks, for instance, or veined marble.

However, the real thing, hardwood paneling, is still the ideal for many of us. Unfortunately, hardwood boards—the rich, lustrous oak, teak, mahogany and so on that paneled formal dining rooms, ducal libraries, board rooms and private clubs of the past—have been almost priced out of the market.

To satisfy this craving, the wood people came up with a satisfactory substitute: hardwood plywood paneling. You can find this paneling with face veneers of some dozen or so species, and a number of color variations of each. The panel may be ungrooved but is usually random-grooved to simulate planking. The better (and more expensive) panelings are surfaced with "mismatched" veneers from a half-dozen different logs, to enhance the effect of a series of individual planks.

If your time is valuable and you want to avoid the mess and bother of staining your own siding, you can buy it prestained—the job is done efficiently and to exact color specifications. (Courtesy of Olympic Stain)

Hardwood plywood, random-grooved to resemble board paneling, in Mediterranean oak. (Courtesy Weyerhaeuser)

A simple way to get paneled effect: milled lumber, surfaced four sides, is applied vertically to a plywood-paneled wall; horizontal members are added to butt against vertical members. The resulting squares are trimmed on the inside with a base cap molding, and the whole wall stained. (Courtesy Western Wood Moulding & Millwork Producers)

You may get an even more believable imitation of solid planks with panels that have been scored crosswise between grooves, resembling end-butted boards. And if you want to go the rest of the way, ask for paneling with all these features, plus deeply embossed simulated square nailheads at each corner of the "plank."

Typical American woods used for hardwood plywood are birch, cherry, elm, hickory, maple, oak and walnut. Premium-quality paneling is also made in imported woods like limba, African mahogany, Honduras mahogany and bubinga.

Some hardwood plywood panels are wire-brushed to emphasize the grain and add dimensional interest.

Be sure to get your properly color-matched nails, putty sticks and moldings at the same time you buy paneling.

Finally, you can also find hardwood paneling that is made with woodgrained paper overlays or decorative patterns printed on the surface.

Softwood plywood is also frequently used for paneling, though its more familiar application is as siding. Any of the textured plywoods are appropriate. Standard sizes are 4x8, 4x9, and 4x10; thickness, 5/16 in. or thicker. These panelings may be painted or stained, but staining is more satisfactory. Or the natural wood color may be left as is. (See "Finishing", in Chapter 7.)

One feature of grooved textured plywood that you will probably appreciate is its ease of application: You may nail it to the stud or furring strip and the nail will hardly show. This is also true when nailing through the groove of hardwood paneling; although grooves are random-spaced, they occur at least every 16 in. so that you can match the groove to the stud.

Both hardwood and softwood plywood may be applied with adhesives over sheathing or, if you are remodeling, over the old wall, providing it is in good shape.

Though wood paneling costs more than the coated hardboard, it will have more impact-resistance and, when properly installed, contribute to the wall's rigidity. It also gives you the satisfaction of knowing you have the real thing. Regarding maintenance, there is not much difference between real wood and imitation. Most hardwood plywood is given a tough, durable synthetic coating, and is about as easy to wipe clean as the plastic or vinyl overlays on other panel types.

All of the above products are as appropriate for paneling a partition as for the basic wall. But if the partition is to bear a load or incorporate storage you will need to choose materials and methods with sufficient structural strength, just as you would do for the wall of the house. And if it is a storage wall, be sure to use shelving strong enough to bear the load of books, TV, stereo components, etc.

MATERIALS FOR BUILT-INS AND STORAGE

Just about any conceivable form of wood, from driftwood to hollowcore doors, can be and is used by the home craftsman. But lumber and plywood are certainly the most standardized, convenient and readily available.

For all those useful home-workshop projects you can send for plans* and if you follow instructions you will get good, dependable recommendations on materials. But a few generalizations may not be amiss.

For cabinetry and interior work you will want finished, kiln dried lumber. Your particular needs and preferences and budget will determine whether you buy select (clear) with no knots or defects, or a less expensive grade. Remember that tight knots and minor defects can usually be filled or concealed by the finish, unless the finish is to be transparent.

In buying lumber, especially hardwood, tell your supplier what you have in mind and he will advise you as to what to buy and how much (based, of course on what he has in stock). Hardwood lumber grades are complex and there is no real need for you to memorize them.

Softwood plywood is a good all-round material for built-ins, storage units and home-improvement jobs. In deciding what kind to buy, refer to the grade-use chart in Chapter 3. For construction that will be highly visible and that requires a perfect, natural finish, look for "N" grade. However, an "A" grade should be adequate for most applications. If you plan to paint the plywood you may select panels with B or C faces. Do not try to use "D" except where it will not show.

Often you will not need to buy a full 4x8 sheet of plywood. In such cases, look at the rack of "Handy Panels" stocked by most dealers. Odd-sized, less-than-full-panel pieces of plywood are available, a natural byproduct of the dealer's willingness to cut to size.

Unless your project is to go outside, or in a bath or laundry where moisture will be excessive, you can

*Or check other *successful* books for particular projects with materials lists.

Formal rectangular arrangement of moldings gives pattern to a wall paneled with rough-sawn cedar plywood. (Courtesy Western Wood Moulding & Millwork Producers)

The Oriental look: Half-round moldings, painted brilliant Chinese red, on walls of clear yellow, with motif repeated on the chest-table. (Courtesy Western Wood Moulding & Millwork Producers)

save money by buying Interior-type plywood rather than Exterior.

You will also need to choose among the various species of face veneer (fir, cedar, redwood, etc.), as well as surface treatments. If you are building shelves, you can make the job easier by using Texture 1-11 plywood for the sides, with grooves running horizontally.

This saves the trouble of installing shelf supports or brackets, or cutting dadoes. Shelves are supported by the grooves and are easy to slide in and out, so they are perfectly adjustable to any height.

You may have some difficulty locating hardwood plywood, if you've set your heart on a certain kind. The hardwood plywood sold for paneling (3/8 in.) may not be as thick as you want for your particular project. But for fine-furniture-quality projects it is worth a search.

The wood-based panel products, hardboard and particleboard, also offer desirable characteristics and should be considered for projects.

Hardboard is useful for sliding doors, drawer bottoms and backs of storage units. Perforated hardboard (pegboard) is deservedly popular as a wall covering for workshops, sewing rooms, pantries, kitchens, or wherever you want to hang things. There is wide variety in the hooks and small shelf supports designed to be used with pegboard.

Use of particleboard may involve two drawbacks: It does not take screws and nails as well as real wood, and it is comparatively heavy. But it is smooth and reasonably priced. It is often sawed into boards and then used as shelving.

What you may decide to build for your home depends so much on your particular tastes, needs and abilities that we can give only general material recommendations. But you will be able to locate exactly what you need, including precise instructions and materials lists for hundreds of useful and decorative projects, from many of the wood associations listed in the appendix.

ACCENTS

Moldings

"Mouldings," as the British call them, have practical and decorative justification. They are simply the milled strips of wood that run around doors and windows, along the line where wall meets floor or where wall meets ceiling. The molding is an ingenious answer to the desire (or need) to cover up joints, with their possible gaps and imperfections.

Vertical grain emphasizes high ceiling and dramatic architecture. (Courtesy California Redwood Assn.; Architect Davidson/Hughes/Franke.) ▶

To vary the pattern, use narrow-width siding on the bias. (Courtesy Olympic Stain)

When properly applied, exterior wood stains can enhance and preserve the wood's original character. (Courtesy Olympic Stain)

In restoration of historic homes, new finishes help preserve the traditional charm of wood siding. An exterior acrylic latex finish completely covered the old paint on this 100-year-old siding. Such finishes can be expected to protect the wood for many more years, because of good adherance and high permeability, which permits moisture to escape. (Courtesy Olympic Stain)

Compatible mantel, bookshelves, paneling show off various textures and shades of wood. (Jamestown Hickory; Courtesy of Weyerhaeuser)

Moldings are easy to apply; they add pattern and elegance to a wall. (Courtesy Weyerhaeuser)

Hardwood Plywood that resembles fine board paneling makes a rich background for a collection of antiques.

Use shakes inside for a pleasant informality.

If you are Henry Moore, sculpt a museum piece; this is Moore's "Bird Basket".

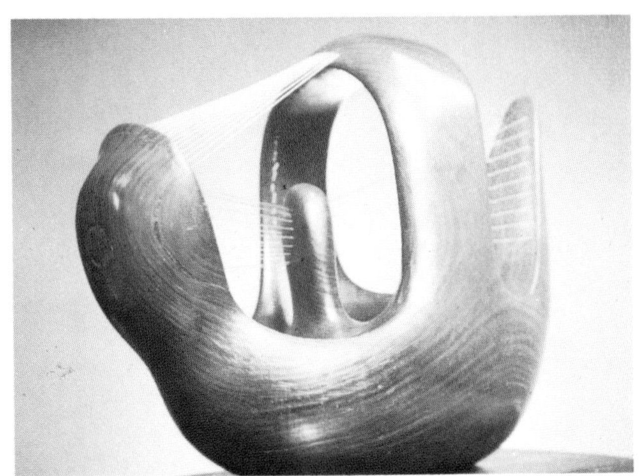

The Colonial Salt Box had a long rakish roofline which evolved from lean-to additions at the rear of early houses. Siding is 6-in. wide Western Red Cedar, narrower than most present-day sidings. (Courtesy Western Red Cedar Lumber Assn.)

Cedar shakes in even courses do a lot for this otherwise plain area.

This handcrafted wood inlay by Stephen Blood used a half-dozen imported and domestic hardwoods, including Benin, pear, figured gum and (for the teeth) holly. (Courtesy John Tessier)

Redwood deck

Reroof your house—install red cedar shakes over the old roof.

Pretreated rustic fencing. Note round tops of posts to prevent seepage into cracks.

Fabricate your own little sailboat. Plans are available from the American Plywood Assn. (Courtesy Family Circle)

Cutting and Fitting Moldings

Basic steps in working with moldings require a little practice before going to the specific job. Try out your techniques on scrap pieces before working on moldings you plan to use. You will want to cover these bases.

Materials. These include many already in your tool kit. They are white woodworking glue, finishing nails, a carpenter's rule, coping saw, fine sandpaper, and a miter box and saw. In addition, you will want to construct a jig with the instructions given below.

Mitering and joining. This is the first step in basic molding carpentry. Set the miter box saw at 45-degrees. Trim the ends of the two moldings to be joined at opposite 45-degree angles. When joined, the two pieces form a tight, right angle of 90-degrees. To make corners that are less than 90-degrees, adjust your miter cuts to an angle wider than 45-degrees. For angles wider than 90-degrees (such as those needed for a hexagon), adjust and miter edges to a narrower-than-45-degree angle.

Coping. Using this shaping method when you want to have one molding butt up to the face of another molding, instead of being mitered with it. This is often used with cove molding. Coping is also a good method for joining cross-members of a complicated molding panel design, while the corners of the outer edge molding might best be mitered.

You want to transfer the profile of one molding piece to the end of the piece that will but up to it for a smooth, tight fit. Here are the steps to follow in cutting a right-side coped molding to fit the profile of a left-side butted molding in a corner. (If you want to have the right side butted into the corner and cope the left side molding, reverse these steps.)

Few home settings offer the year-round beauty enjoyed by the residents of this home looking across Puget Sound to Vashon Island and the Kitsap Peninsula beyond. Architect Ralph Anderson selected redwood for the total exterior. (Courtesy California Redwood Assn.)

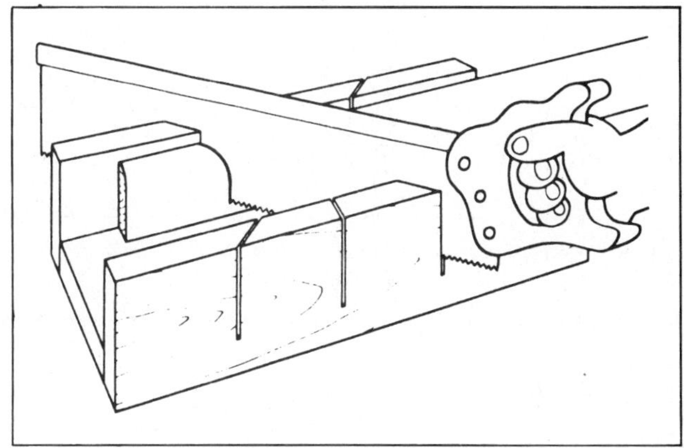

To miter a molding, start by cutting both ends on 45 degree angles in opposite directions

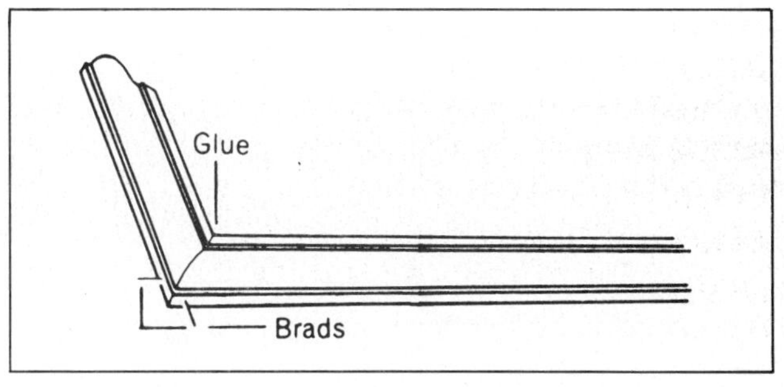

Glue the raw ends of both pieces together and secure the corner with brads

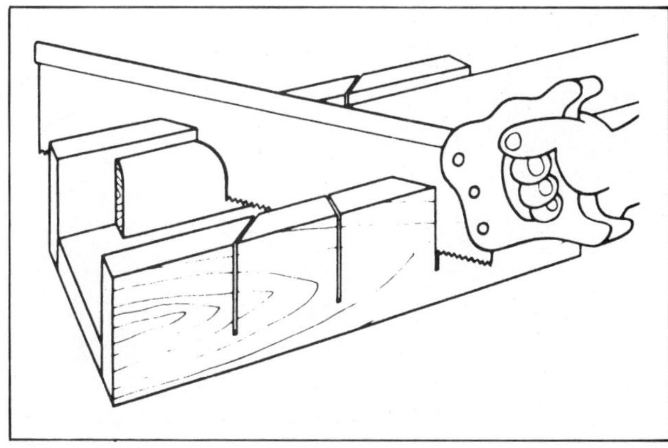

To cope a molding, make a 45 degree cut, angled so that a slanted raw edge shows from the front

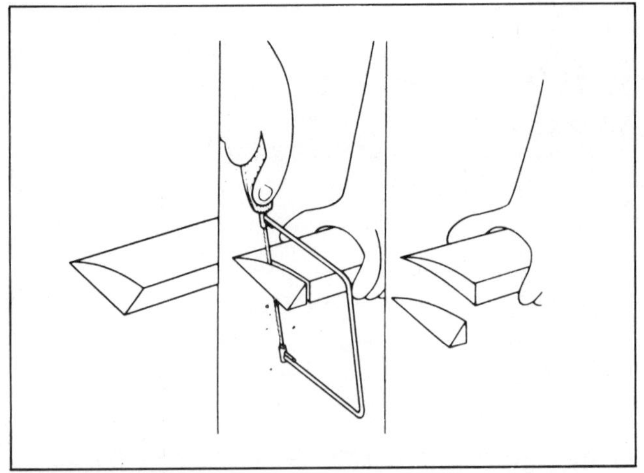

Cut straight back across the molding so that all of the slanted, raw wood is removed

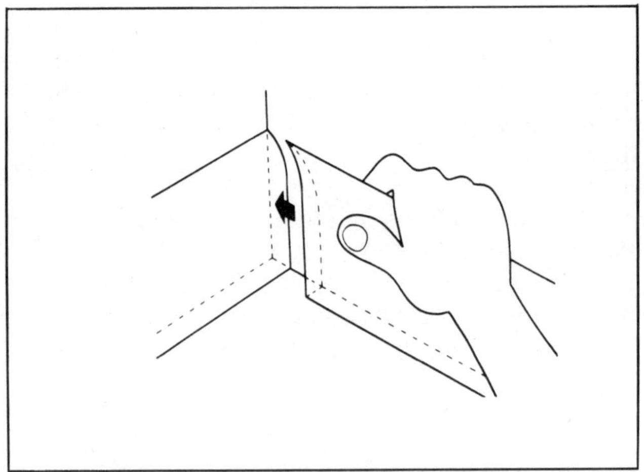

Remaining trimmed molding end will fit snugly to matching molding

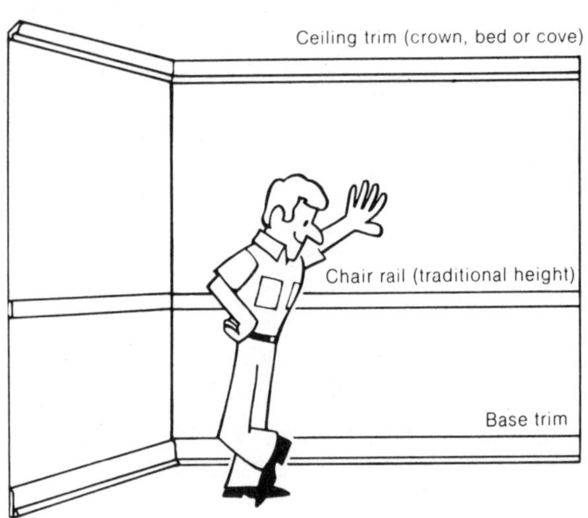

Wood Moldings Add A New Look

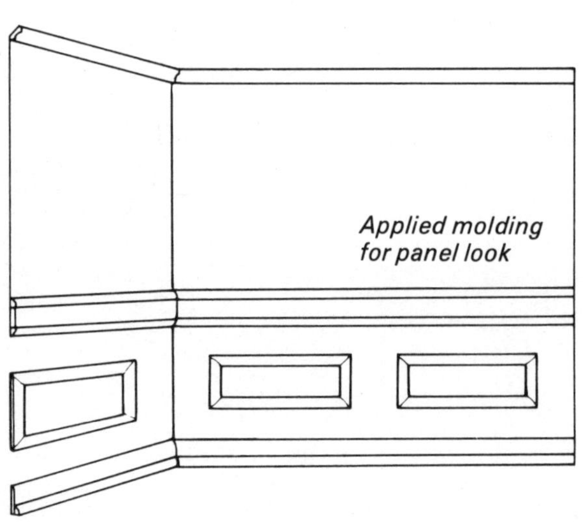

When applied to paneling, furniture, cabinetry, ceilings and doors, they are also a subtle way to give pattern and dimension to these flat surfaces.

The inspiration is said to go back to the Greeks, who adorned their marble columns with marble moldings. The wood molding reached its highest flowering in the 18th century and in Colonial America. Since Colonial architecture and furniture are still so popular, moldings live on.

The most common wood species used is Ponderosa pine, followed by Douglas fir and white fir. Some lauan appears but relatively little other hardwood now finds its way into the moldings market.

When buying, you will find that your lumber dealer has lengths from 3 to 16 ft. Always measure what you need and round off to the next highest foot, rather than risk coming out short. If you plan mitered joints, add the width of the molding to the length of each piece to be mitered. For example: if your molding is 3 in. wide and you will have two miters, add 6 in. and then round off to the next highest foot.

Moldings are really quite easy and rewarding to work with. The Western Wood Moulding and Millwork Producers will be glad to provide information and instructions, even how to make picture frames.

Only a few of the more common of the hundreds of types are shown here.

For window interiors, you may use stool molding, mullion (middle) casing, side and head casing and apron. The same casing may be used for head and side and apron.

Baseboard molding covers the joint between floor and wall, and a shoe molding may be added to cover the joint between baseboard and floor. The shoe is not always necessary but does make floor cleaning easier.

The chair rail saves wear and tear on the wall.

The crown covers and decorates the joint of wall and ceiling.

Quarter-rounds and half-rounds are often used in cabinet and shelf installation.

The chair rail is one of the commonest moldings, with practical justification: it saves wear-and-tear on the wall. Note also, in this reproduction of a Williamsburg room, the typical heavy base and crown moldings. (Courtesy Western Wood Moulding & Millwork Producers)

Use Moldings for Variety

Following are the primary types of stock wood moldings found in the WP/Series Molding Patterns catalog. Each is defined for basic use. Numbers following the definitions indicate special idea applications which are keyed at the beginning of this section.

Decorative Use Key:
1. Picture Framing
2. Unfinished furniture embellishment
3. Toys
4. Games
5. Cabinet face trim
6. Flush door face trim
7. Decorative wall molding
8. Decorative ceiling trim, such as surrounds for light fixtures
9. Wall applied bed headboards
10. Grids for recessed lighting
11. Garden storage sheds
12. Garage door embellishment
13. Garden Gazebos
14. Trellis work
15. Plate Rail
16. Fireplace trim and decoration
17. Room divider Screen
18. Miscellaneous small projects such as rosettes, medallions and display pedestals
19. Chair rail

Back Band: A rabbetted molding used to surround the outside edge of casing. (Decorative use key: 1,2,3,4,9,16.)

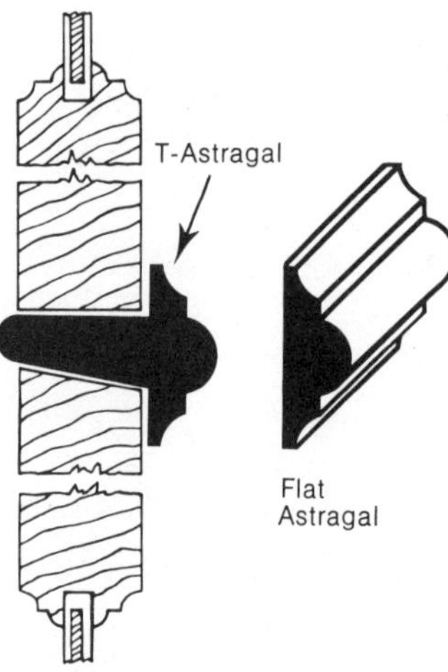

Astragal: This molding includes two different types, a T-Astragal and a Flat Astragal. The "T" is attached to one of a pair of doors to keep one door from swinging through the opening. The flat astragal, which in classic Greek architecture was a bead around a column below the cap, is used for decorative purposes. (Decorative use key: 2,3,4,5,6,7,8,9,16,17,18.)

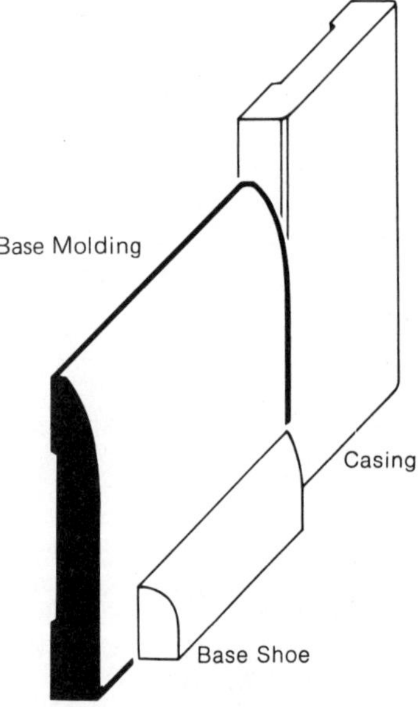

Base: Applied where floor and walls meet, forming a visual foundation. Protects walls from kicks and bumps, furniture and cleaning tools. Base may be referred to as one, two or three member. The **base shoe** and **base cap** are used to conceal uneven floor and wall junctions. (Decorative use key: 1,2,3,4.)

Base Cap: A decorative member installed flush against the wall and the top of an S-4-S baseboard. Also a versatile panel molding. (Decorative use key: 1,2,3,4,5,6, 7,8,9,12,16,17,18.)

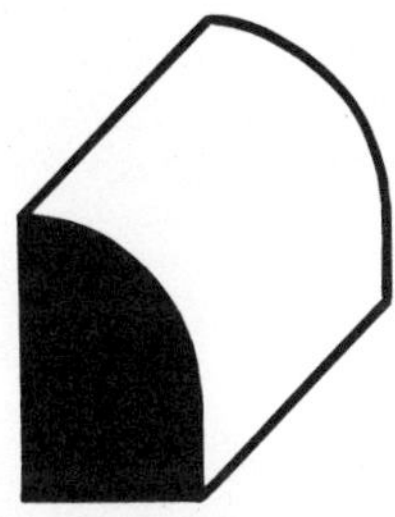

Base Shoe: Applied where base molding meets the floor. Protects base molding from damage by cleaning tools. Conceals any uneven lines or cracks where base meets the floor. (Decorative use key: 1,3,4.)

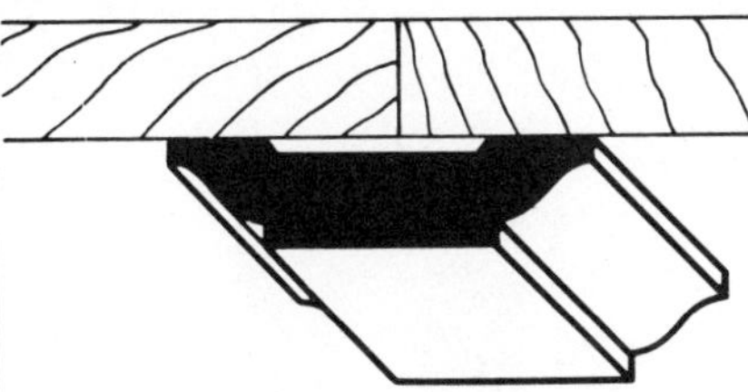

Batten: A symmetrical pattern used to conceal the line where two parallel boards or panels meet. (Decorative use key: 2,3,4,5, 6,7,8,9,12,16,18,19.)

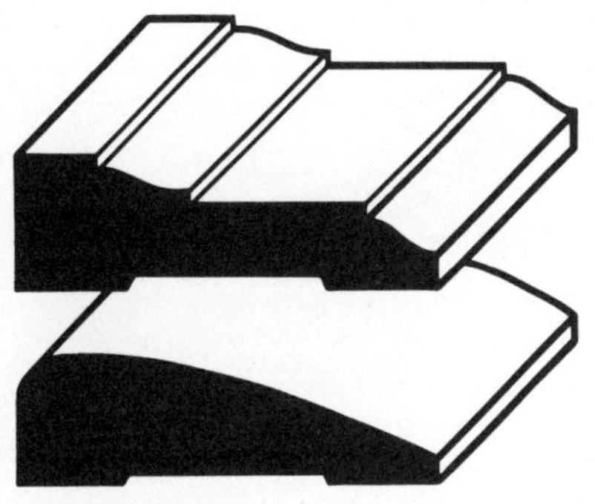

Casing: Used to trim inside and outside door and window openings. (Decorative use key: 1,2,3,4,5,6,7,8,9,11,12,13,16, 18,19.)

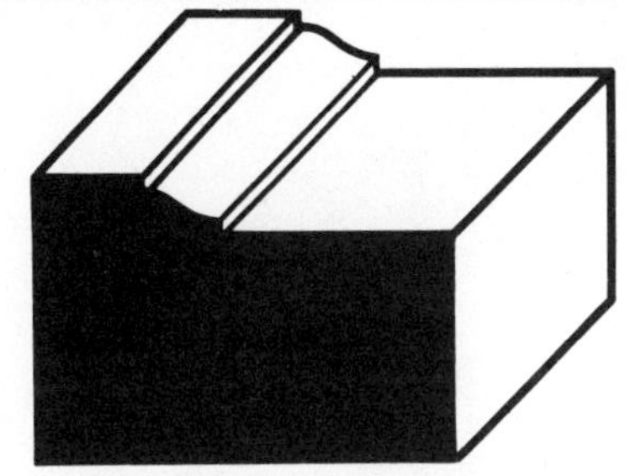

Brick molding is used as exterior door and window casing. It is a thick molding, providing a surface for brick or other siding to butt against. (Decorative use key: 1,2,3,4,5,6,7,8,9,11,12,13,16, 18,19.)

Chair Rail: An interior molding usually applied about one third the distance from the floor, paralleling the base molding and encircling the perimeter of a room. Originally used to prevent chairs from marring walls. Use today is as a decorative element or a divider between different wall covering such as wallpaper and paint or wainscoting. A key decorative detail in traditional and Colonial design. (Decorative use key: 1,2,3, 4,5,6,7,8,9,12,16,18,19.)

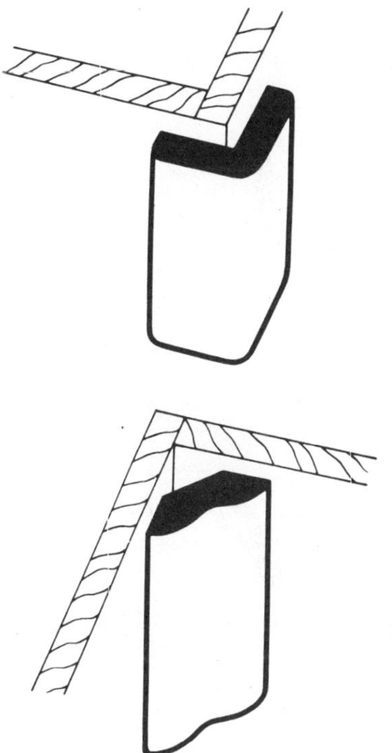

Corner Guard: Outside (OS) corner guard is used to protect corners or to cover the ragged edge where wallcovering and painted surfaces meet at an outside corner. Inside (IS) corner guard covers uneven joints or ragged lines where wallpaper, paneling or other covering materials meet with painted or contrasting surfaced walls at an inside corner. (Decorative use key: 1,3,4,18.)

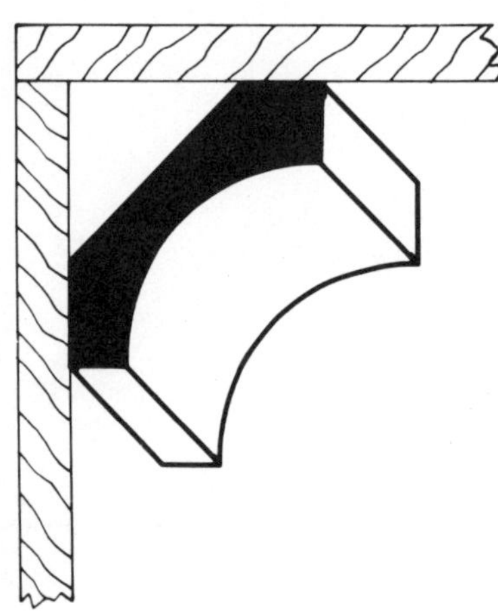

Cove: A molding with a concave profile used at corners, particularly as a ceiling cornice. Small coves may be used as inside corner guard. (Decorative use key: 1,2,3,4,5,6,9,10,11,15,16,18.)

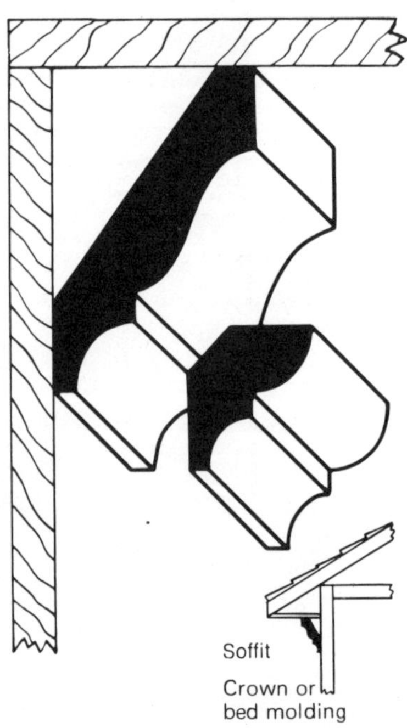

Crowns/Beds: Most often used where walls and ceiling meet. Crown moldings are used to cover larger angles. Crowns are always "sprung" while beds are either "sprung" or plain. A "sprung" molding has the interior corner beveled off to better fit a right angle joint. (Decorative use key: 1,2,3,4,15,16.)

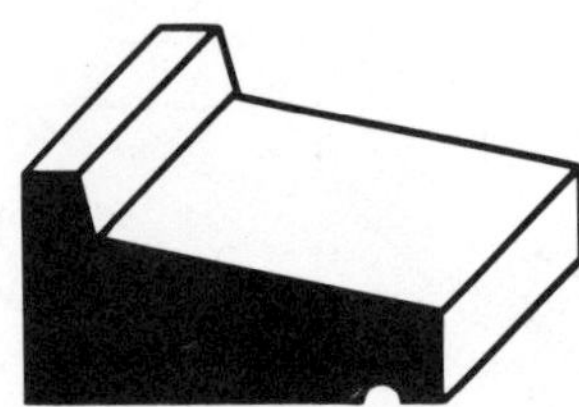

Drip Cap: Applied over exterior window and door frames, this molding keeps water from seeping under the siding, also directs away from window glass. Makes an attractive contemporary interior door and window casing. (Decorative use key: 1,3,4,9, 18,19.)

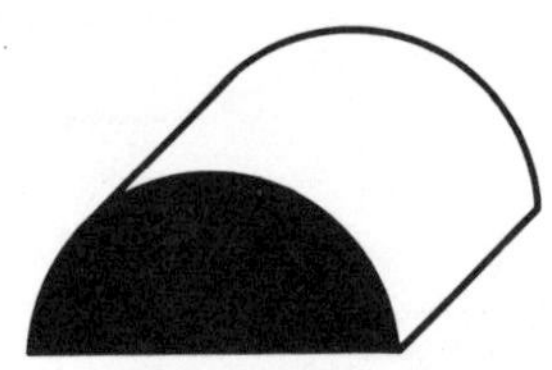

Half Round: A molding whose profile is half a circle. May be used as a screen molding or bead, shelf edge or panel mold. (Decorative use key: 2,3,4,5,6,9, 11,12,13,18.)

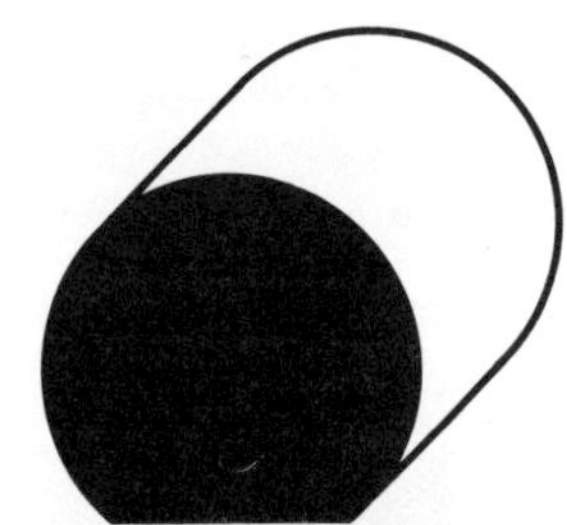

Hand Rail: Used as a hand support in a stairwell.

Glass Bead: Also called glass stop, cove and bead, putty bead, glazing bead and staff bead. Used to hold glass in place. (Decorative use key: 1,2,3,4,18.)

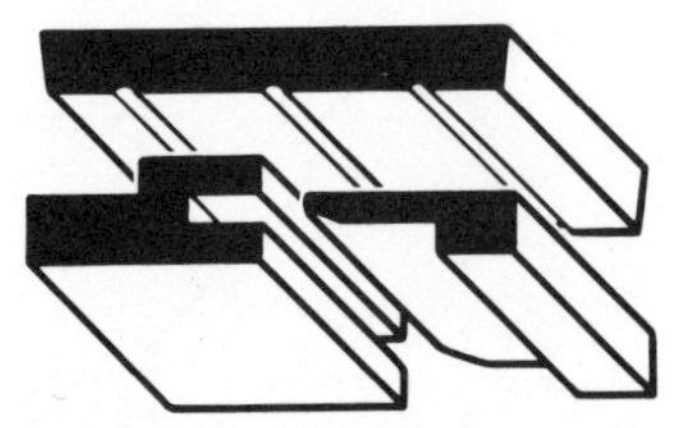

Jamb: The top (header) and two sides (legs) of a door or window frame which contacts the door or sash. Flat jambs are of fixed width while split jambs are adjustable.

One-piece flat jamb.

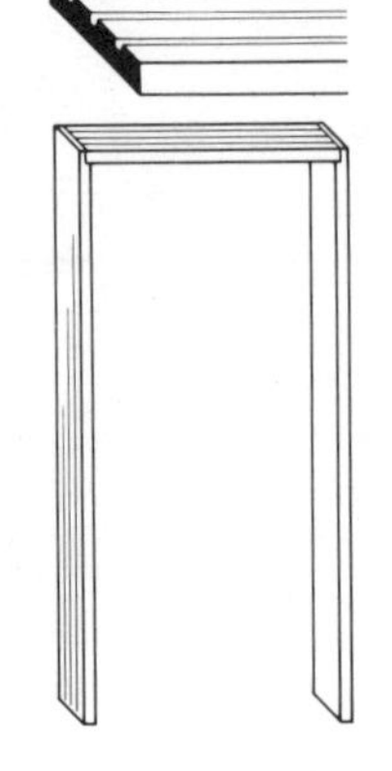

Two-piece adjustable or split jamb.

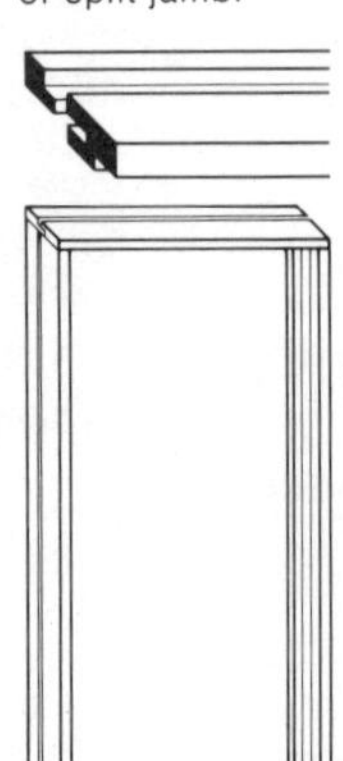

Lattice: Originally used in trellis work, this small, plain, S-4-S molding is among the most versatile of profiles. (Decorative use key: 1,3,4,7,9,10,11,13,14,17,18.)

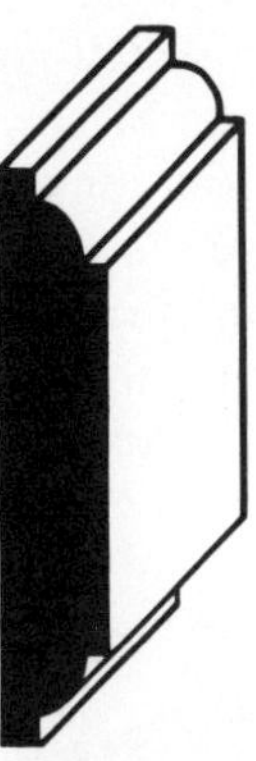

Mullion Casing: The strip which is applied over the window jambs in a multiple opening window. Sometimes called a panel strip, used for decorative wall treatments. (Decorative use key: 1,2,3,4,5,6,7, 8,9,18,19.)

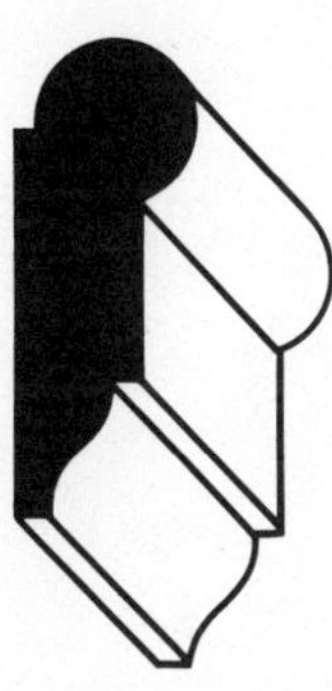

Picture Mold: Used.to support hooks for picture hanging. Applied around a room's circumference near the ceiling line. (Decorative use key: 1,2,3,4,5,6,7,8,9,16,18,19.)

Quarter Round: Versatile quarter round may be used as a base shoe, inside corner moulding or to cover any 90° recessed junctures. Often used to cover the line where roof and siding meet on exteriors. (Decorative use key: 1,3,4,18.)

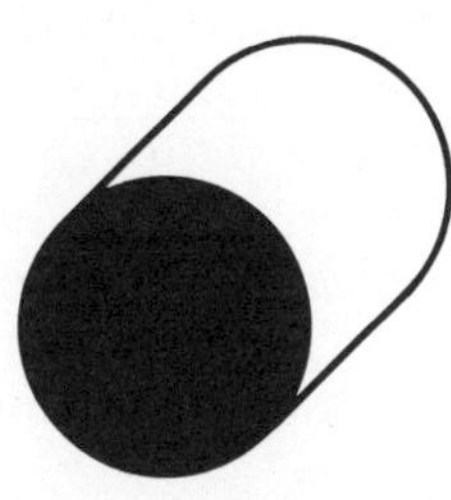

Round: A 360-degree round molding, most often used as a closet pole. (Decorative use key: 3,4,18.)

Screen Mold: A small molding which covers the seam where screening is fastened to the screen frame. Also used as a shelf edge. (Decorative use key: 1,2,3,4,18.)

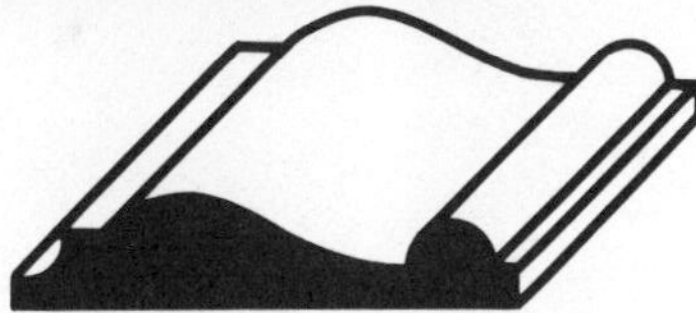

Panel Mold: A panel molding is a decorative pattern, originally used to trim out raised panel wall construction. It is most useful fabricated as a frame, surrounding attractive wall covering for a paneled effect on walls.
Shingle Molding may be used in similar ways but originally was used on the rake of a building or around exterior window frames. (Decorative use key: 1,2,3,4,5,6,7, 8,9,16,18,19.)

Stool: A molded interior trim member serving as a sash or window frame sill cap. (Decorative use key: 3.)

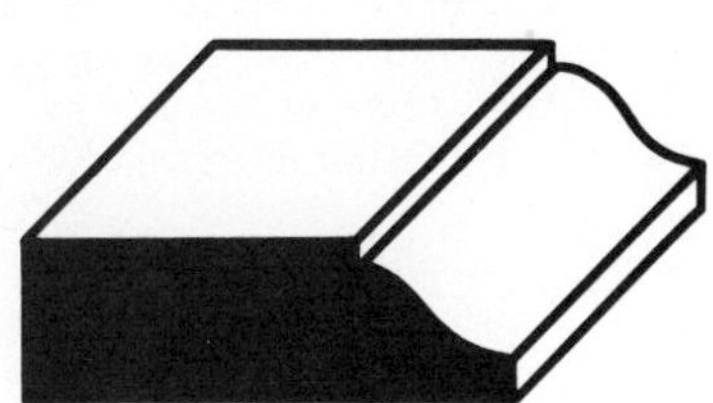

Stop: In door trim, stop is nailed to the faces of the door frame to prevent the door from swinging through. As window trim, stop holds the bottom sash of a double-hung window in place. (Decorative use key: 1,2,3,4,5,6,7,8,9,10,11, 12,13,14,16,17,18.)

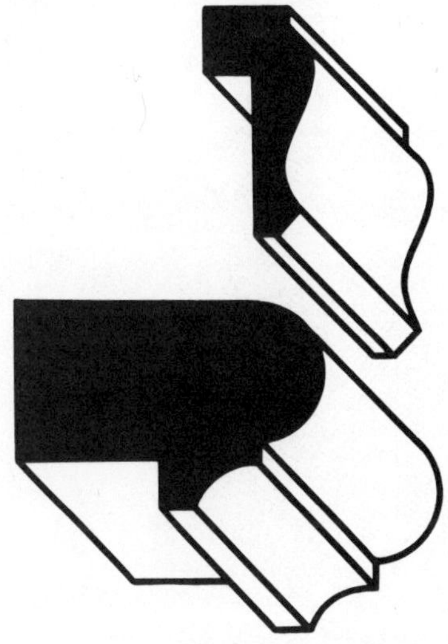

Plycap: Covers and beautifies plywood's rough sandwich edge in installations where it is exposed to view.
Wainscot Cap: Sometimes called a dado cap, this trims out the upper edge or top of a wainscot. Also called a wainscot molding. (Decorative use key: 1,3,4,5,9,16.)

Doors

It is unlikely you will build your own, though you may paint or stain them. The same procedures for interior or exterior finishing of other wood products apply.

When selecting a door, do not settle for the first one that comes along. Your front door, especially, represents you and your personality to every one who approaches your home. With such a wide choice of woods and patterns, take time to look around.

Both hardwoods (such as birch, oak, walnut, lauan) and softwoods (fir, hemlock, Sitka spruce, pine) are used for doors. They may be of solid plank construction, or solid core (perhaps with particleboard core), or hollow core. Some have special core construction to provide sound or fire resistance.

Juxtaposition of verticals, horizontals and diagonals in this entry is given focus and stability by the darker, eye-catching door. (Courtesy Western Wood Products Association)

To a rather ordinary door you may add the stamp of individuality with a carved initial framed with wood moldings. (Courtesy Western Wood Moulding & Millwork Producers)

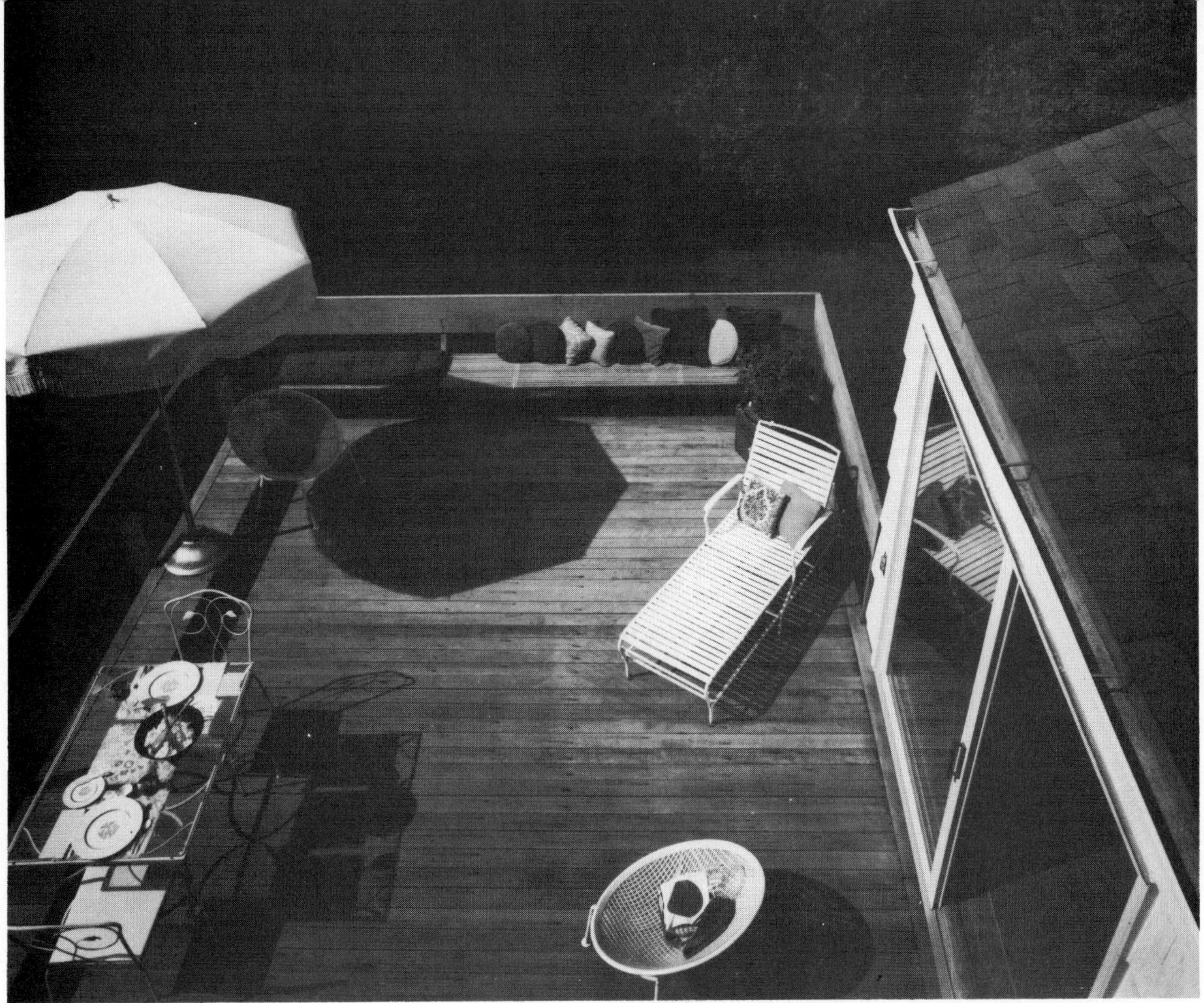

Redwood lumber, versatile and durable, is used for benches, decking, and rail of this Connecticut outdoor room. (Courtesy California Redwood Association)

OUTDOOR USE

Laminated Decking

This useful product gives homeowners a flooring board that can span 7 ft. or more between supports. It is also widely used in schools, churches and commercial construction.

The decking consists of three pieces of kiln-dried lumber glued together in a staggered arrangement so the finished piece of lumber has a tongue-and-groove shape.

It is made in nominal widths of 6 in. and 8 in.; thicknesses from 2¼ in. to 4½ in.; in lengths ranging from 8 ft. to 20 ft.; and in several softwood species (Ponderosa pine, hemlock, fir).

Before using laminated decking for long spans, be sure to check with your lumber dealer, or study information from the manufacturer as to what loads it can be expected to bear.

Laminated Beams

Made of individual pieces of lumber, glued with grain parallel, these beams may be straight or curved.They are not commonly seen in home building, though they are sometimes for barns. However, most of us have been impressed by soaring glued-laminated arches supporting roofs of churches, gymnasiums, and other large buildings. Curved "glulams," as they are often called, can span more than 300 ft. Straight beams are used as posts and horizontal timbers; they may be as deep as 7 ft. and may span more than 100 ft.

Fences and Posts

Fence-building offers a wide-open opportunity for those with imagination and energy and patience. But it will help to know something about a few of the choices you have in methods and materials.

Five variations on the post-and-rail:

(A) Two-rail, with hexagonal rails (Courtesy Weyerhaeuser);
(B) Two-rail, with conventional round rails (Courtesy Weyerhaeuser);
(C) A chestnut post-and-rail fence built before the blight wiped out the chestnuts. Note mortise-and-tenon joints and tapered ends of rails (Courtesy U.S. Forest Service);
(D) A corral fence in Montana of lodgepole pine. Fencing was one of the earliest uses of this fine straight tree (Courtesy U.S. Forest Service);
(E) Ingenious double-post fence requires very little fastening (Courtesy U.S. Forest Service).

A

Wood fences, by far the most popular type, may be categorized as post-and-rail, and all other types. The variations are numberless.

Post-and-rail Earliest fences of the pioneers were made from the trees cut down to clear farmland. They used the trunks of small trees as is, or if they were larger, split them into rails. Because there was plenty of raw material, they could be extravagant in its use. And since they had plenty of other demands on their time, they devised labor-saving fence designs that required no fastening.

One such was the post-and-rail fence with the rail resting on the crotch of two crossed posts. Another did not even need posts: the common zigzag-patterned "boundary fence." Rails were stacked so the end of one lay atop the end of the adjoining one.

You may still build fences like these. But, as our 19th-century predecessors did when timber began to get scarcer and lumber more plentiful, you may turn to different forms of wood. You will probably secure rail to post, even if only by fitting the rail into a groove cut in the post.

If you are buying posts you may look for round or square or, just to be different, hexagonal ones. The latter are often used for stockade fencing because they are easier for fastening necessary hardware.

B

Posts with round or pointed tops are likely to last longer than flat-topped ones because water tends to run off, rather than run down cracks in the post and freeze, causing splits.

For the rails, you may use dimension lumber or boards; or round or hexagonal rails sold especially for fencing; or, if you are lucky enough to find them, split rails or railroad ties.

Other types of fences are, in general, variations on the post-and-rail theme. To rails, or stringers, between posts you attach various kinds of "siding"—pickets, boards, grapestakes, louvers, slats, lath or plywood.

Picket fences Also associated with American development, these are still very prevalent. The word picket comes from the French, meaning pike or pointed stake. In this respect it recalls the days when such a fence really repelled invaders or discouraged enemies, as did the early settlers' stockades. Today it is simply a friendly way to mark a property line or boundary.

Pickets (typically 1x3 boards) need not even have pointed tops. Traditionalists still search for some of the intricately shaped pickets that used to be stocked by lumber dealers. But you may have to end by making your own if you want an out-of-the-ordinary

E

C

D

The "zigzag" fence is popular everywhere; New Englanders call it a "lazy man's fence." (Photo by the author)

picket shape. In any case, be sure you paint your picket fence white, if you wish to carry on the Colonial tradition.

Boards Board wood used for fencing need not be top-quality, kiln-dried lumber, unless it will bear loads or span long distances without support or bracing. Boards may be applied horizontally or vertically; some people like them on the bias. The fence may be quite open in its pattern, suggesting privacy, or have solid boards that protect from sun and wind as well as inquisitive passersby.

Grapestakes The split stakes that support grapevines in vineyards make fine fencing and can be used many ways. They are especially good for rustic, informal fences because of the rough splintery edges; if they are redwood (as most are) they will weather to a soft natural gray. The stakes are about 2 in. square, and you may find them 3 to 6 ft. in length.

Plywood You can save a lot of time in fence building using any plywood siding, such as roughsawn, Texture 1-11, and the various grooved patterns. Buy it preprimed or prestained or natural. If you wish an opaque, decorative fence or screen, you might use overlaid plywood and paint the panels in bright or muted colors, then frame with narrow dimension lumber and attach them to stringers between posts.

Finishing fences requires more than the ordinary painting or staining you give to other outdoor wood structures. Paint and stain will be beneficial in preserving the wood, but fence posts, and any part of the fence that touches or will be within a foot of the ground, must be preservative-treated to protect from decay and termites. Only redwood and cedar, naturally resistant to decay, may not need this treatment.

Though you can do the treating yourself (see the pointers on pages 126 and 127), the American Wood Preservers Institute warns that there may be potential harm to the user with certain formulas. To play safe, buy posts which are already pressure-preservative treated, and which the manufacturers say are protected against decay for 25 to 30 years.

Poles and piling It takes tens of millions of wood poles to support the power and communications lines that keep this country in business. Though metal or concrete poles are becoming more common, and though much wiring nowadays is going underground, the wood poles still march across the plains and along the highways, tying the country together.

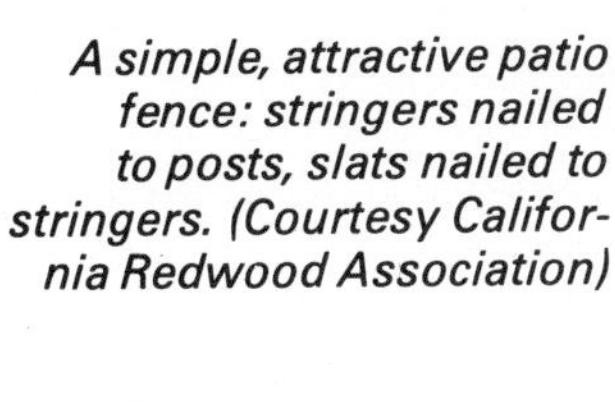

A simple, attractive patio fence: stringers nailed to posts, slats nailed to stringers. (Courtesy California Redwood Association)

There are more ways to build a fence than you can shake a stick at. Here's one way they do it out west—a juniper-post fence in Utah. (Courtesy U.S. Forest Service)

Of more interest to the ordinary citizen, who takes phone and power poles pretty much for granted, is the use of poles for supports for farm buildings and homes—especially hillside homes. The same qualities that suit the wood pole so well to its utility-line job make it a good building support too: it is widely available, comparatively low-cost, able to support heavy loads, and when preservative-treated it is remarkably long-lived. A properly treated pole should last 50 years.

Only certain species combine the required strength with the ability to accept and retain the preservative. These include several pines, Douglas fir, western red cedar, western hemlock and western larch.

Pole manufacturing steps include peeling, air drying, turning (for spars or masts), incising (punching holes so the preservative will penetrate) and impregnation under pressure with the treating material.

The preservative may be pentachlorophenol or as it is familiarly known, penta; creosote; or water-borne salts. Creosote, which stains brown and has a distinct odor, is used mostly for applications where appearance is least important such as pilings and railroad ties. Penta, cleaner and less smelly, is used for transmission poles, guardrail posts. And water-borne salts are for situations where cleanliness and paintability are desirable, such as visible supports for homes and buildings. Water-borne salts are recommended for any use where the pole will pass through the interior of an enclosed living space.

Most pole manufacturers adhere to the preservative standards of the American Wood Preservers Association.

Piles or pile timbers, used as columns for support of heavy structural loads, are made much the same as poles. Besides the softwood species mentioned above, a couple of exotic hardwoods from South America have special qualities that show promise for marine installations such as ferry slips, docks and wharves. These include demerara greenheart and angelique. Both are said to resist attacks of teredos or marine borers. If you are building a dock or float you might investigate them further.

At one time this was the only way to preserve fenceposts. Many people still treat posts in vats or troughs, but in most cases pretreated ones are more dependable. (Courtesy U.S. Forest Service)

Juniper's longevity is attested to by this 80-year-old fencepost in Nevada. Unemployed miners at a silver-mining camp built the fence by simply drilling holes in the posts and passing the wires though. (Courtesy U.S. Forest Service)

VI. Working with Wood

Success with wood has two prerequisites: understanding the material, and planning the job before even picking up the first tool.

A true understanding of wood, in spite of the guidance you can get from books, comes only with experience. But it *will* come. If you seriously wish to master woodworking, look into courses offered at vocational schools. In any case, the sooner you get to work on an actual project the better.

First, assemble your materials. Then make a checklist of the steps you must carry out to complete the project; take an inventory of your tools and equipment, to see if you have on hand what it takes to accomplish the job.

BASIC EQUIPMENT FOR THE HOME SHOP: HAND TOOLS AND MACHINE

A good home shop need not be loaded with power tools, though they speed up the work and usually do a more precise job. But the familiar carpenter's tools still belong.

Recommended basic equipment for an efficient home workshop (geared to working with wood) is described below, with tips on usage.

Measuring and Marking Tools

Accurate laying-out or setting-out (measuring and marking) is absolutely essential to good workmanship, no matter how simple the project.

Folding rules Sizes most helpful are 2 to 8 ft. long, especially when measuring long pieces of lumber. Lay the rule flat, not on edge, if measuring more than 2 ft.

Tape measure The best tape measure is of flexible steel, usually 12 ft., with a 2-in. or 3-in. base on the case. If the tape has automatic recoil, make sure it can be locked into the extended position.

Try square Consisting of two parts at right angles to each other it has a thick wood or metal handle and a thin steel blade, from 2 to 12 in. long. It is used to check the squareness of surfaces and edges and to lay out lines perpendicular to an edge.

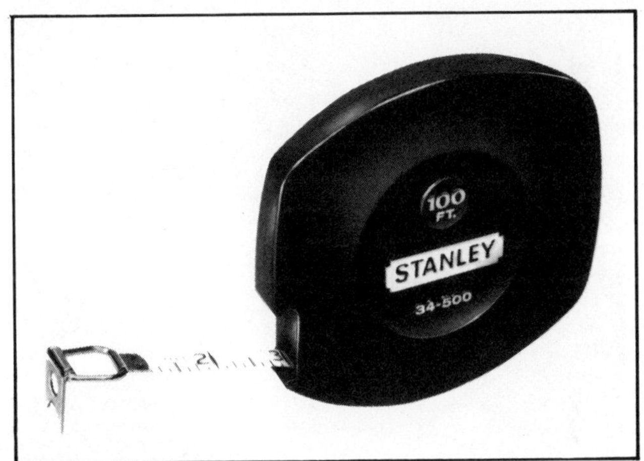

Steel measuring tape

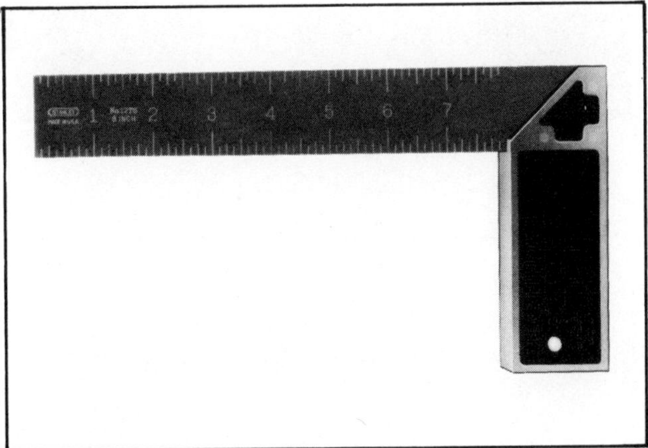

Try square

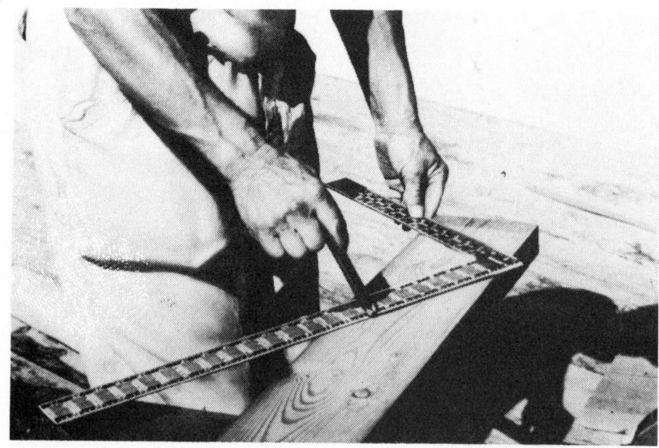

Carpenter's square

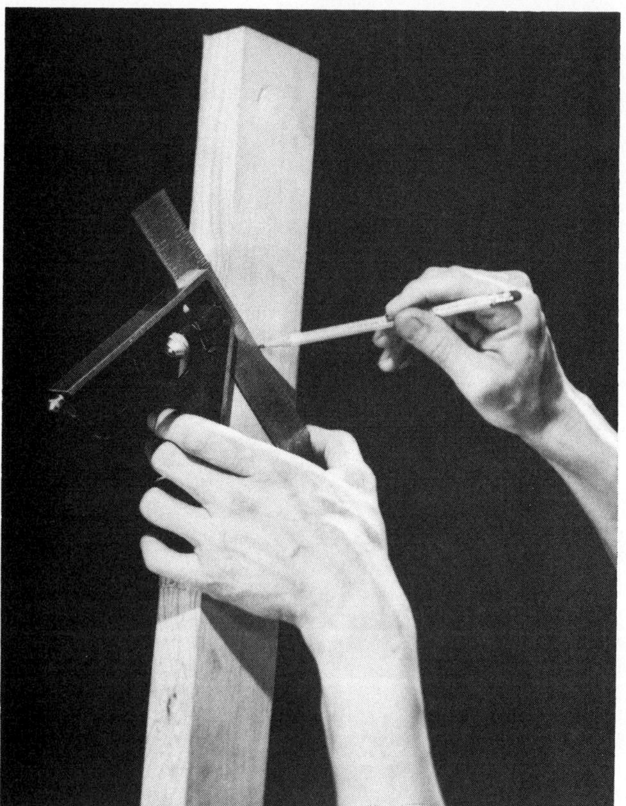

Combination square

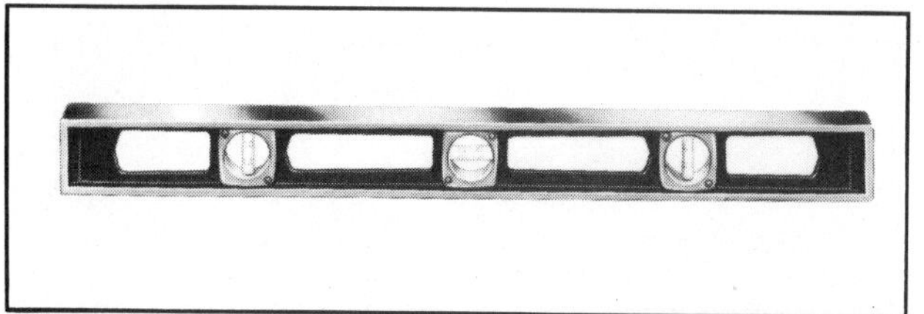

Spirit level

Combination square So called because it does so many things—serves as miter gauge or try square, scribes, and makes short (up to 12 in.) measurements and corner measurements—its head is adjustable and may be slid along the blade and fastened at any position. Some combination squares incorporate a "spirit level" (see below).

Bevel square Another very useful tool, the bevel square cn be used for checking other angles besides a right angle.

Steel carpenter's square Also called a "rafter square," it is larger than most —at least 12 in. one direction and 16 in. the other. Besides inches, it has scales and tables that the professional builder needs (but you probably won't).

Wing dividers or compasses These instruments are used to transfer measurements, as well as to draw circles or arcs to be cut. They may be fitted with pencils.

And speaking of pencils, be sure yours is always sharp when you draw lines or make marks. It should preferably be sharpened like a chisel blade so you can hold the point against the rule or square.

For the accuracy needed in cabinetwork, it is best to scribe with the tip of a knifeblade or with a scratch awl. (The latter is often used to punch starter holes for small screws or nails.) Do not scribe unless the mark will not show or will be cut away by the saw cut. You cannot erase a scratch.

Spirit level Use a spirit level to find out if your shelves or other horizontal surfaces are level, and whether vertical supports are plumb (straight up-and-down). The *plumb bob* is also used for this latter purpose.

Cutting Tools (hand)

Find out ahead of time just how much precutting, if any, your lumber dealer will do for you for a small fee. This saves you from working with long or unwieldy pieces, such as 4x8 panels of plywood; however, you will still need a good arsenal of sharp saws, chisels and planes in your workshop.

The most versatile of handsaws is the crosscut saw. It can be used to cut across or (with a little more difficulty) along the grain. Use it for lumber, plywood, hardboard, etc. The number of teeth per inch are called "points." The more points, the smoother and slower the cut. Look for the point measure on the corner of the blade near the handle. An 8-point blade is suitable for rough work. For finish work or finer cutting you may use a 10-point saw. A blade 26 in. long is a good choice for average demands. If you have to make cuts in spots where you do not have much room to maneuver, get a shorter, supplementary saw.

Keep your saw sharp, dry, and rustfree. Like other cutting tools, it will dull rapidly when used on hardboard and particleboard.

Other handsaws do special jobs well, but none is a substitute for the crosscut saw.

Ripsaw This tool excels at one thing—cutting along the grain. It does this much faster than a crosscut saw because the teeth are coarser: 5-½ to 6 per in.

Backsaw Shorter and rectangular with metal reinforcing along its back to keep it rigid, it also has finer teeth (standard is 15-point) than the crosscut saw or ripsaw. If you do much cabinet and furniture work and need accurate angles or square cuts in moldings or narrow pieces of wood, the backsaw is a big help—especially when used with a miter box. The backsaw has a narrower, shorter brother, the "dove-tail saw," used for undercutting and flush-cutting in tight places.

Coping saw Featuring a very thin blade with fine teeth, it looks almost like a toothed wire and can be used for cutting curves and making sharp turns. But the distance you can cut in from the edge is limited by the C-shaped metal frame that holds the blade.

Keyhole saw This saw is short with a pointed tip and is used to start a cut in the middle of a board or panel, from a predrilled hole. The "compass saw" is similar, but a little larger.

Miter box You should have a miter box to make saw cuts for miter joints, that is, joints where you do not want end grain to show, as in picture frames and moldings around windows. A metal miter box with attached saw permits adjustment of the saw to any angle from 30 to 90°. Or you can make your own wooden miter box: fasten two pieces of dimension lumber to a base; with a sliding T bevel, lay out at a 45° angle in both directions. Usually this and a 90° angle are all the angles needed.

Power Saws

You can step up your productivity enormously with electric saws, but be careful; they are not playthings.

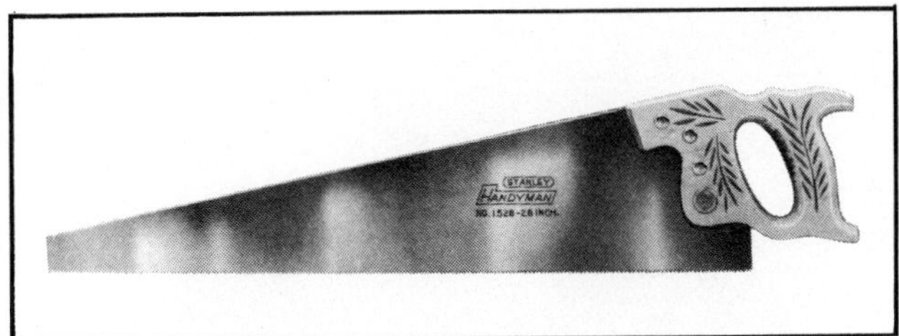

Crosscut saw

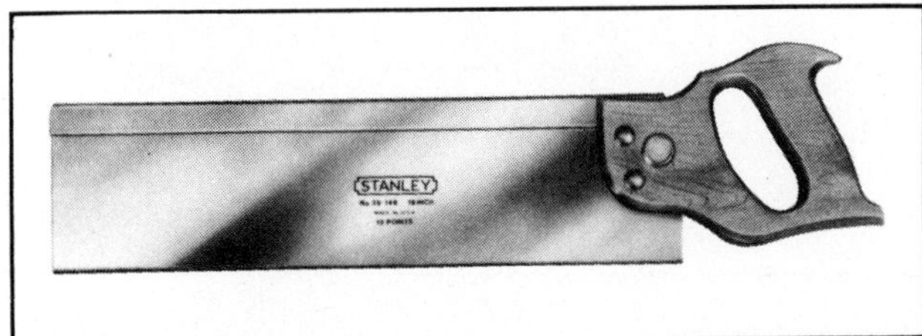

Backsaw

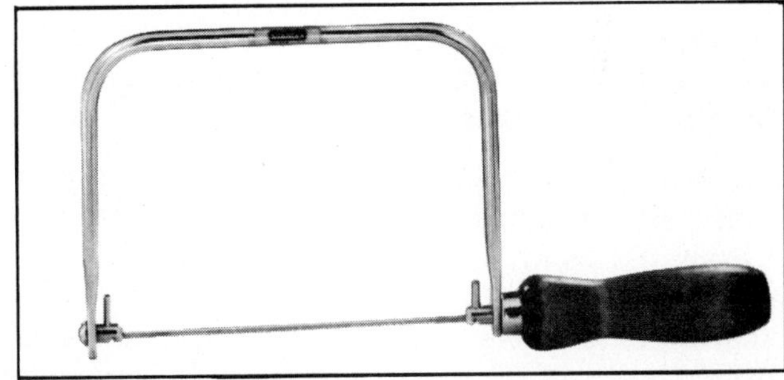

Coping saw

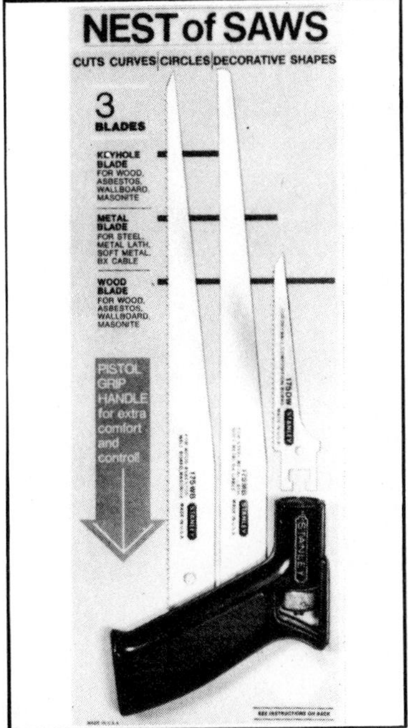

Set of keyhole saws

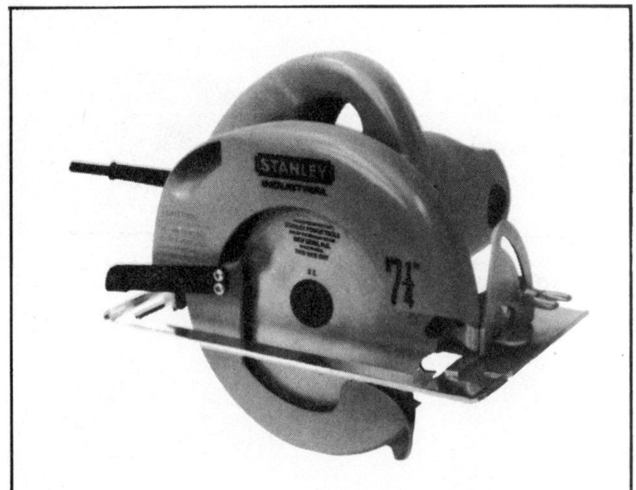

Portable power saw

Portable circular saws You buy these with a variety of blades for different jobs. A 7-in. blade, designed to do both crosscut and rip sawing, suffices for most home workshops.

Saber saw (bayonet saw) This one saw combines the functions of several handsaws: crosscut, ripsaw, band saw, keyhole saw, hack saw (used to cut metal) and jigsaw. Blades with a variety of sizes and spacing of teeth are available. For general purposes use a blade with 10 teeth per in. Use a saber saw for straight, bevel or curved cuts.

Table saw (circular saw) For larger and more accurate cuts, use a table saw and position the wood to suit the saw rather than move the saw across the wood. If you do a lot of cutting and cabinet work this saw is a worthwhile investment. Common sizes for the small workshop are 8-in. and 10-in. tilt arbor saws. (The arbor holds the blade.) With a combination blade you can use it for ripping, crosscutting, beveling, rabbeting and many other operations.

Radial arm saw Another versatile stationary saw, its main advantage over the circular saw (which has the cutting blade below the work) is that you can see the blade and the cut. This makes it easier to keep the blade aligned with the cutting line. The radial arm saw does the basic sawing operations and, with accessories, can shape wood, make dado cuts and moldings, and work as a sander or router.

Chisels

A chisel has a sharpened blade that is beveled on one side. Use it to cut grooves and notches and

A dozen woodworking operations, from simple crosscutting to sanding to compound mitering, can be performed by an experienced craftsman with a radial arm saw. (Courtesy Rockwell International)

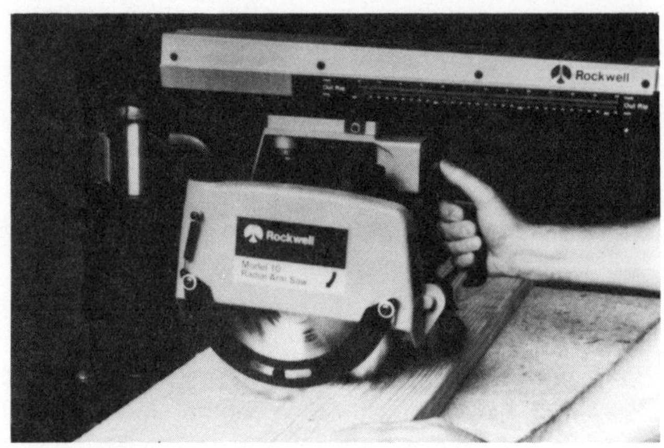

Cross cutting

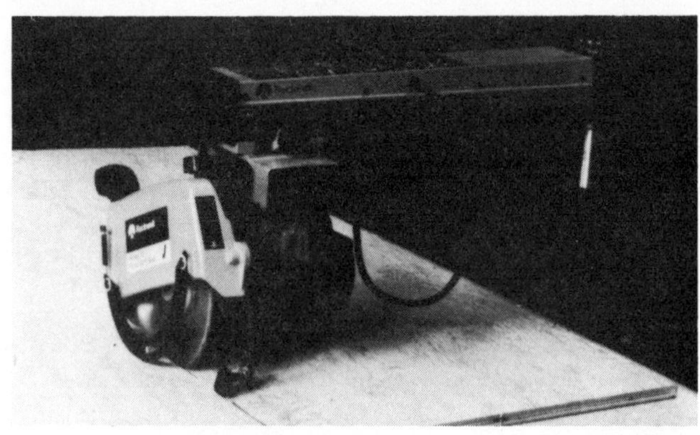

Ripping

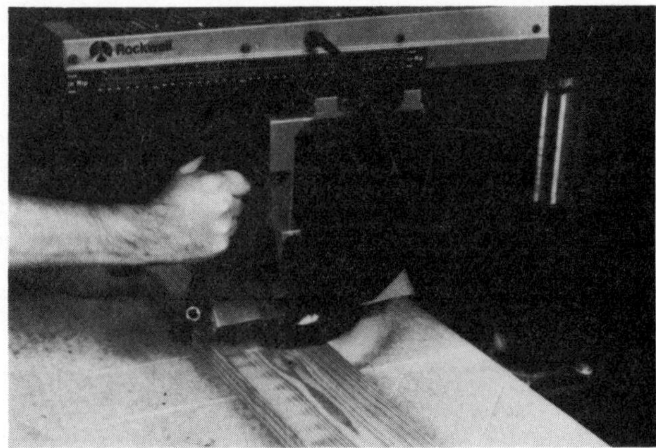

Bevel cross cutting

Bevel ripping

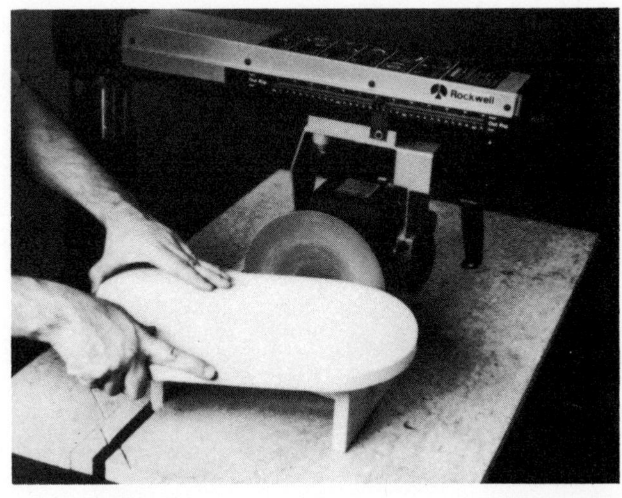

Disc sanding

Shaping

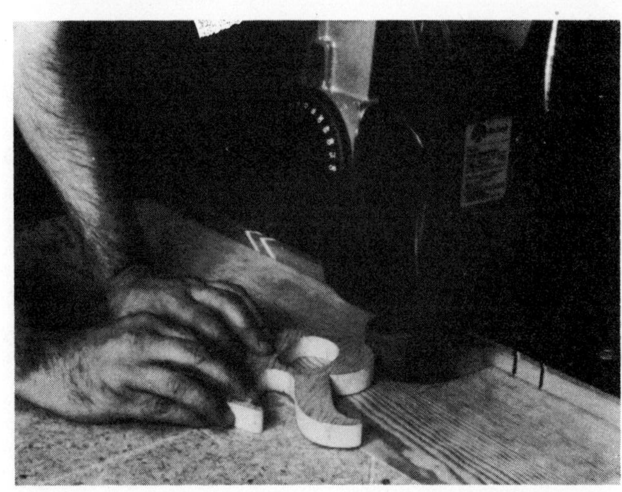

Drum sanding

Making moldings

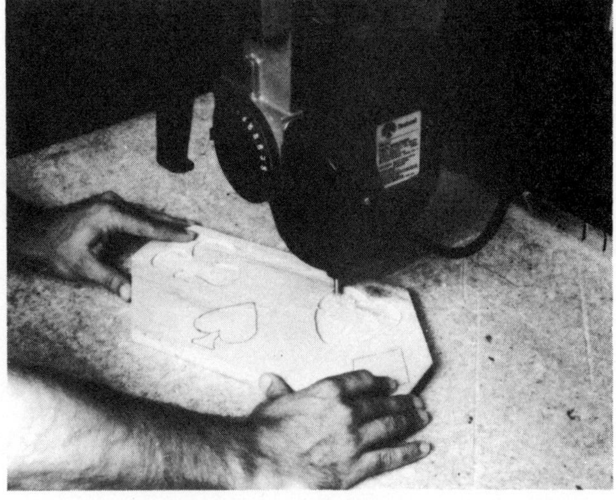

Routing

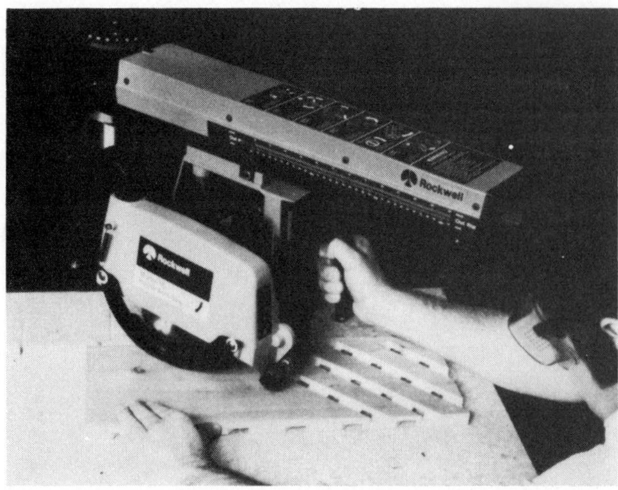

Making dado cuts

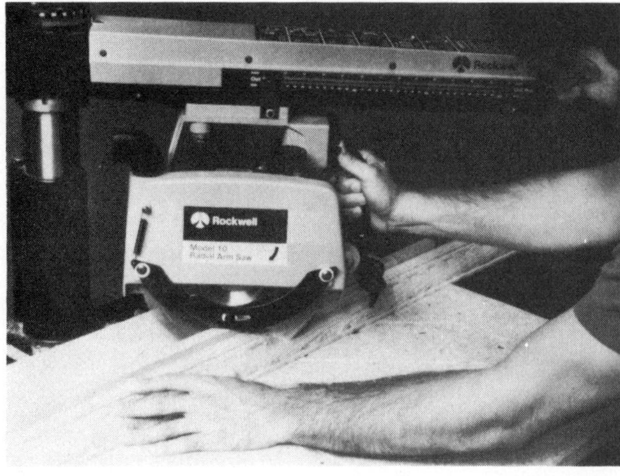

Mitering

Compound mitering

mortises, as for hinges. A set of four, with blade widths ranging from ¼ in. to 2 in., is recommended.

Chisels are made with several kinds of blades, suitable for different jobs. The "paring" chisel, with a comparatively light thin blade, is a good all-round tool for hand chiseling or cutting fine shavings. Another often-used type is the "firmer" chisel, with a long strong blade that can do both heavy and light work.

Buy a chisel with a metal cap on the handle if you will be driving it into wood with a mallet. (Never use a metal hammer to drive a chisel.)

A few tips on working with chisels: first, safety. There are probably more chisel wounds than any other kind in the workshop. So to avoid gouging yourself, always keep both hands back of the cutting edge. Secure the piece you are chiseling so it cannot move. Never cut toward yourself. If you can, cut with the grain. Cutting against the grain leaves the wood rough.

When feasible, use other tools (saws, planes, augers) to remove as much of the waste wood as possible before using the chisel. Do not hurry, or try to do too much with one cut. And never try to use a woodworking chisel on metal.

Planes

You will need at least a couple of these slicing, smoothing tools in your carpentry.

Block The smallest plane, it is used to smooth a board's end grain and to shave down rounded surfaces.

Bench planes Used to shave and smooth with the grain, along a board's edge or length, they come in three sizes. The largest is the "fore" plane, for smoothing long surfaces. Then the "jack" plane, often used to get most of the irregularities off before finer smoothing. Finally, the smaller "smooth" plane, which is the one to buy if you will be getting only one plane.

There are more types of planes for special jobs like routing and grooving and rabbeting. As you get farther into woodworking you will discover whether you need them.

Other Smoothing Devices

Files and rasps Toothed tools commonly used to abrade metals and plastics, they also come in types that smooth wood, particularly for small and curved, internal areas. The larger the teeth, the

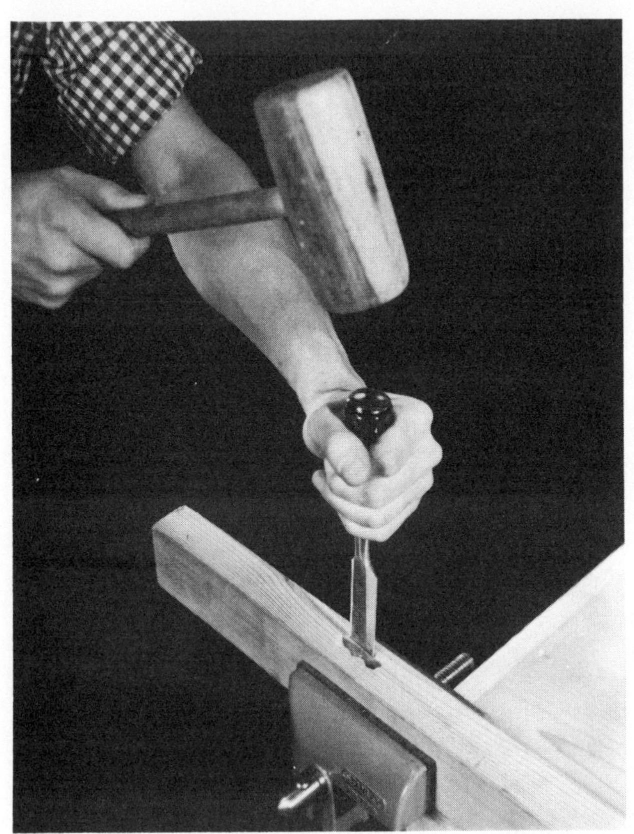

Tips for Using Chisels

Use a wooden mallet when extra force is needed.

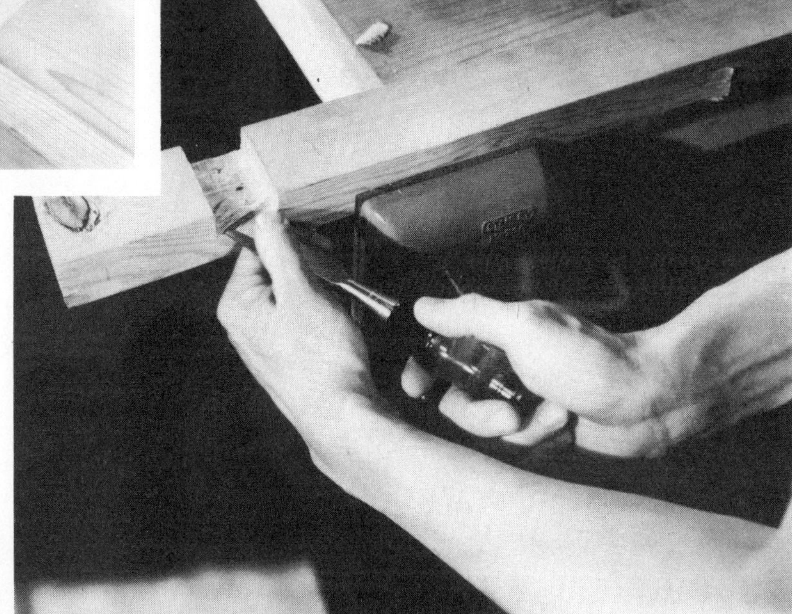

Always keep work firmly clamped.

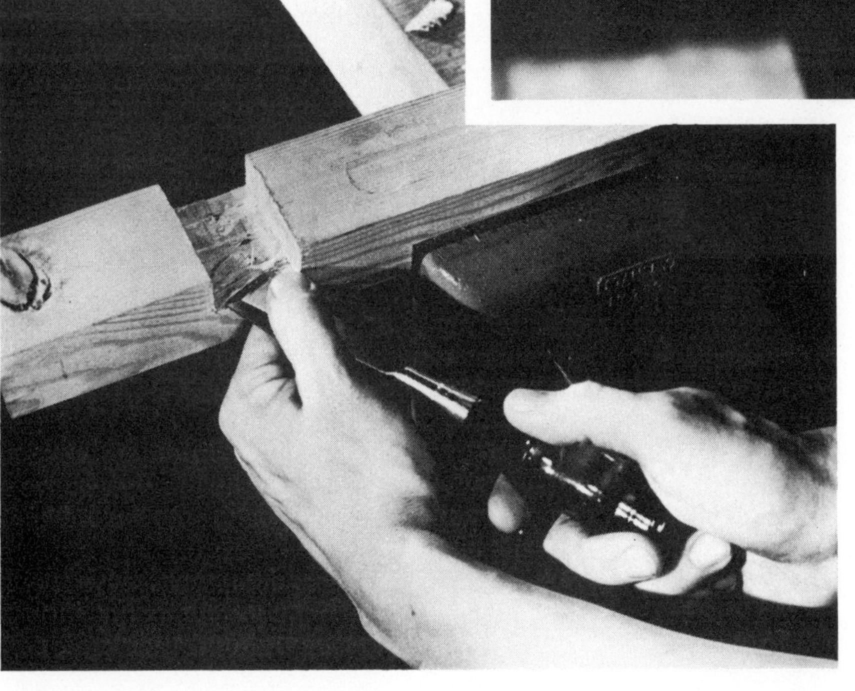

Keep both hands back of the cutting edge. (Courtesy Stanley Works)

rougher the result. A rasp, with its individually shaped teeth, removes wood faster than a file.

Scrapers Used a lot in fine furniture making and cabinetry, these take off finer shavings than a plane. The "cabinet scraper", a beveled blade set in a two-handled frame, makes a smooth cut against the grain. The "spokeshave" is similar and is used to plane convex and concave shapes. (It was originally used to shape spokes of wheels.) The "hand scraper," something like an oversize razor blade, produces an even finer shaving. It is used on veneers and is the most satisfactory tool in refinishing furniture.

Sandpaper Do not forget to keep a good supply of sandpaper on hand. Sandpaper is made with different abrasives, which may be recognized by their color.

Flint, or quartz, is yellowish and the most common type. It is used as an all-purpose paper for hand sanding.

Garnet, reddish brown, is harder and sharper, long-lasting and fast-cutting. Use it on hardwoods.

Aluminum oxide is reddish brown or white and good for either hand or machine sanding.

Silicon carbide is shiny black, very hard and sharp; use it to sand lacquers and shellacs.

You may see sandpaper, except the flint type, numbered by the old grit-size system or the new mesh number. In either case, the higher the number, the finer the sandpaper. Flint sandpaper is simply graded from Extra Coarse to Extra Fine.

GUIDE TO SANDPAPERS

Coarseness	Garnet (old system)	Garnet, Silicon carbide and Aluminum oxide (new system)
Very fine	8/0	280
	7/0	240
	6/0	220
Fine	5/0	180
	4/0	150
	3/0	120
Medium	2/0	100
	1/0	80
	½	60
	1%	50
Coarse	1½	40
	2%	36
Very coarse	2½	30

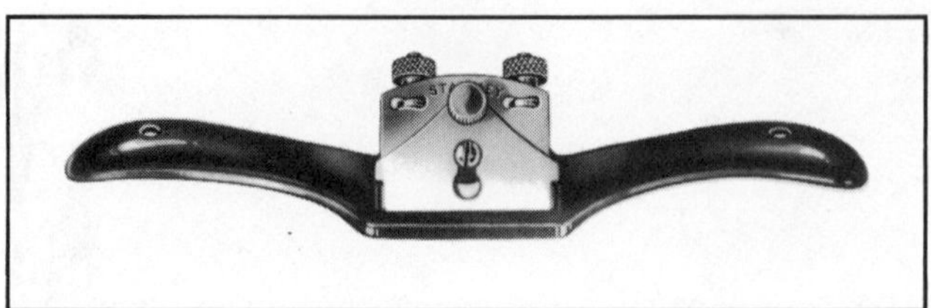

Spokeshave

Fasteners

Nails Nails are available in a thousand or more sizes and types. Here are a few useful terms.

Penny. Abbreviated "d," penny is the measure of length. It is said to go back to when you bought 100 nails of a certain size for a penny; 1-penny nails referred to that size. Now nails come in sizes from 2d to 60d. A 2d nail is 1 in. long, a 16d nail is 3-½ in. long. You get about 830 2d common nails to a pound, 49 of the 16d size.

Common, box nails. Nails with flat round heads are common and box nails. Common nails are used for rough framing. Box nails, thinner, are used for lighter work and for toe nailing (driving the nail obliquely through the end of one piece into the side of another).

Ring nails. Threaded, they hold almost as well as a screw but you can't remove them without damaging the work.

Casing nail. Small-headed, it is used for fine carpentry, such as attachment of door and window casings.

Finish nails. These have "brad" heads (very small heads) and are thinner than casing nails. These last two nails are meant to be driven slightly below the surface with a nail set (a short metal punch) and the hole filled with wood putty and sanded before the wood is finished.

Brads. Small in diameter, bradheaded nails are used in cabinet making and fine furniture.

Corrugated fasteners. Also called "wiggle" nails, these are useful for holding joints and in repair work. You often see them used in picture frames.

Here are a few helpful hints concerning nails:

- Use rustproof nails (aluminum, galvanized or stainless steel) for outdoor work.
- Use double-headed or scaffold nails for temporary work. You drive the nail in as far as its lower head, and pull it out later by the easily accessible upper head.

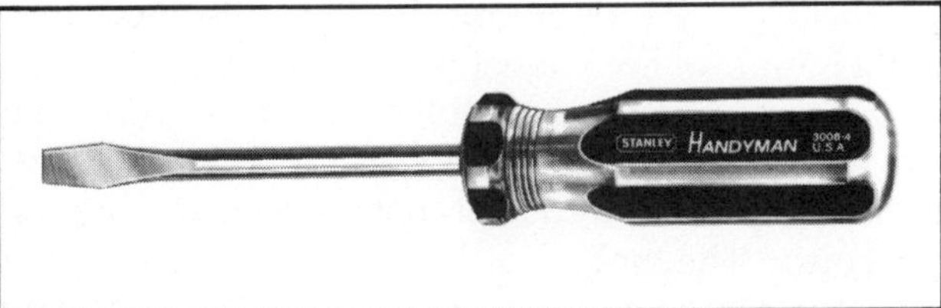

Screwdriver

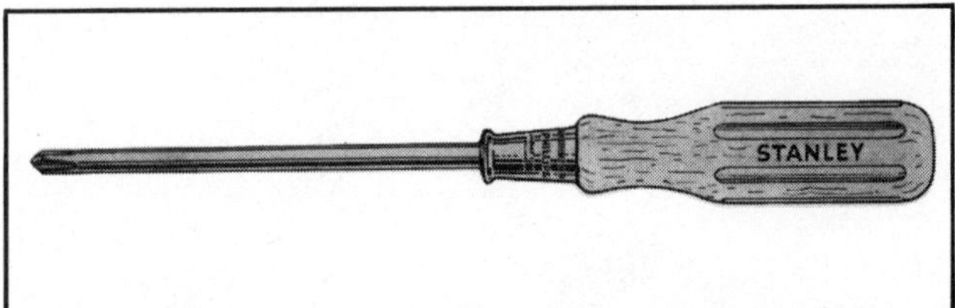

Phillips screwdriver (Courtesy Stanley Works)

- If you drive a nail at a slight angle it will hold better.
- If the nail begins to bend as you pound, remove it and start over with a new one. Do not waste time and risk damaging your work by trying to straighten it with the hammer.
- When removing a nail, put a piece of scrap wood under the hammer after engaging the nail head with the claw and pulling it part way. The wood protects the surface of your work and gives you more leverage with the hammer.

Screws Some have rounded heads; some flat (to be flush or counter sunk below the surface of the wood); others have oval heads, or lag (square) heads. They are measured by gauge (thickness): smallest is 0, with a diameter of .060 in., and length (¼ in. to 6 in.).

Why use screws? They have greater holding power than nails, you do not need as many, also, they can be easily removed if need be. But they take longer to install, and they cost more. You will want to use screws for fine cabinet and furniture work.

How do you use screws? First you need a starting hole. In softwood, this may be made with an awl or push-pull drill (yankee drill). The hole in the top piece of wood should be the same diameter as the screw shank (the smooth cylindrical section just below the head). The pilot hole in the bottom piece of wood should be slightly smaller than the diameter of the core of the screw.

The screw you select should be long enough so that at least half its length will penetrate the bottom piece of wood.

To recess flathead or ovalhead screws so they are flush with the surface of the wood you will need to countersink a beveled hole the same diameter as the screwhead. Or, to conceal the screw entirely, you may drill a counterbore hole so the screw is recessed below the surface. Cover its head with a wood plug (you can buy decorative ones, if you like), or with putty, plastic wood, etc.

Bolts Like screws, bolts have threads. But they do not grip the wood and do not have pointed ends. You must drill a hole all the way through the wood before inserting a bolt. You always fasten it with a nut. You may need to put a washer under the head and also under the nut; for self-anchoring or countersunk bolts, put a washer under the nut only.

Bolts are generally zinc-plated steel and come with many kinds of heads, including self-anchoring (carriage bolts). They are more likely to be used for heavy, outdoor construction than in cabinetry and furniture making. However, when hanging or fastening cabinets or shelf assemblies to hollow walls, you should use the types known as toggle bolts or Molly bolts.

Other Essential Tools

Wrenches Useful for tightening the nut or the bolt, they can also be used for dozens of other jobs. You may buy an adjustable open-end wrench or a set of graduated open-end or box wrenches.

Screwdrivers There is no such thing as an all-purpose screwdriver. You will need several sizes in your workshop—and maybe one or two more in the kitchen so that people who tend to use screwdrivers as can openers or crowbars or tools to force open a stuck window can ruin their own rather than yours. A blunt, bent uneven screwdriver blade can be devastating to the screw's head and to your temper.

Always use a screwdriver whose blade approximates the width of the slot in your screw or bolt. Do not scrimp on screwdrivers. Buy the kind with well-tempered steel for maximum life.

You should have a Phillips and a Reed Prince screwdriver for the two kinds of screw with criss-crossed slot. With these, the screwdriver cannot slip out of the slot and gash the wood.

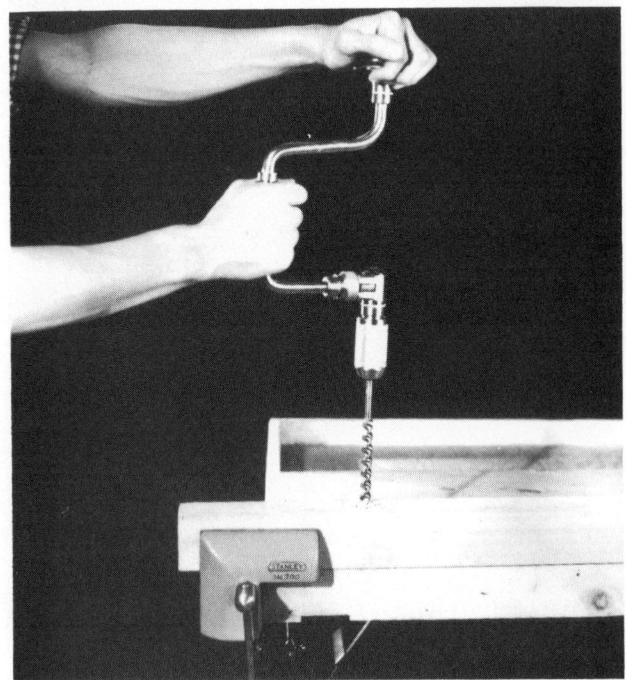

Brace and bit

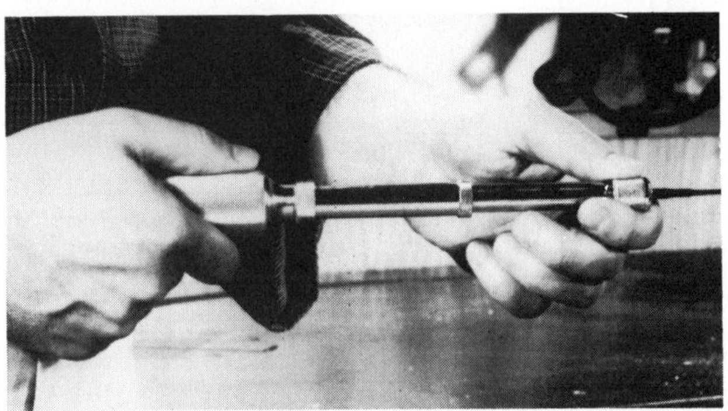

Hand drill

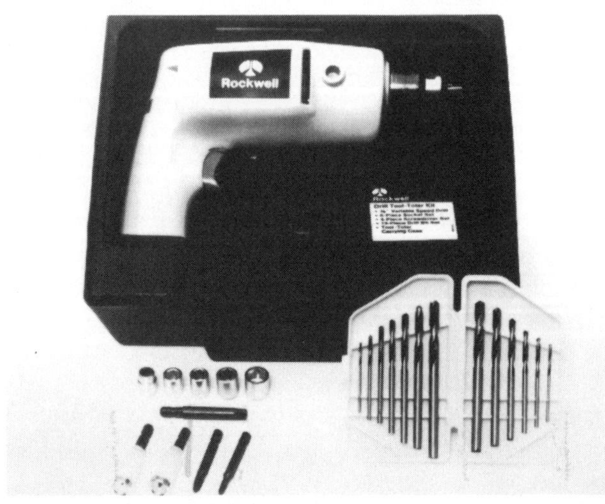

An electric drill kit that fills most needs includes a six-piece socket set, four screwdriver bits and 13 twist drills. (Courtesy Rockwell International)

Pliers Pliers belong in any self-respecting workshop. Like an extension of your hand, they do many things well, such as pulling out loose or broken nails. (But do not use pliers to loosen or tighten nuts—that's for a wrench.) Most pliers have a built-in wirecutter. The long, needle-nosed pliers are handy for getting into spots where your hand can't go and retrieving dropped screws or nails or keys or dollar bills. Channel-lock pliers have the head at an angle and an adjustable bite.

Bores and drills Use a bore for a hole larger than ¼ in. in diameter and a drill for any smaller hole.

The brace-and-bit bores holes in wood from ¼ in. to 2 in. in diameter. If the brace has a ratchet you can bore holes in tight spots where there is not sufficient room for the brace to make the complete circle. The auger bits come in many shapes and sizes; keep a good assortment so you can drill neatly through thin panels, heavy timbers, hard wood, gummy wood or whatever. For example, the single twist and straight core auger bits bore fast and clear themselves of chips more quickly than the double twist, and bore hard woods better; but the double twist cuts more accurately and smoothly and is better for soft woods.

For small holes you will need: the hand drill (which works like an eggbeater), to make holes up to ½ in., and the automatic or push drill, which usually has a hollow handle to hold extra assorted drills. It punches holes rapidly through thin wood and is frequently used to make pilot holes for screws for hinges, locks and other hardware.

In all drilling, mark the hole position first with a scratch awl.

Electric drills These do all the above things faster and easier and can be fitted with many attachments. In fact, if you were to buy just one power tool this would be a wise choice. But before you buy, make sure it will take the accessories you may want later. And pay attention to horsepower; a good ½-in. drill should develop at least ⅔ horsepower. Speeds of approximately 1,000 rpm are best for woodworking.

Common sizes for electric drills are determined by the "chuck," the neck that clamps around the bit. A ⅜-in. chuck is adequate for ordinary demands.

Your power drill can, with appropriate accessories, drill a hole from the size of a pin on up, in 1/64-in. increments; drill a countersunk hole; saw round holes with a hole saw; do power sanding; have it fitted with a chisel to make grooves in soft wood; drive or remove screws. You can even saw ¾-in. plywood; plane boards or keep your tools sharp with a grinding wheel attachment.

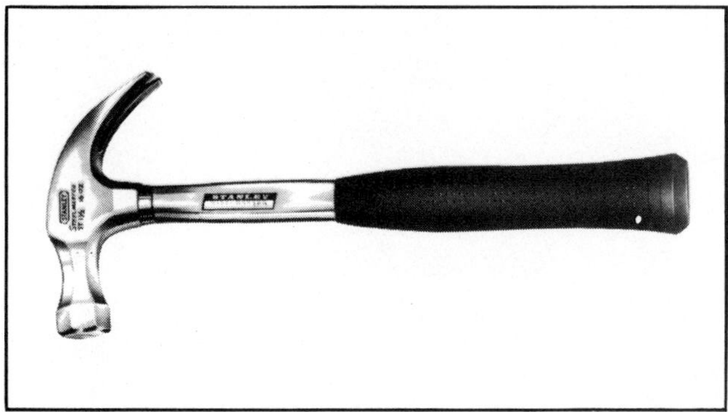

Claw hammer

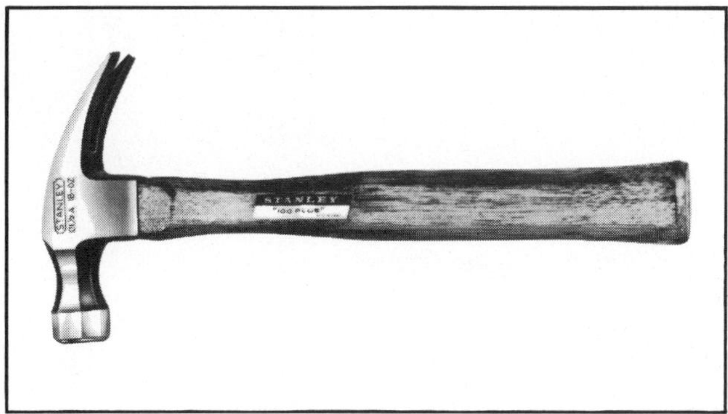

Ripping or framing hammer

Clamps Use clamps to keep things in place while you work on them, and also keep two pieces tightly pressed together while the adhesive sets. C-clamps, most versatile, have jaw widths from 3 to 16 in. Keep plenty on hand. To protect wood surfaces, use wood shims between clamps and the wood on which you are working.

Other clamps you might need include spring-clamps, good for small work and delicate jobs; adjustable hand screws; and a woodworker's vise.

Hammers Your hammer should have a curved claw if you use it for nail pulling. A straighter claw characterizes the ripping hammer, useful for ripping assemblies apart. (Anyone can make a mistake.)

A slightly convex face (the part of the hammer that hits the nail) will help you to hit only the nail, not dent the wood. Hammer sizes range from 5 to 20 ounces; a 13-ounce head is good for general-purpose work. A hammer that is too light will require more muscle power and wear you out if you are doing a lot of nailing, as in framing a house.

As for handles, you may choose metal, fiberglass or wood. The first two may last longer, but many carpenters and craftsmen do not feel comfortable without their favorite hickory-handled hammer.

TECHNIQUES FOR WORKING WITH WOOD

The first and most formidable task faced when working with wood is to change its size and form by various cutting tools. There are many ways to attack the shaping of wood.

Often we start by sawing. But before there was the saw there was the axe, with which wood can be cleft.

The cleaving of wood does not lend itself to anything very fancy in the way of woodworking, or fine shaping. But it is a fast and time-honored way to turn a log into pieces that are far stronger than sawn wood, which can then be shaped further into tools and other products. It is also the technique familiar to every woodchopper and kindling splitter.

To cleave is simply to reduce a log to planks or palings without use of a saw, in order to leave the wood fibers intact—which means you will end up with a very strong piece of wood. The skilled craftsman drives an axe blade or wedge into the end-grain of the log exactly along one of the rays—the lines of storage cells that radiate from the center of the log. The two half-cylinders are then cleft into pieces (as for shakes) or flat boards, using axe or froe. The strong grain, preserved uncut, gives the wood a toughness and durability not found in sawn wood.

In our country the cleaving of wood as a means of shaping goes back to the days when colonists cut down trees, then quickly made them into fence posts, palings, gates, planks for cladding of houses, and shingles for roofs.

Cleft wood, usually ash or hickory, was thus prepared for shaping into tool handles by early Americans and the technique is still widely used. It requires only the simplest of tools, but it does take strength and skill.

Sawing

Sawing is the most common method of reducing a large piece of stock (that is, wood) in the shop. As we have seen, you may use handsaws or machine. Here are some suggestions—which will seem elementary to some readers, but which are important in view of the crucial nature of the sawing process.

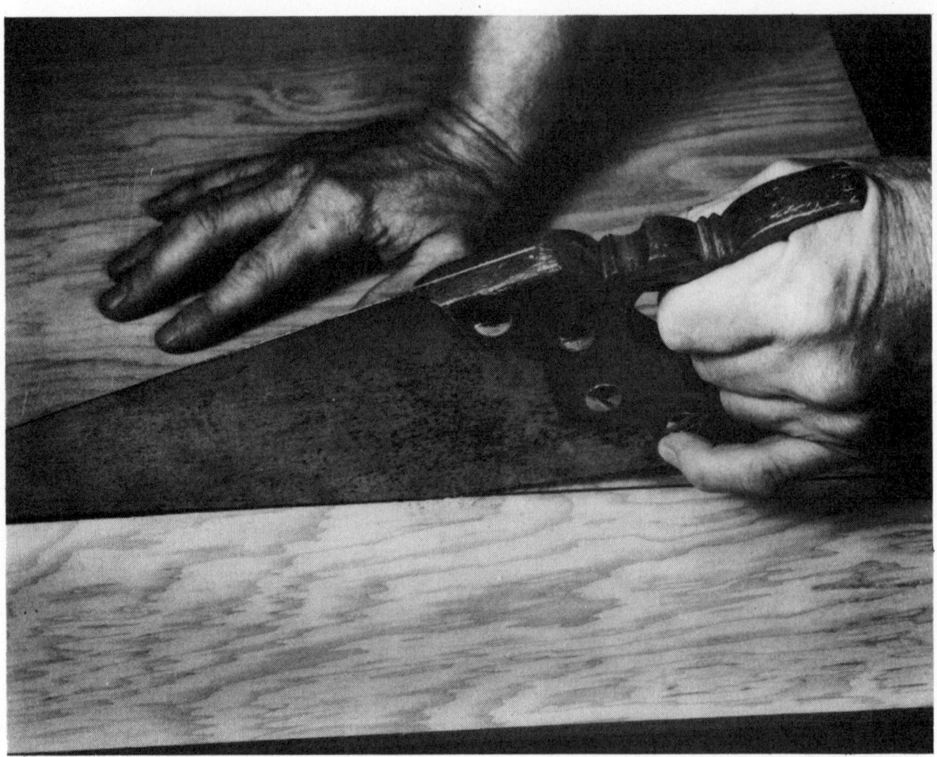

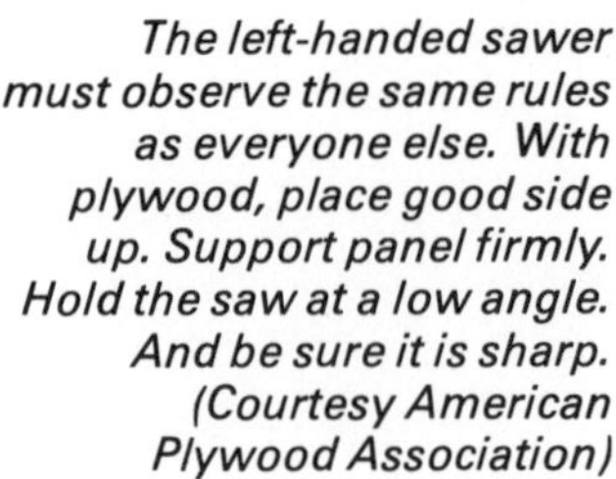

The left-handed sawer must observe the same rules as everyone else. With plywood, place good side up. Support panel firmly. Hold the saw at a low angle. And be sure it is sharp. (Courtesy American Plywood Association)

Mistakes can be extremely costly, in both time and money.

Hand sawing First, mark the cutline. Then place the teeth of the crosscut saw nearest the handle at the starting point of the line. Make a short upward stroke to score the wood. If your wood is hard you may need several such light strokes to make a starting groove. Then start sawing with full strokes, holding the saw at a 45° angle. To keep your saw from straying from the straight and narrow, clamp a straight board along the cutting line so the saw can ride against it.

You must allow for the width of the saw and the "kerf" or saw cut, so do not saw exactly on the marked line, but on the waste side. Always support wood and plywood firmly during cutting. When you get nearly through, hold the end of the cut-off piece so it will not break and splinter.

Use the same procedure with a ripsaw which, as you recall, is used to cut along the grain, not across it. If your saw is a coarse one with a few fine teeth at the point, use that end for starting the kerf. And it works best to hold a ripsaw at a 60° angle.

Since the cutting action of the handsaw's teeth takes place only on the forward or pushing stroke, do not apply pressure on the return, or pulling, stroke.

Final note: keeping the flat surface of the blade at right angles to the work is vital. Until you get a feel for it check yourself now and then with a try square.

The above suggestions apply to simple perpendicular cuts, which are no problem with a handsaw. You are better off using a power saw for other types of cuts, such as:

Bevel This is an angle cut completely across the edge or end of a piece, required when one piece is set at an angle to another.

Chamfer This cut, used mostly as a decoration on an edge or an end, is an angular cut that reaches only part way across the corner or edge.

Mortise-and-tenon When making a mortise-and-tenon joint, you will need to shape the end of one piece to fit into a hole that you have cut into another piece.

Dado The dado cut is a groove cut across the grain, to receive the end of a joining member.

Machine sawing The chances of a serious accident when using a power saw or other machine are so great that you cannot be too careful. Pay attention to these safety rules, and see that others who frequent your workshop do also.

- Have plenty of room to maneuver. Keep the shop off-limits to sightseers and visitors, when you're working.

When using a table saw, keep good side of wood up. Let the blade protrude just the height of teeth. (Courtesy American Plywood Association)

- Be sure the room is well lighted, dry and not cluttered. Don't let lumber scraps accumulate on the floor. Clean oil spills at once.
- Read your equipment manual carefully, and refer to it before starting any new, unfamiliar process.
- Make sure your machine is properly grounded.
- Don't wear loose clothes; tuck in ties and scarves; remove rings, wristwatches, pins and other jewelry; tie back long hair, or better, tuck it under a cap.
- Use safety glasses.
- Never stand in line with a revolving blade or wheel.
- Let the machine do the work—don't force material into it faster than it will cut.
- Always examine wood for nails or other impediments. If there are knots, feed more slowly.
- Disconnect power plug and remove switch key when saw is not in use.

So much for safety and good sense. Now to the work at hand: how to make best use of your portable circular saw and saber saw.

The general procedure is to grasp the handle firmly, with forefinger ready to operate the switch. Don't turn on the switch until the saw is resting on the work and the guide mark is aligned with the cutting line. Let the motor reach full speed before feeding the saw into the stock. Release the switch as soon as the cut is finished, but do not move the saw until the motor stops.

If using a saber saw, however, always turn on the switch before bringing the saw blade in contact with the wood.

Keep the good side of lumber and plywood down, because the saw blade cuts upward. This means you will mark the cutting pattern or line on the back.

To saw plywood more manageably tack a 2x4 to the top of each sawhorse. These will support the panel while you saw and permit you to saw into the 2x4 without damaging the sawhorse. To keep the cut straight, use a straight-edge to guide the saw across the wood.

If you have a circular table saw (as differentiated from a portable), you should keep the following precautions and pointers in mind.

- Be sure the blade is sharp, and is the right one for the job.
- Be sure your machine has a guard for the saw blade.

- Always stand to one side of the saw blade, never directly in back of it, so if a piece kicks back it won't hit you. Kickbacks can happen when your saw blade is not properly sharpened.
- Never place your hand between the saw and the ripping fence.
- Before you start to saw, set the blade so it is ⅛-in. to ¼-in. above the stock to be cut.
- Never cut stock freehand, but always use the proper guide.

Safety precautions for the radial arm saw are much the same: be sure that the blade is sharp and guard is in place, and keep your hands away from the path of the blade.

With all power tools, refer frequently to your manual; do not guess at your procedure. This is especially important with table saws, which account for the most serious home workshop accidents. You could lose a finger, or even a hand.

Planing and Smoothing

Having cut your stock to approximate size, you must plane it to the exact dimensions and cut off the rough spots. The types of planes you may need were described earlier in this chapter.

In planing a surface that will show, always select the side of wood with the most interesting grain and fewest flaws.

Then lock the board securely in a vise, lengthwise. (Because with larger planes you need to use both hands.) Always plane in the direction of the grain —planing against the grain roughens the surface. As your wood becomes smooth, check frequently with a straight edge to see if it is true.

In planing end grain, work from each edge toward the center. If you worked all the way across or from center to edge, you would find corners and edges splitting off. End grain is harder to plane than faces or edges which you plane with the grain. Especially when working with end grain, be sure your planer iron (blade of the plane) is very sharp.

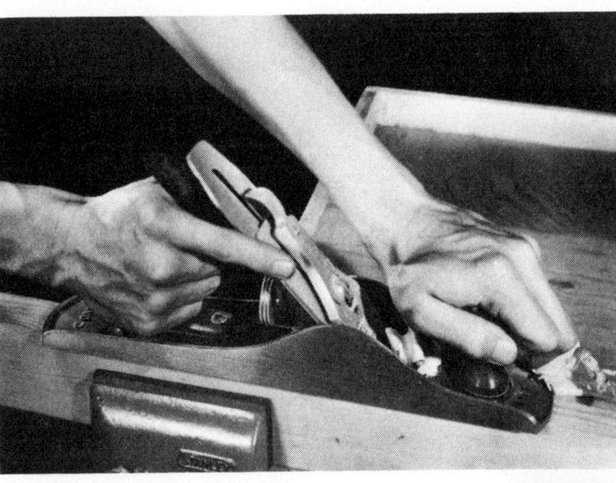

Planing is the first step in smoothing the wood. (Courtesy Stanley Works)

Two variations on the useful surform tool. Numerous sharp teeth bite into the wood, and chips and shavings pass through the blade without clogging the work. Use these to cut, shape, shave, smooth, file, rasp and form. (Courtesy Stanley Works) ▶

If you are working with plywood, never plane the surface; that has already been done for you. But you may need to plane the edge. If so, take shallow cuts from both ends of the edge toward the center.

The next step in smoothing the wood may require use of a scraper or a file or rasp, and almost certainly will require sandpaper.

Scrapers work best on hardwoods and, like other cutting tools, should be very sharp. Set the blade just deep enough to form a thin even shaving. If you get dust instead of shavings, it is a sign your blade is dull.

Secure the work in a vise, hold the scraper in both hands, and either pull the tool toward you, or push it as you would a small plane. You get a finer shaving when you pull.

Use files and rasps on wood only as a last resort; other cutting tools usually do a better job. But sometimes when you need to smooth a spot that you cannot reach any other way, these may be the answer. Clamp the work tightly in a vise. Hold the tool handle in your right hand and the end of the tool in your left, and stroke forward evenly. Never use a file without a handle. And clean tools often.

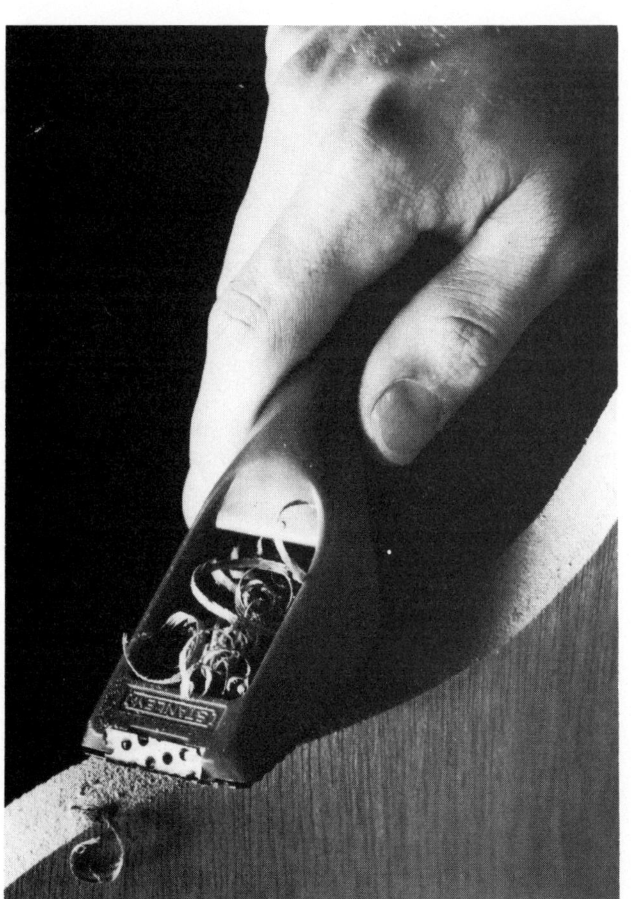

Now we assume the wood has been smoothed to your satisfaction. Next, take a careful look for nailholes, cracks, or dents that need filling. Use wood dough, plastic wood or stick shellac in a color to match the wood (if it will keep its natural color) or the color that the wood will have after staining (it's a good idea to experiment with a bit of scrap wood first). If you plan to paint you may use spackling compound or putty to fill holes, since color won't matter.

Fill the knots too. After sanding, you will seal them with shellac, to keep sap from seeping through.

Now you are ready to sand. Even if you have a power sander, you should do the final touches by hand. And almost everything you make with wood should be sanded, even after painstaking planing or scraping.

You almost always sand with the grain. Take great pains to sand all parts of your work evenly, not neglecting the hard-to-get-at spots. Fold the piece of sandpaper into a manageable size, or cut it, or wrap it around a piece of carpet, a block of wood, or a piece of cork. A sandpaper holder may be purchased which will hold the paper tightly and save your fingers. And there are many power sanding attachments.

Start your sanding with a coarse paper, then proceed with finer and finer grades. You will perhaps end up with a paper between 3/0 and 6/0 (120 and 220, new system; see chart).

Very important Clean the sanded area thoroughly before applying a finish. Use a vacuum for large areas; a tack cloth is also highly recommended for picking up all remaining dust. (This is a piece of cheesecloth or cotton rag, moistened with thinned varnish and then squeezed almost dry.)

Shaping

Wood shaping , refining the preliminary cutting and sawing, may involve carving, turning or bending. All are within the ancient tradition of fine craftsmanship.

Wood carving is the oldest wood-shaping craft —or art. It is far from dead, being still actively pursued and even taught.

Wood can be carved with nothing more complicated than the whittler's pocketknife. Or you may go to the other extreme and do free-hand carving with a drill press. Most likely, if you are serious about it, you will want to have a matched set of carving tools which would include, besides knives, a skew (flat chisel); a parting tool (to cut triangular shapes); a veiner or very small gouge; and assorted gouges and fluters.

These are the basic carving techniques:

Whittling This technique takes little more than wood with workable softness, a sharp knife, patience and imagination. Cedar and white pine were favored by the whittlers who produced so much of the American folk art: toys, decoy ducks, ships in bottles, weather-vanes. And it was basically whittling that was responsible for early American "treen"—woodenware necessities such as platters, bowls, drinking cups, ladles. They were made by carving hardwoods such as oak, sycamore and cherry. Surviving items are treasured antiques. But you can make your own if you like.

Chip carving The term covers cutting of geometric shapes in the wood surface.

Relief carving A difficult procedure, it requires the cutting away of the background so the design stands out in three-dimensional form.

Wood sculpture The most difficult technique of all, it is the field where creativity and artistry are most called on. But a mundane pointer: you may use routing bits and carving burrs on your drill press and do the rough shaping, before you start the painstaking work with knives and gouges.

White pine is a rewarding wood if you are a beginner because it is easy to cut and is relatively straight-grained. Other favored woods for carving are mahogany and walnut.

Wood turning Another venerable but still lively art, it dates at least from the Egyptians, the first to create decorative turned legs for chairs and stools. Early wood turning was done by holding the wood between two pointed centers, looping a cord around it, and attaching the cord to a bow worked by hand or foot to make the wood revolve. The tool was held against the wood and the cut made while the wood spun around. Later came the pole lathe. Motive power was a treadle.

The main tools for wood turning were (and are) gouges, chisels and scrapers; and, of course, sandpaper is essential.

The two turning methods were (and are) cutting and scraping. In cutting, the tool is held at an angle so its cutting edge digs into the revolving stock and peels off shavings, much as a hand plane does. In scraping, you hold the tool at right angles to the surface, and it scrapes away particles of wood rather than shavings.

Cutting is faster, produces a smoother surface, and is more dangerous. Scraping is a completely satisfactory method and is recommended for the beginner.

Basically, these were the tools and techniques used by the craftsmen who produced the beautiful, decorative table and chair legs of the elegant furniture of the 17th century. Some were further carved once turning was completed.

Today the powered wood lathe makes it easier to perform many shaping operations. The common cutting tools you would want to own include: the gouge, to make rough cuts; skews; a spearpoint, to make V-grooves; a roundnose, for concave curves; a spear and a parting tool, to make grooves; and good measuring tools (rule, calipers, dividers). Get advice from your lathe supplier as to sizes and varieties.

With these, and considerable practice, you can turn a rectangular chunk of wood into a smooth cylinder; or make it tapered, concave, convex; or give it beads and coves, etc.

Wood turning is addictive. You may start with rolling pins, then candlesticks, then lampstands, then bedsteads, then legs for tables you haven't even made the tops for yet, and proceed to a set of ebony chessmen.

Bending This is another way to change the shape of wood. You may bend wood by softening it first in steam or boiling water; however, this requires a heating tube, equipment few home shops would include.

An alternative is kerfing, which calls only for careful saw work: cutting deep, closely spaced parallel saw cuts across the grain of a strip of wood to render it flexible. This weakens the wood, so it will need support;try gluing it to a strip of plywood.

Lamination is another technique: simply slice a piece of wood into very thin veneers, then glue them back together, clamping them in a curved form and maintaining pressure until the glue is thoroughly set. Unlike plywood, which is cross-laminated, these veneers have grain running all in the same direction. The finished product is very strong because the wood grain is parallel to the curve, and the glue stiffens the assembly.

Laminated wood is less likely to warp, split or check than regular wood. Some examples of uses for your laminated woodwork: furniture parts such as chair arms and backs; headboards for beds; small kitchen necessities like salad servers and spatulas; magazine racks; trays; and, how about making your own water skis?

Hardwoods are best for bending; try mahogany, walnut, ash, birch, maple or oak. Redwood and white cedar, among the softwoods, work well and result in handsome finished products.

Fastening: Joints and Corners

There are hundreds of ways to join one piece of wood to another. Generally you use nails or screws, often along with adhesives. Try to select the simplest method that will do the job. These are the most common methods.

Edge joint The simplest of all, edge joints are nothing but two pieces of wood fastened together to make a wider piece, as when narrow boards are joined to make a table top. Adhesive is nearly always needed here. Dowels and splines help too.

Dowels are round wooden pins, placed in matching holes where the two members of a joint meet. Dowel rod is usually birch, and may be found from ⅛ in. to 1 in. in diameter.

A spline is also a small piece of wood securing two larger pieces to each other, but is flat and inserted into grooves cut in adjoining edges of the two members.

If you nail close to an edge, predrilling the hole may avert disaster. Drill bit should be slightly smaller than diameter of nail you will use. (Courtesy American Plywood Association)

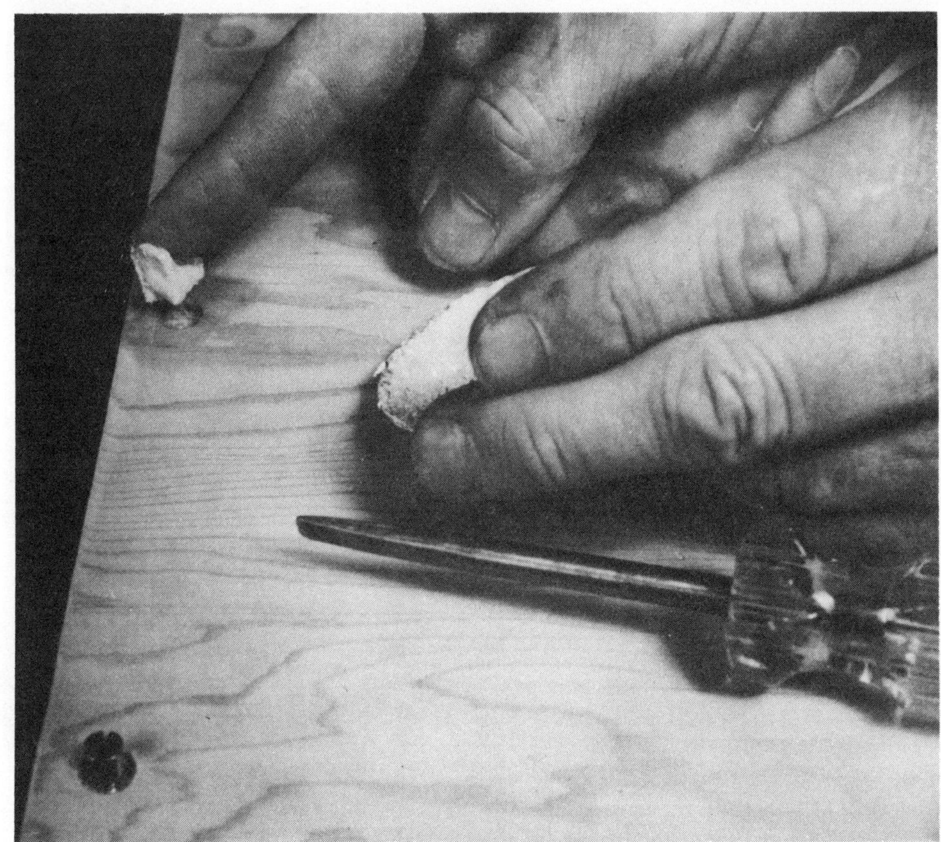

For work that will show, take pains. Countersink screws and nails, fill the holes with wood dough or putty. When dry, sand to level of wood. (Courtesy American Plywood Association)

Butt joints are simple. Left, ¾-in. plywood needs no reinforcing block, as thinner plywood on right does. For strongest joints use glue as well as nails or screws. (Courtesy American Plywood Association)

Butt joint Another simple joint, where the end of one member is connected to the flat surface, edge or end of the other member. The two parts must be flush against each other. Sometimes, to strengthen a butt joint, you need to add a corner block. Adhesive applied to the mating surfaces before fastening will give added strength.

Rabbet joint Made by cutting a rectangular slot in the edge or end of one piece and fitting the end or edge of the second piece into it, it is often used in drawers, chests, cupboards and boxes. You may make the cuts with a hand backsaw, then trim excess wood with a chisel.

Dado joint Similar to a rabbet joint, but the slot or groove is not at the end of the board. It is a common joint where a cross-piece must support considerable weight, as in shelves, bookcases and stairsteps. It may be made by cutting several adjacent saw kerfs, then routing out waste wood with a chisel. But a power saw with dado blade is faster and easier.

Miter joint The miter joint is familiar to any one who has made or taken apart a picture frame. Its peculiar advantage is that it insures that no end grain will show on the finished product. In principle it is similar to a butt joint, but the joining parts ae cut at less than a right angle, usually 45°. While not a very strong joint, it can be beefed up with dowels or a spline across the corner. A miter box is essential to make accurate cuts. Secure the joint with both glue

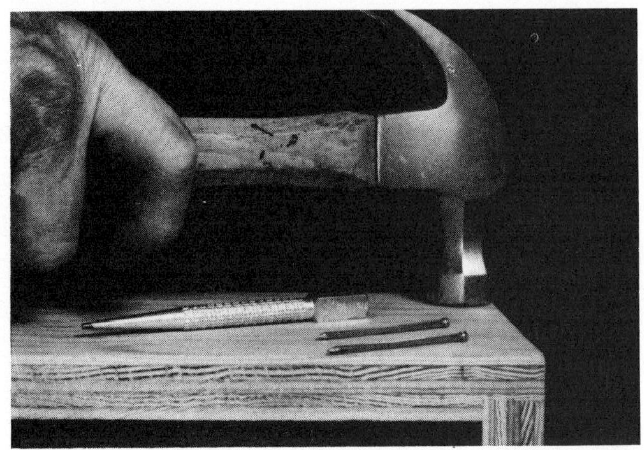

This is a rabbet joint, neat and strong and fairly easy with power tools. Note nail set, used to recess nail head below surface. (Courtesy American Plywood Association)

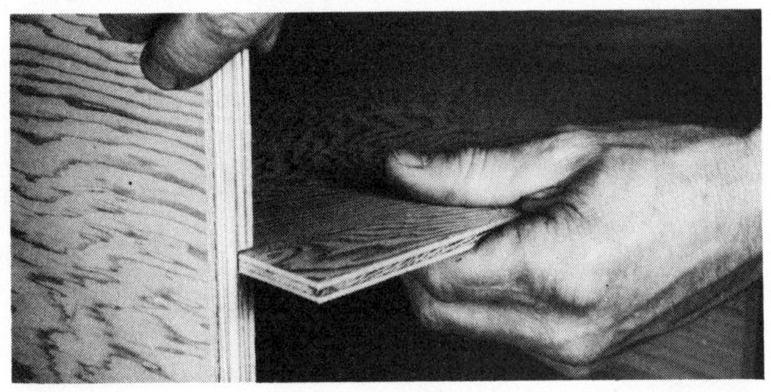

Dado joints are commonly used for shelves. (Courtesy American Plywood Association)

and nails (finish nails or brads). The same procedures are followed for any miter joint, whether with plywood or lumber in cabinetry, or with wood moldings for picture frames.

Mortise-and-tenon joint Used in fine furniture, this joint is hard to do successfully without power tools. There are many variations, but the basic idea is to fit a projecting piece (tenon) of one member into a corresponding hole or notch (motise) of the other. These joints are usually glued.

The commonest joint in chair and table construction is the "blind" mortise-and-tenon, where a rectangular projection on the end of a rail fits into a rectangular hole in the leg, and where the mortise is "blind" or hidden and the end grain of the tenon does not show.

In another and easier type, the "through" mortise-and-tenon, the hole for the mortise is cut entirely through the leg. This means you will have end grain of the tenon exposed, so you would not use this type of joint where a uniformly finished surface is desired, because the end grain may stain unpredictably and may not match the rest of the leg.

If you are making something that calls for one of these joints, your plans will almost certainly include cutting and fitting instructions and diagrams.

Adhesives

Glued joints are strong and reliable; when properly made, they will last as long as the wood itself (or longer).

There are several kinds of glue, each with a different set of qualities. So your key to success will be picking out the one suited to your project, and remembering these basic steps.

1. Make sure both surfaces are clean and dry.
2. If glue is to be mixed, be sure it is of proper thickness.
3. Mark all pieces to be glued, and run through a trial assembly first to make sure everything fits.
4. Follow instructions carefully as to working temperature, amount to mix, whether to let it become tacky, how soon it must be used, etc.
5. Have clamps ready.
6. Apply glue to both surfaces.
7. Clamp parts together securely.
8. Wipe off excess glue.
9. Allow ample drying time (varies with different glues).

Here's an abbreviated guide to glues. (In all cases follow manufacturer's directions for application methods and recommended uses.)

Animal Also called hide glue, it is not much used now, since new synthetics have proliferated. It is available premixed in squeeze bottle, or you can mix your own. This glue makes a very strong joint, sets slowly so you can take your time in assembly, and fills gaps in imperfect joints. Disadvantage: not waterproof; never use for exterior work.

Casein glue You have to mix the powder with water. Quite a strong adhesive, it is not expensive and has fairly good strength. More moisture-resistant than animal glue, but not waterproof. It may stain some woods. Non-toxic.

Contact cement This comes ready to use straight from the can, and is often used to bond plastic laminates to wood (countertops, plywood edging). You apply it to both surfaces, let dry 30 minutes, then assemble and hope you have aligned everything correctly, because it will adhere permanently in an instant.

Epoxy This is the kind of glue which you mix from two tubes and use it at once; do not mix too much. Unlike some glues, it sets at a relatively low temperature and when conditions are moist. It is effective for gluing wood to other nonporous materials (metals, glass, plastic).

Polyvinyl resin glue (white glue) This familiar glue is sold in plastic squeeze bottles. It dries at room temperature, is colorless, and sets quickly. Good for small jobs and indoor use, it is only moderately moisture-resistant.

Resorcinol resin You mix a powder with a liquid and the resulting adhesive forms a very strong, slightly flexible waterproof bond. Use it for outdoor funiture, boats and any application where you're using exterior plywood. But since it costs more than other types and is somewhat harder to mix, don't use it unless you really need its unique qualities. It fills gaps well.

Urea-resin or urea-formaldehyde This comes as a powder which you mix with water. It makes very strong joints, is almost waterproof but is not for indiscriminate outdoor use. It doesn't fill gaps well, so make sure joints fit perfectly.

Hot-melt glue For use in glue gun, it comes in a stick. This glue bonds quickly; use for small areas. It is moderately strong.

Glue has more uses than securing joints. For instance, laminating is a bending technique discussed previously. And woodworkers frequently laminate pieces of wood, edge to edge, to create a larger surface as for a small table top. Or wood may be laminated face to face to produce a thick planklike piece which may then be worked into the desired result.

In such operations, if you are using clamps on wood with a surface you wish to protect, be sure to use cleats or small pieces of scrap wood between the clamp and the wood.

Oak slices were laminated, face-to-face, to make this knife rack. (Courtesy Ann Roush)

Distinctive grain pattern of oak is featured in drawing board made in a home shop. (Courtesy Ann Roush)

Shaker-style table is simply a pegged-together plywood top on trestle supports. (Courtesy of American Plywood Association)

You don't need to be an experienced craftsman to build furniture. This table and chair call for modest investments in time, materials and skill. You can make them with standard lumber sizes and grades, such as fir or pine, using hand tools (though a power drill and circular saw will save time). Turned wood buttons are recommended to cover screw holes. (Plans for Lumberyard Furniture available from Western Wood Products Association)

Small commercial woodworking operations, increasingly threatened by highpowered mass production, have traditionally depended on local wood availability and survival of handed-down skills. Here are two such cottage industries that have prospered well into our century. (Courtesy U.S. Forest Service)

A Missouri craftsman uses a drawknife—a long blade with a handle at each end—to cut strips of white oak for baskets.

The oak strips are then woven into baskets for roadside sale.

Another small-scale woodworking operation: shingled birdhouses created by a North Carolina craftsman.

VII. Finishing Wood

Wood finishing is the last step in the long process of turning part of a tree into an object that will bring grace or utility or both into your life. Properly done, it justifies all the previous steps.

Though your newly built or installed furniture or cabinetry may be flawless in your eyes, you have one more obligation: to give it a finish coat, for two good reasons. First, for the wood's sake: to protect it against stains and dirt and even, with some tough finishes, aagainst dents and scratches, and to make it easier to clean. Second, for the esthetic reasons: to enhance the wood's beauty by bringing out its distinctive grain pattern and giving it a richer color, or changing the color entirely.

There are eight basic steps to a complete wood-finishing job. You need not go through each step for every item you make or work on, but do try to be familiar with them. And remember, these are only general procedural suggestions. In all cases, read and follow manufacturer's instructions for all the products you use.

INTERIOR WOOD FINISHING

First, let us digress a moment and discuss furniture per se. Fine furniture construction and finishing are deeply rooted in tradition. Basic methods have not changed drastically for 3,000 years, when the Egyptians used primitive tools to perform many of the steps we still go through: joining, turning, carving, veneering, painting. The quality of their workmanship is dramatically demonstrated by the few precious examples that have survived.

A piece of fine furniture still warrants special treatment. Whether you have constructed a headboard, bought an unfinished desk, found a neglected chest in the attic, or snapped up a bargain Early American secretary at a roadside antique stand, you will want to give it the respectful, loving attention that good wood deserves.

In the cases of the furniture from the attic or the antique store you will almost certainly need to remove the old finish. So it is pertinent now to bring up stripping—the common term for removing the old finish, as well as all the old wax, polish and dirt that have built up—to reveal the bare wood.

Boxwood and ebony chair from Egypt's New Kingdom (1st and 2nd millenia B.C.). Center figure in carving on back is the god Bes. (Courtesy of Seattle Art Museum)

General tips on stripping wood:

- Always work in a well ventilated room; a fan is a good idea.
- Do not be in a rush. Most finish-removal processes include several periods during which you must wait for the wood to dry. Your job could take two days to a week.
- Be prepared to use a good deal of muscle.
- Keep containers tightly capped when not in use, to avoid loss through evaporation, and to avoid breathing possibly toxic fumes.
- Wear plastic or rubber gloves.
- Don't smoke; many removers are highly flammable.
- Avoid using sandpaper, especially on really fine old wood. Remember, we discussed sandpaper

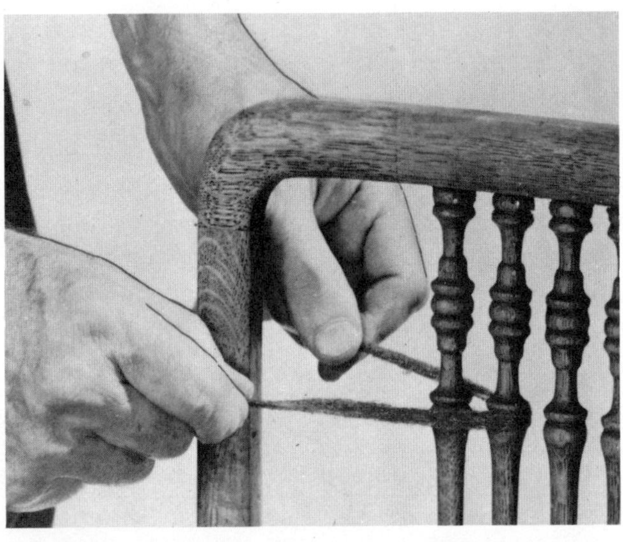

Steel wool entwined with ordinary string can be used for removing finish from spindles. Place steel wool over electrician's black tape. This provides a simple way to remove paint from curved surfaces.

An old lollipop stick with steel wool wrapped around its tip lets you remove finish from carvings and intricate moldings.

A fine steel brush should be used to remove debris from sanding and any other foreign matter present.

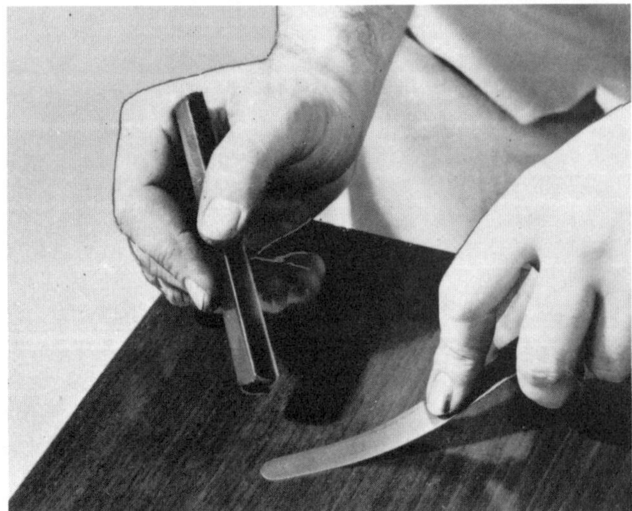

Use stick shellac or wood putty to fill small holes. Gently smooth fill material with a flexible spatula or knife. To smooth dents dampen a cloth, put over dent and apply a hot iron until dent is out.

earlier in the section on cutting tools. That is your clue that it will actually remove not only the old finish but a thin layer of wood as well. Thus you destroy the aged-in patina, the soft, velvety, rich finish that is typical of old woods. (Of course, if you plan to use paint or some other opaque finish, you may sand; you need not even strip the wood.)

Since stripping wood is hard work, you may want to have it done commercially. Take your piece of furniture (unless it is a grand piano) to one of the places that will dip it in a tank of solution; the job is practically done. It is also possible for you to use this method for small pieces at home, but you need a large tub and a lot of remover solution.

Brushing on the remover is the usual and preferred method. Your remover may be the liquid no-wash type; or the wash-off type, which may be liquid or paste. If the latter, you will do well to move the job outdoors because the easiest way to wash off the remover is with the garden hose. This takes a little longer than the no-wash type, because of the drying time after the washing.

Formerly, many people removed paint (not varnish, etc.) with lye. You are advised not to try it unless you are thoroughly familiar with the essential precautions, such as use of safety glasses, and keeping lye from getting on grass or anything it could kill or damage. You should also allow 4 or 5 days for the job. The newer removal products are fully as effective, though maybe more expensive.

As you brush on the remover, work on a small area at a time. If you are using a liquid the surface should be in a horizonal position so the remover won't run off. Brush remover on generously, without skips. In a few minutes, perhaps 3 to 6 (depending on previous finish and type of remover) wipe off the sludge that the remover and the old finish form. Very cautious use of a putty knife, with rounded corners and a dull even blade, will help to push the dissolved finish off the surface. Be careful not to scrape or gouge the wood.

After wiping off the residue gunk, very fine steel wool (grade 1 or 2) can be used to loosen finish in recesses and turnings. For carvings and other hard-to-get-at grooves, use an old toothbrush or a skewer with a piece of steel wool wrapped around the point.

You may need to repeat this several times to get all the old finish off. It is all right to reuse the remover, but only on sections you have not worked on yet. For the final application, use a fresh clean supply and a fresh brush. Otherwise you are adding more dirt than you are getting off. Also be careful not to let remover spatter onto other areas; it will leave stains that you will have to bleach out.

When all the old finish is off, some removers require washing the entire surface with a neutralizer.

If you have used steel wool, every shred must be removed, perferably with a vacuum. And allow plenty of drying time.

Stripping does not remove old stain, just the old finish. If you want to lighten a stained color, bleaching is the next step. It may also be necessary to get rid of old water stains, ink spots, etc., that have penetrated the wood. (Unless you prefer to let them stay, as proof that the piece really is an antique.) For either purpose, laundry bleach is fine, or a solution of oxalic acid. The latter is more hazardous and requires mixing. Do not *ever* inhale the dry oxalic acid.

You will probably need to apply bleach to the whole surface (top or side) where the stain occurs, to avoid having a light-colored blotch that contrasts with the rest of the surface. After use of bleach, a borax solution is recommended as a neutralizer.

It may take several applications to get a spot out. Do not become impatient. Give the bleach time to work, and the wood to dry, before you decide another treatment is needed. The stain may be evident for four hours, then disappear as drying continues. When satisfied, still wait overnight or 24 hours to make sure wood is completely dry, before beginning the next step.

Suppose you have successfully removed the old finish on a piece of furniture that had not been stained. You are down to the bare original wood. And suppose—though it is unlikely—that you want to change the color of the wood itself. With fine furniture woods like walnut, mahogany and cherry, the only good reason for wanting to change color is if you discover that two dissimilarly colored woods were used for a table top or for legs, etc. In that case you would need to bleach the mismatched section in order to restain it in the color of the rest of the piece. This is tricky. Do not use the bleaches referred to above; use instead a wood bleach, and follow instructions carefully.

Repairs

Now, stripped and perhaps bleached, your piece of furniture is ready for repairs, if any are necessary. This may well be the case with an elderly example. You may need to reglue loose joints, for instance. If so, take the old joint completely apart, clean all parts thoroughly, make sure surfaces match well, apply glue according to instructions, and hold the joint tightly while glue dries. This can be done with brads or screws that you may remove later, or with clamps. If you employ clamps, protect your wood surface by placing wax paper and then a piece of wood scrap, between wood and clamp.

Veneers You may also need to repair or replace veneers. The simplest veneer problem is separation from its base, usually at an edge. You probably don't know what kind of glue was used originally if you are working on an antique, so you might as well hope it was the heat-sensitive type, easiest to fix.

(1) Clean dirt from inside of the separated area.

(2) Cover with waxed paper and then several layers of newspapers.

(3) Press with a warm dry iron, checking frequently to see if anything is happening.

(4) If the veneer seems to be sticking, place weights over the spot until the glue cools and check again.

If this doesn't work you'll have to reglue, being conscientious about getting glue well into the separated area's recesses.

If veneer has separated in the middle of a table top or other surface, making a bubble or blister, you may carefully cut down the middle, pry up the two edges and insert glue. Or insert a little instrument like a hypodermic needle. Then apply pressure until it's set.

Splits in veneer are a bit more difficult to fix and require very careful gluing and fitting together. If pieces of veneer are actually missing you are better off replacing the entire surface.

Other Repairs Repairing boards that have split or cracked—or two boards that have separated—also calls for cleaning the surfaces, getting glue into every crevice and applying pressure.

Sometimes drawers in an old piece of furniture will stick. Check the drawer guides first—the small strips of wood in the drawer opening that guide the drawer in and out. They could be worn, broken or even missing. Most often, if they're imperfect, it's easier to replace than repair them.

Finally, you'll often want to repair a burned spot. Use steel wool or for deeper burns, scrape the spot gently. Then you can usually count on your stain and finish to mask the remaining discoloration and fill the slight depression.

For more pointers on these and other refinishing repairs to fine furniture, see the helpful discussion in Savage's book on furniture refinishing, listed in the Appendix.

From now on, your furniture refinishing calls for primarily the same steps as other interior wood finishing, as with bookshelves, built-in cabinets, paneling, doors, etc. The eight basic steps are outlined below.

Finishing Steps

1. Sand and patch, to eliminate indentations in the surface of new wood.
2. Bleach, only if you want to make dark wood lighter or to even out the color. But as discussed above, you can not make a dark wood like mahogany look like birch (and why should you?)
3. Fill. With porous woods (oak, mahogany, walnut, teak, rosewood, for example) you will need to use a paste wood filler to fill the pores and to be sure of getting a supersmooth surface. No filler is needed for small-pore woods such as basswood, cedar, fir, pine, poplar, spruce and willow. You brush the filler on, wipe off the excess, let it dry and wipe again. Allow plenty of time for this step, and follow manufacturer's instructions. Some people stain first, then fill.
4. Seal. This is next if you do not intend to apply stain. Otherwise it follows staining, and seals both filler and stain. The purpose of sealing is to prevent bleeding through of the sap or stain, and to create a nonabsorbent base for the final finish. The sealer is usually a mixture of shellac and denatured alcohol.
5. Stain. Skip this step if you plan to preserve the wood's natural color or to cover it with paint or enamel. Wherever possible test your stain first on a scrap of your wood, or on a spot underneath or on the back of your furniture. Many inexpensive woods may be stained to a close approximation of fine hardwoods. For example, you can stain black gum or tupelo to resemble mahogany or maple. Birch is a veritable chameleon among woods, and can be stained to look like walnut, cherry, mahogany or maple. Other woods that can be disguised as walnut include red or sap gum, tupelo, magnolia or Southern willow. With experimentation you can custom-mix your own stain to achieve the exact shade you wish. But

remember that if you want a realistic result, grain as well as color is important. You will never, for example, get pine or fir to look like walnut.

6. Topcoat. This may be: a clear finish like shellac, varnish or lacquer; a penetrating resin or oil; or paint or enamel.
7. Rub-and-buff. Most of the above finishes require wet-sanding, rubbing and/or buffing to bring out all the latent beauty of wood-plus-finish. Follow directions for your particular kind of finish. Buff with paste wax to add life to the finish and protect it. Don't skip or stint on this step—it makes all your previous hard work worthwhile.
8. Or you may paint, if your wood is not the kind you want to show off. You must still carry out steps 1 through 4, but from then on things are easier. You generally need an undercoat, then apply paint or enamel. Paint, either oil-based or synthetic, does not give as high a gloss as enamel or as hard a surface. Enamel is either oil-based or latex; the latter doesn't cover or withstand wear and tear as well as oil-based enamel, but dries much more quickly and is easy to clean up with water. You can buy enamels with semi-gloss or high-gloss finish, in every imaginable color. You may need two coats.

Stains & Other Finishes

Stains A brief guide to wood stains follows.

Penetrating oil stain. The color soaks into the wood. You apply stain with a cloth or brush, and wipe off excess. If you decide you don't like the color, you can bleach it out and start over. You have a wide choice of wood colors, including fruitwood, light or dark walnut, light or medium or dark oak, mahogany, cherry and rosewood.

Pigmented oil stain. More opaque, for when you want to obscure the pattern, darken the wood, or give two different, adjacent pieces of wood a uniform color. Apply as above.

Water-based stain. You mix an aniline dye in water, or buy it ready-mixed. It is less expensive than other types and gives an even color. But it raises the grain and is slow to dry.

Alcohol stain. Like water stains, but the solvent is alcohol. Fairly costly, and rather tricky to use. These stains come in attractive colors, and are very quick-drying.

Sealer stains. Combination products, that penetrate the wood and also produce a good finish. Brush on, wipe off excess. You still need to apply a final protective finish topcoat.

Varnish stain. Actually, this is a colored varnish (see topcoats, below). You don't wipe off the excess but let it dry, as with varnish.

Topcoats Here is a condensed guide.

Shellac. A good durable coating, and quick-drying. It may darken light-colored woods, so get the bleached (white) shellac for these. Takes a nice shiny polish. But shellac is not proof against alcohol or water—so glasses or vases left on shellacked wood will produce those unsightly white rings.

Varnish. This is a very hard finish, resistant to alcohol, heat and water. But it's slow to dry and may collect dust before fully dry. You should apply two or three coats, sanding lightly between coats. Polyurethane varnish is quicker-drying; may be clear or colored.

Lacquer. It may be sprayed or brushed and produces a very hard finish. Dries very quickly and has a flat or high luster finish. No need to sand between coats. It's best when used over bare wood—never use it over paint or varnish.

Penetrating resin. Soaks into the surface and protects the wood from within. There are quite a few different multipurpose, wipe-on finishes of this nature that seal, stain (or not—your choice), and give a fine furniture finish. Three coats are generally necessary, but they are quick-drying.

Danish oil. This is a well-known example of the penetrating finishes, to be used on natural or stained wood. You'll need several coats, and it won't protect wood against dents or marring, but it gives a beautiful, lustrous finish.

Finishing fir plywood Due to the very pronounced grain pattern of smooth, sanded interior plywood, its finishing takes special attention; otherwise it will look like a "flat zebra," as furniture doctor and author George Grotz warns us.

One way to even out the wild grain in fir plywood and other such woods is to use a product called a color leveler, which should be applied before staining. Because it tones down the contrast between the winter and summer growth patterns, it can make fir plywood look practically like cedar or redwood, when stained.

Finishing sanded softwood plywood Here are the recommendations of the American Plywood Association.

Natural finishes: Assuming you want to tone down but not obscure the natural grain (though few people are that fond of this effect), you may use light stain finishes in either of two ways.

Color toning may be achieved in one step, with a nonpenetrating sealer tinted with a companion stain. Apply by brush or spray, let dry and sand lightly. You may add a coat of clear finish to give luster and durability. Best grain masking is achieved with tones of light gray, brown or tan.

Light staining is a more complicated process, entailing:

(1) applying a pigmented resin sealer to whiten the plywood;
(2) wiping off the sealer before it becomes tacky;
(3) applying clear resin sealer;
(4) drying;
(5) lightly sanding;
(6) adding color (with tinted undercoat, thin enamel, pigmented resin sealer, or light stain) and wiping to get the proper color depth;
(7) drying and lightly sanding;
(8) applying satin varnish or brushing lacquer to give luster and durability.

Painting Far easier than the above, this is your best choice if you do not want any vestige of the plywood grain.

APA says to use oil or alkyd resin (solvent thinned) paints where washability and durability are of prime concern. They can be scrubbed repeatedly, have good hiding properties, and can be brushed, rolled or sprayed. Some are self-priming on wood and are the kind to use on Medium Density Overlaid plywood.

Latex paints are not as washable.

Prime plywood with an oil or alkyd primer, or a stain-resistant latex primer (depending on type of paint you use), which will prevent grain raise and minimize staining.

You may use gloss and semigloss enamels if you want the utmost washability, as in kitchens, bathrooms, cabinets and trim. Apply over the manufacturer's recommended primer.

Finishing textured woods The above refers to finishing sanded, smooth plywood. For textured plywood, stain finishes are beyond any question the preferred method for retaining the natural, woodsy look. Apply in one or two coats, as the manufacturer directs. Stains should be brushed on or worked in with a rag to help work the finish into the wood's surface. Or you may apply by roller, using a long-napped covering.

Stains recommended for use on textured woods and plywood may be of the oil (solvent thinned) or latex emulsion (water thinned) variety. Both types provide excellent performance and are available either semitransparent or opaque. Emulsion stains dry quickly and care is needed to avoid lap marks from double coating previously stained areas. Depending upon the appearance desired, two broad types of stains are available.

Semitransparent or penetrating stains provide maximum grain and color show-through and display of surface texture. The stain penetrates the surface to provide protection, but leaves little surface film. One or two coats may be used to obtain the depth of color desired. This is the favored finish where desirable grain characteristics are to be displayed.

Opaque or heavy-bodied stains are used where masking of all substrate characteristics except texture is desired. These highly pigmented stains usually require only one coat for adequate coverage. Opaque stains penetrate the surface to protect the wood but leave a thin coating of uniform color on the surface. Use where maximum masking is desired on textured plywood such as rough sawn and Texture 1-11.

EXTERIOR WOOD FINISHING

Wood used outside requires different treatment, because it may be affected by sunlight, moisture and wind-carried abrasives. So here is guidance for finishing your siding, your carport, your fence, your planter box, your doghouse—whatever exterior wood construction you wish to protect and preserve.

If you are fortunate enough to have an innately good-looking siding like redwood, Western red cedar or Philippine mahogany, you will probably wish to keep its natural appearance. (See page 124 for special redwood pointers.)

One commonly used finish in such cases is water-repellant preservative, which reduces swelling and shrinking of the wood and protects against mildew and decay but hardly changes wood color—only darkening it very slightly. However, this is a temporary measure and you will need to repeat it in perhaps six months. The actual time lapse will depend on how damp your climate is. If you decide to stain after use of this product, be sure to wait at least 90 days after its last application.

Above all, if you are interested in preserving the original color of your siding, never use a clear polyurethane sealer-type finish, thinking it will protect the wood and keep it looking natural. These products are for interior use only and when subjected to outdoor conditions will crack and craze. Your siding will suffer and so will you.

A much-recommended means to keep cedar, fir, redwood or pine siding looking its beautiful best is to use natural-tone stains, which come in enough variations to match your original color with great fidelity and which last for three to five years before you need to repeat.

If you want to get a jump on nature and achieve a weathered look immediately, you may bleach. You will avoid the darkening that may occur when wood weathers naturally.

Or use weathering stains, which act chemically to change wood color to a silver-gray weathered tone, with uniform results on all four sides of the house. (With completely unaided weathering, different exposures change color at different rates.)

Successful restaining or repainting of siding requires a clean surface with no loose paint or rough spots. (Courtesy of Olympic Stain)

Brushing is the best way to apply stain, to make sure enough gets worked into the wood. Don't apply stain in direct sunlight–it may dry too rapidly. (Courtesy of Olympic Stain)

Edge-sealing of plywood siding is easiest when panels are still stacked. (Courtesy of American Plywood Association)

Suppose you wish to change your wood's color but not its texture or grain: Use a semi-transparent stain (also called light-bodied penetrating stain). This will eventually need a repeat coat.

To completely obscure natural color and grain, a solid color or opaque (heavy-bodied) stain is the answer. This is frequently used on textured wood and plywood sidings. These stains come in all wood tones. They're also made in paint-like colors, from pastels to dark, if you wish to get away from the natural-wood category of finishes.

Most kinds of wood siding may be either stained or painted. Even Medium Density Overlaid plywood, which is preprimed and designed primarily for easy painting, may be given an opaque stain. And textured plywood, though preferably finished with high-quality stain, may be painted.

And while we're on the subject of plywood, there are a few special tips for exterior finishing, mostly having to do with edge sealing. Since end grain surfaces pick up and lose moisture far more rapidly than side grain, all panels should be sealed to minimize possible moisture damage. It is easiest to do this while panels are stacked. If plywood is to be stained, the best way is to liberally apply a good water repellant preservative, compatible with the finish you will be using. If you plan to paint, simply brush your exterior house paint primer on all edges; don't be stingy.

No matter what your choice of wood siding, in deciding on a finish remember that paint, when properly applied, protects wood better against weathering than stain. And it has the wider selection of colors. Your choice of finish will depend, finally, on whether or not you care to have the natural look of wood.

In any case, you are advised to follow the stain or paint manufacturer's directions conscientiously. Also, see the appendix for helpful publications.

Exterior Finishing of Redwood

These tips are based on recommendations of California Redwood Association.

An easy-to-build planter box of redwood. The trickiest part is correct mitering of joints: plan carefully before you cut. (Plans available from California Redwood Association)

No finish at all Permit the redwood lumber or plywood to weather naturally. In a damp climate and over a period of years you may expect the wood to first darken, then (as darkening is rinsed off by rain) to weather-bleach to a soft driftwood gray. But if the siding is sheltered from rains it may stay dark. In a drier climate it is not likely to darken at all, but to turn a silvery tan. A naturally weathered redwood house may have many variations in color because of different amounts of sunlight and rain that reach different areas—and the distinctive character of individual boards. If you wish to speed the weathering, spray the wood with a fine mist from the hose now and then.

Water repellants This modifies the effects of weathering and eliminates the darkening stage. Wood gradually changes from reddish-brown to a buckskin tan, then stabilizes. It may eventually bleach to driftwood gray. An advantage of this treatment is that it is easy to apply another finish without major surface preparation. You may buy redwood siding that has been pretreated with water repellant, or you may apply it yourself by brush or dipping (not spray gun). It usually takes two coats. Make sure the water repellant contains a mildewcide. And if used on planter boxes, let dry one week before planting.

Bleaches This hastens redwood's natural color changes and produces a permanent driftwood gray color, faster than natural weathering. Add gray stain to the bleaching oil if you wish to achieve instant weathering. Again, to guard against discoloration, be sure the bleach oil contains a mildewcide.

Stains Light-bodied penetrating stains, or opaque heavy-bodied stains (see above) are both appropriate, depending on how much of the wood grain you wish to obscure.

Paint Redwood holds paint better than any other wood, because of its open cellular structure and complete absence of pitch and resins. For the prime coat, you are advised to always use an oil or alkyd base paint, but top coats (two are recommended) may be any type: oil or alkyd or synthetic base, or water emulsion. Just make sure it is for exterior use.

How Much Stain Will You Need?

Stain	New wood		Re-do	
(in sq. ft. per gal.)	Rough surface	Smooth surface	Rough surface	Smooth surface
Solid color oil base stain	100-200	300-400	200-300	300-400
Solid color acrylic latex stain	100-200	200-300	100-200	200-300

Measure the distance around your house and multiply this by the height from foundation to roofline; if your home has gables, add 2 ft. before you multiply.

Subtract the area taken up by large windows, doors, etc., that won't be stained.

Then divide the total by the coverage in square feet per gallon indicated in this table (may vary according to surface characteristics of wood). Table courtesy of Olympic Stain)

SIMPLE METHODS OF WOOD PRESERVATIVE TREATMENT FOR POSTS

Treatments of Low First Cost

If you cut your own posts, have no help, and want to spend as little cash as possible, you may be willing to settle for a shorter post life—just so the treatment saves you money and work in the long run.

If so, preservatives such as water solutions of zinc chloride or chromated zinc chloride may work best for you, since the dry chemicals cost only 10 to 20 cents a pound and a pound will usually take care of one post. These chemicals are fairly clean to handle and are not dangerous to people or animals. They can be bought in dry form and mixed with water just before use, so that you get away from heavy freight charges. They can also be bought in the form of strong water solutions that call for extra water before using. These are easier to use and store than the dry form and may be practical where the freight haul from the supplier to you is not too long.

End-Diffusion Treatment on Green Unpeeled Posts

The end-diffusion or trough method of treating with zinc chloride is quite simple and has been given considerable study by the South Carolina Agricultural Experiment Station at Clemson College, the Forest Products Laboratory, and others. It consists in standing freshly cut unpeeled posts in a tub or other container into which you have poured a measured quantity of 15- to 20-percent zinc chloride solution or chromated zinc chloride solution. Copper sulfate is sometimes used but it is not recommended because it is highly corrosive to staples and fencing wire and has not done as well as zinc chloride in service.

About 5 pounds or approximately ½ gallon of 20-percent (by weight) zinc chloride solution is recommended for each cubic foot of post treated. The posts are allowed to stand with the butts down in the solution until approximately three-fourths of the solution has been absorbed—which may take from 1 to 10 days or longer. After treating with butts down the posts are turned over, and the tops are allowed to absorb the remaining solution. They are then stored for at least 30 days with the tops down to permit distribution of the preservative within the post before it is set in the soil

The South Carolina Agricultural Experiment Station reports that the treatment works well with southern pine posts. The Forest Products Laboratory in Wisconsin has obtaind fair to good penetrations and retentions in the treating of aspen and jack pine under the following conditions: (1) Posts cut during summer and early fall seasons, (2) treatment started within 7 days after cutting trees, (3) temperatures above freezing.

An average life of 8.5 years was estimated from 4 tests of birch and southern pine posts treated with either zinc chloride or copper sulfate by end diffusion while the average life of untreated posts of these woods was 4.4 years. Of 5 species treated with zinc chloride and tested in Mississippi, posts of slash pine and red oak were in serviceable condition after 4 years while those of sweetbay, sweetgum, and tupelo were estimated to have an average life of from 3 to 4 years.

The advantages and disadvantages of end-diffusion treatment can be summed up as follows:

Advantages	*Disadvantages*
Low first cost.	Protection limited
Peeling not necessary.	Results of treatment not uniform.
Preservative may be bought and shipped dry or in concentrated form.	Water-borne preservatives subject to leaching.
Requires little equipment.	
Does not call for surplus of preservative.	
Can be used conveniently for small batches of posts.	

Tire-Tube Treatment

Tank soaking treatments, except for end diffusion treatments, are somewhat wasteful of preservative since they end up with leftover preservative. A treating method that gets you away from most of this loss is the so-called tire-tube treatment with water-dissolved preservatives as developed by the Forest Products Laboratory. This consists in setting posts on a slant, butt end up, with sections of old truck tire inner tubes slipped over the upper end, pouring a measured amount of zinc chloride solution into the supported tubes, and letting gravity force the solution lengthwise through the post, to replace the sap with treating solution. The method works only with green, round posts with the bark still on. It does not work with split or sawed posts. The posts preferably should be treated soon after cutting.*

The tire-tube treatment on posts of several species has provided an average life of 10 to 15 years.

Steeping Treatment

Another low-cost method of using water-dissolved zinc chloride to treat farm timbers is the simple tank steeping method. In this treatment either green or seasoned peeled posts or timbers are soaked for 1 or 2 weeks in unheated 5-percent zinc chloride solution. When time is very limited, the soaking period can be shortened to 3 days with fair results, but the longer treating times are better.

As with other methods of treatment, the results of steeping vary with different woods and with different exposure conditions. Posts of woods such as hickory, southern red oak, sweetbay, sweetgum, and water tupelo have not shown a significant increase in life as a result of steeping in zinc chloride, particularly when tested under warm moist climatic conditions. Southern yellow pine posts similarly treated perform somewhat better under these conditions. Western red cedar posts last reasonably long without treatment and no significant increase in service has been noted in posts of this species treated by steeping in zinc chloride. Treatment by steeping has been found to be definitely beneficial in the case of round posts of ash, jack pine, lodgepole pine, ponderosa pine, red pine, and Scotch pine tested in Wisconsin, Nebraska, and Montana. Posts of various species treated by steeping and included in 43 different installations have an estimated average life of 15.8 years.

Brushing is also considered suitable only for preservative oils. It is generally advisable to apply two coats of the preservative by flooding rather than brushing it over the wood surface. The oil should be heated if it is not sufficiently fluid at the prevailing temperature. Special care should be taken to fill every check and crevice in the wood and to apply the preservative liberally to the end grain. The first coat should be allowed to dry completely before the second coat is put on.

The advantages of the brushing method over the others are its simplicity and the small quantity of preservative that is used. Sapwood pine 2 by 4 inches treated by brushing two coats (with creosote) showed a retention of 0.76 pound per cubic foot or about one-half that resulting from dipping 3 minutes in the same preservative. Brushing requires little equipment and you need have no excess of preservative left over after the wood is treated. Brushing is more time-consuming than dipping, however, and is therefore more costly. You will find it of value in treating parts of large sticks if they cannot be tank treated, and in treating timber at joints and all points of contact where decay is likely to occur. As mentioned before, brushing or dipping adds less to decay resistance than do the other treatments that result in real penetration.

Like dipping, the brushing method is suitable only for use on peeled, thoroughly seasoned, and dry timber. It is best to use it in warm weather. In cold weather, the preservative is cooled and penetrates less readily. Penetration in any event will be shallow.

The apparatus for treatment consists only of a pail and a suitable brush. A small soft broom might be substituted for the brush if desired.

Although brush applications of preservatives are often beneficial when the wood is not used where it is likely to be moist for long periods, service tests on posts indicate that the treatment has doubtful value when applied to wood used in contact with the ground. In 10 tests of posts of various species such as Douglas-fir, red oak, white oak, northern white-cedar, lodgepole pine, and spruce, the estimated average life of the treated posts is only 9.5 years while the average life of untreated posts of these woods is approximately the same. Of these 10 tests only 1 showed a definite increase in post life due to the brush treatment.

STORAGE OR RE-USE

It would be a misfortune, and a waste of your investment, to let your valuable wood products deteriorate before you are ready to use them. Your own common sense, and the facts we have already dis-

*Complete details of the tire-tube treatment are available in Report No. 1158, Tire-Tube Method of Fence Post Treatment, which can be obtained free from the Forest Products Laboratory, Madison, Wis. 58705.

cussed as to what can damage or threaten wood's integrity, will guide you. But here are a few elementary rules for proper storage.

Lumber

The first precaution is something like making sure the mother stays healthy before the baby is born. Satisfy yourself that the lumber is seasoned properly when you buy it. For example: lumber graded by the Western Wood Products Association will include in the grade-stamp information as to degree of dryness: S-DRY indicates moisture content not exceeding 19 percent; MC-15 means moisture content not exceeding 15 percent; and S-GRN means moisture content is over 19 percent. Similarly, Southern Pine grading rules require this information to be readily evident: S-DRY means moisture content does not exceed 19 percent while M-15 means not exceeding 15 percent.

The reason for seasoning is to bring the lumber close to the moisture content at which it normally stabilizes after the house is built, that is, from 12 to 15 percent. This safeguards you from the annoyance, and maybe replacement costs, of lumber that warps, twists or cracks, and prevents nails that pop away as well as the pulling-apart of floor or ceiling joints.

You have to trust your dealer for storing lumber properly in his yard. But once you have brought it home it's up to you. Carelessness could permit moisture content to become excessive.

Of course, ideally you will use your lumber as soon as you bring it home. But even if you have to store it only for a short time, observe these precautions.

Whether stored in a building or outside, framing lumber should not be in water or mud. If untreated, it should not be in contact with the ground at all, but raised on stringers so air can circulate underneath. Many people stack lumber with the first layer in one direction, the next at right angles, and so on.

If you store it outside, cover it to protect it from rain and snow but do not use plastic coverings for long-term storage; they do not permit moisture trapped inside to get out. Be even more attentive to siding and exterior finish lumber, and keep them in an enclosed, unheated area.

As for interior materials—flooring, millwork, cabinet lumber—they should also be kept in an enclosed space, preferably where you may turn on some heat to keep the proper moisture content during damp weather.

Plywood

Once again, treat with thoughtful care: store it in a cool, dry place out of sun and weather. If you have a large quantity to store and it is delivered strapped together, loosen or cut the straps. If stored outdoors, cover as with lumber.

If it will be a while before you actually put the plywood in place, at least give it the first coat and the edge sealing as soon as possible, to minimize moisture penetration.

For safety's sake, avoid storing wood (including firewood) next to and touching exterior wood walls of homes or buildings.

Recycling Wood Products

The thrifty woodperson re-uses as much material as possible. Lumber and especially plywood left over from concrete formwork can find good use in structural applications—framing, sheathing, flooring—where they will not show and will still serve you well.

Most of us are familiar with the appeal of old barn boards for siding and interior use. In fact, they have become so popular that there are thriving little businesses devoted to making new boards look like old boards, complete with moss and lichen.

You may get more satisfaction out of finding your own supply. When you see a tumbledown deserted cottage or farm building, it is possible, with a little research and time, to find out who owns it. Do not be instrusive or aggressive, but chances are the owner will be glad to entertain your offer to take it down and carry off the pieces, if you also make a moderate payment.

Beaches are another good hunting-ground for reusable bits of wood. Collect well-weathered beach boards and use them on walls, where they are a pleasant change from some of the ultra-smooth look-alike panelings.

Sometimes you can find an old cask or barrel to cut in two and use the halves as planters. Whiskey barrels are especially suitable. Warning: these "tight-cooperage" barrels really are watertight. So be sure to drill a few holes in the bottom, to insure proper drainage.

Aside from the aesthetic satisfaction you get from a well-seasoned piece of wood, there is much to recommend reuse from the conservation standpoint: Wood products are getting scarcer and costlier. But wood does not wear out readily, and any way we can extend its useful life may keep a few more trees standing a little longer.

Appendix 1:

Major Commercial Wood Species: Domestic and Imported

Based on nomenclature and classification of U.S. Forest Service in Agriculture Handbook No. 72, revised 1974. However, a few species have been added which, though not produced commercially, are known to and used by many workers in wood.

DOMESTIC HARDWOODS

Alder, red (Alnus rubra). Most abundant hardwood along Pacific Coast, Alaska to California. Wood is almost white, to pale pinkish brown; turns orange-brown after cutting. No boundary between sapwood and heartwood. Moderately lightweight, intermediate in strength, low in shock-resistance and shrinkage. *Use.* Furniture, pulpwood and fuel, mainly; also sash, doors, millwork, panel stock. European alder is much used for plywood.

Apple (Malus pumila). Native to Europe and western Asia, but now grown almost worldwide. Moderately heavy wood, often with spiral or distorted grain if from a tree with a misshapen trunk. May warp and split in drying, but once dry is stable in use. Hard, strong, tough. Saws, machines, takes stains and polishes well. Not decay-resistant. *Use.* Not a commercial wood, but suitable for crafts and small-shop production. Turns extremely well, good for carving.

Ash: Eastern species (Fraxinus americana, F. Pennsylvanica, F. quadrangulata, F. nigra, F. profunda); Western species (F. latifolia, Oregon ash). Eastern half of the U.S., except Oregon ash which grows along the Pacific Coast and is mainly a fuelwood. Heartwood is brown; sapwood nearly white. Heavy, hard, strong, stiff with high shock resistance. Species vary considerably in character. *Use.* Tougher wood for handles, oars, baseball bats, cricket stumps, other sporting equipment. Lighter, less strong woods for cooperage, furniture, containers. Some use for veneer paneling.

Aspen: bigtooth (Populus grandidentata), quaking (P. tremuloides). In commercial use, sometimes confused with cottonwoods and poplars. Wood of aspens and cottonwood sometimes mixed and sold as poplar ("popple") or cottonwood. Northern Lake states, Rockies. Heartwood is grayish white to light grayish brown, merges gradually into lighter sapwood. Straight-grained, fine uniform texture, easy to work, lightweight, soft, low strength. *Use.* Lumber for light structural work; pallets, boxes, crating, pulpwood, particleboard, matches (cut from veneer).

Basswood: American (Tilia americana), white (T. heterophylla). Sometimes called linden, linn, beetree. In Europe, known as lime, often seen as decorative trees along avenues and in parkland. Eastern half of U.S. Heartwood pale yellow-brown with darker streaks, merging gradually into wide, white sapwood. Soft and lightweight, fine and even-textured, straight-grained, easy to work. Large shrinkage, but does not warp in use. Not strong. *Use.* Sash and door frames, Venetian blinds, woodenware (because it is odorless and tasteless, often used for dairy and domestic utensils), boxes. Some use as veneer, cooperage, pulpwood. One of the best woods for carving; Grinling Gibbons used lime (basswood) for his flower and fruit carvings in the 17th century.

Beech, American (Fagus grandifolia). Central, Middle Atlantic states. Close, uniform texture, not much figure. Color varies from nearly white sapwood to reddish-brown heartwood in some trees. Wood is heavy, hard, strong, highly shock-resistant. Works well, takes a good finish. Large shrinkage. *Use.* Flooring, furniture, handles and woodenware (it turns well), containers, cooperage. Treated, as railway ties.

Birch: yellow (Betula alleghaniensis), sweet (B. lenta), paper (B. papyrifera). From Canada through Northeast and Lake states; yellow and sweet birch also along Appalachian Mts. to North Georgia. These two are heavy, hard, strong, have good shock resistance, fine uniform texture, considerable shrinkage. Yellow birch has white sapwood, light reddish-brown heartwood. Sweet birch sapwood is light-colored, heartwood dark brown tinged with red. Paper birch is lower in weight, softer, weaker. *Use.* Yellow and sweet birch lumber and veneer are used in furniture, boxes, crates, woodenware, cooperage, doors. Birch plywood is much used in cabinets and furniture. Paper birch—first notable through use of its bark for canoes—is now used for turned products: spools, handles, toys.

Buckeye: yellow (Aesculus octandra), Ohio (A. glabra). European horse-chestnut (A. hippocastanum) is widely grown in Europe as an ornamental tree. Appalachians of Pennsylvania, Virginia, N. Carolina west to Kansas, Oklahoma, Texas. Uniform textured, straight-grained, lightweight, soft, low in shock resistance. White sapwood merges gradually into creamy or yellowish-white heartwood. Does not machine well. *Use.* As lumber, used for same purposes as aspen, basswood, sap yellow-poplar. Used for pulpwood; and boxes, planing mill products.

Butternut: white walnut, oilnut (Juglans cinerea). From southern New Brunswick and Maine, west to Minnesota; south to Arkansas and east to N. Carolina. About same weight as Eastern white pine (moderately light), soft, not very stiff. Narrow, nearly white sapwood and light brown heartwood. Machines well. *Use.* Lumber, veneer for cabinets, furniture, paneling.

Cascara: buckthorn, polecat tree, bitter bark, wild coffee (Rhamnus purshiana). Pacific Northwest, British Columbia to California. Wood is light brown with a reddish-orange tinge, soft and fairly heavy, and has no commercial use because of the small size of the tree. *Use.* Important for its bark, which is peeled and dried to make the well-known medicine cascara sagrada.

Cherry, black: wild black cherry, wild cherry, chokecherry (Prunus serotina). Scattered, from southeastern Canada throughout eastern U.S. Heartwood is light to dark reddish brown with distinctive luster. Sapwood narrow, white. Uniform texture, machines well; moderately heavy, strong and stiff. High shock resistance. Dimensionally stable after seasoning. *Use.* Furniture, fine veneer for paneling, caskets.

Chestnut, American, sweet chestnut (Castanea dentata). Once grew from New England to northern Georgia, but most has been killed by a blight. Some standing dead timber is still harvested. *Use.* Was used for poles, railway ties, furniture, boxes, fences; very durable for outdoor uses. Some "wormy chestnut" now seen in paneling, trim, picture frames.

Coast live oak, evergreen oak (Quercus agrifolia). Southern California north to San Francisco, in valleys and along coastal mountains. Wood tends to warp and check. *Use.* Little or no commercial value.

Cottonwood: eastern (Populus deltoides), swamp cottonwood (P. heterophylla, also known as swamp poplar), black (P. trichocarpa), balsam (P. balsamifera). Eastern and swamp cottonwood grow throughout eastern half of U.S. Black and balsam poplar grow from Alaska across Canada, and in northern Lakes states. Sapwood is whitish and merges gradually with grayish-white to light-brown heartwood. Uniform in texture, straight-grained. Not a very strong wood, and some is difficult to work with tools because of fuzzy surfaces. *Use.* Lumber and veneer for boxes, crates, baskets, pallets. Also pulpwood and fuel.

Elm: American (Ulmus americana), slippery or red elm (U. rubra), rock, cork or hickory elm (U. Thomasii), winged elm or wahoo (U. alata), cedar elm (U. crassifolia), September or red elm (U. serotina). Eastern U.S., but supply severely threatened by Dutch elm disease and phloem necrosis. Sapwood nearly white, heartwood light brown. The hard, somewhat heavier elms are rock, winged, cedar and September; soft varieties are American and slippery elm. Both have excellent bending qualities. *Use.* Lumber for boxes and barrels; furniture; veneer for decorative paneling.

Hackberry (Celtis occidentalis). Lumber from sugarberry (C. laevigata) also known as hackberry. Hackberry grows east of the Great Plains, from Alabama, Georgia, Arkansas and Oklahoma northward. Sugarberry, from southern range of hackberry, throughout southern and South Atlantic states. Sapwood is pale yellow to greenish- or grayish-yellow. Heartwood darker. Wood is moderately heavy, stronger in bending than compression. *Use.* Lumber for furniture, containers.

Hickory, pecan: bitternut hickory (Carya cordiformis), pecan (C. illinoensis), water hickory (C.

aquatica), nutmeg hickory (C. myristicaeformis). Central and South Central U.S. Considered inferior to true hickory, which wood it resembles. Heavy, large shrinkage. *Use.* Tool and implement handles, flooring. Lower grades used in pallets. Higher grade logs sliced for veneer for furniture and paneling.

Hickory, true: shagbark (Carya ovata), pignut (C. glabra), shellbark (C. laciniosa), mockernut (C. tomentosa). Southern Canada and throughout eastern U.S., with most commercial production in Middle Atlantic and Central states. Sapwood white and thick, heartwood reddish. Wood is exceptionally tough, hard, heavy and strong. Considerable shrinkage. Hard on saws and cutting tools because of weight. *Use.* Tool handles (because of high shock resistance); ladder rungs, athletic equipment, agricultural implements, dowels, furniture. Lower-grade (because knotty) hickory is used for pallets, blocking. Sawdust and chips used to flavor meat by smoking.

Holly, American: white holly, evergreen holly, boxwood (Ilex opaca). Natural range is along Atlantic Coast, Gulf Coast, Mississippi Valley. Heartwood and sapwood white. Uniform, compact texture. Heavy and hard, high in shock resistance. Can be dyed (dyed black, substitutes for ebony). Works well, cuts smoothly. *Use.* Not enough production for wide commercial use. But some for scientific and musical instruments, furniture inlays, athletic goods. Burns well. Best known for shiny leaves and red berries as Christmas decorations.

Honeylocust (Gleditsia triacanthos). Natural range is eastern U.S., except New England, South Atlantic, Gulf Coast plains, but has been extended by planting. Sapwood wide and yellowish, heartwood light red to reddish-brown. Very strong, hard, stiff, shock-resistant. Attractive figure. Unfortunately it is very scarce. *Use.* Not much commercial use because of scarcity. Used locally for fenceposts, lumber.

Locust, black: Yellow locust, white locust, green locust, post locust (Robinia pseudoacacia). From Pennsylvania along Appalachians to northern Georgia, and in a small area in northwestern Arkansas. Narrow, creamy-white sapwood and greenish-yellow to dark brown heartwood which darkens on exposure. Very heavy, hard, highly shock-resistant, high in strength and stiffness. Moderately small shrinkage. Heartwood highly resistant to decay and termites. *Use.* Much used for mine timbers, fenceposts, railroad ties, poles, stakes. Also fuel.

Madrone, Pacific: madrona (Arbutus menziesii). Pacific Coast, British Columbia to California. Wood is reddish-brown, heavy, brittle, has high shrinkage and is easy to work but warps readily. *Use.* Not a valuable timber species. But madrona logs are used locally for fencing and fuel. Experimentation indicates it could produce good rotary-cut veneer.

Magnolia: Southern magnolia, evergreen magnolia, big laurel, bull bay, laurel bay (Magnolia grandiflora), sweetbay, swamp magnolia (M. virginiana), cucumbertree (M. acuminata). Natural range of Southern magnolia is from North Carolina to Texas; of sweetbay, along Atlantic and Gulf Coasts from Long Island to Texas. Cucumbertree grows from Appalachians to Ozarks, and northward to Ohio. Most commercial production is from Louisiana. Sapwood of Southern magnolia is pale, heartwood light to dark brown. Wood is close-textured, generally straight-grained, like yellow-poplar. Moderately hard and stiff, with good shock resistance, below average in bending and compression strength. Sweetbay similar. Cucumbertree is like yellow-poplar and marketed with it. *Use.* Lumber for furniture, boxes, pallets, Venetian blinds, sash, doors, millwork, veneer.

Maple: sugar (Acer saccharum), black (A. nigrum), silver (A. saccharinum), red (A. rubrum), box-elder (A. negundo), bigleaf or Oregon (A. macrophyllum). Grows extensively throughout the U.S., but most commercial production is from Middle Atlantic and Lake states. Wood of sugar and black maple is known as hard maple; that of silver and red maple and boxelder is known as soft maple. Sapwood is white with slight reddish-brown tinge. Heartwood is light reddish-brown, sometimes darker. Hard maple has a fine, uniform texture, is heavy, strong, stiff, hard, shock-resistant. It has large shrinkage. Sugar maple, when not straight-grained, is known as "birdseye," "curly," or "fiddleback." Soft maple is less heavy. *Use.* Principally lumber, veneer, crossties and pulpwood. Hard maple, because of abrasion resistance, is an outstanding flooring material, especially where floors get hard use—dance halls, gyms. Maple is also used for furniture, boxes, pallets, crates, shoe lasts, handles, woodenware, spools and bobbins. Though substitutes and imitations have made inroads, maple sugar and maple syrup from New England's sugar maples are still produced and prized.

Oak (red oak group): northern (Quercus rubra), scarlet (Q. coccinea), many others. Most production from Southern and Central states, and Atlantic coastal plains. Sapwood is white, heartwood brown with a tinge of red. Considered inferior to white oak because it is more permeable and less durable. It is heavy and harder to saw and machine. It is less suitable for exterior use. *Use.* Lumber, veneer, flooring, furniture, boxes, pallets, crates, boxes, agricultural implements, caskets, handles. When preservative-treated, used for railroad ties, mine timbers, fenceposts.

Oak (white oak group): white (Quercus alba), chestnut (Q. prinus), overcup (Q. stellata), chinkapin (Q. macrocarpa), live (Q. virginiana), others. Most commercial production is from Southern, South Atlantic, and Central states. Heartwood is grayish-brown; sapwood is nearly white. Wood is heavy, heartwood has good decay resistance, and heartwood of most species is impenetrable by liquids. Among them, the oaks account for more standing timber in the nation than any other hardwood. *Use.* Lumber, railroad ties, fencing, posts, veneer, railroad car and truck flooring. Because of decay resistance of heartwood, it is used for planking and bent parts of ships and boats. High-quality white oak is especially sought for tight cooperage, as in whiskey and sherry casks. Historically, oak has a distinguished record as a structural and decorative material.

Pear (Pyrus communis). A northern temperate tree, with most usable timber from old orchard trees. Pale pinkish-brown to rosy-red wood has uniform, very fine texture, straight- or irregular-grained according to shape of trunk. Properties similar to apple; may blunt saws. *Use.* Limited supply and not much commercial use. Turns well, as for bowls and handles. Good for carving because of very fine texture. Takes a good finish. Veneer used in cabinetry, inlaying, especially (previously) in French furniture.

Sassafras (Sassafras albidum). Most of eastern half of U.S. Wood resembles black ash. Sapwood is light yellow, heartwood dull grayish-brown or dark brown, sometimes reddish. Moderately heavy, hard; weak in bending and compression; shock-resistant; decay-resistant. *Use.* Not an important commercial wood, but well known for use of bark as sassafras tea. Indians prized sassafras wood for dugout canoes and some lumber is still used for small boats. Locally, used for fenceposts and rails, containers, millwork.

Sweetgum (Liquidambar styraciflua). From southwestern Connecticut westward into Missouri and southward to the Gulf. Sapwood and heartwood are differentiated—former is lightcolored; latter (known as red gum) is lustrous and reddish-brown and has a ribbon-stripe pattern due to interlocked grain. This is desirable for its uses as furniture and interior finish. Wood is moderately strong, heavy, stiff and shock-resistant. *Use.* Lumber, veneer, plywood, slack (dry) cooperage, railroad ties, fuel, pulpwood.

Sycamore, American: sycamore, buttonwood, buttonball tree, planetree (Platanus occidentalis). From Maine to Nebraska, southward to Texas, and eastward to Florida. Central states rank first in production of sycamore lumber. Heartwood is reddish-brown, sapwood lighter. Wood has a fine texture and interlocked grain; is moderately hard, stiff, strong, has good shock resistance. Saws well but has slight tendency to bind. *Use.* Lumber, veneer, railroad ties, slack cooperage, fenceposts, fuel. Lumber is used for pallets, furniture, flooring, handles, butchers' blocks. Veneer is used for fruit and vegetable baskets, some decorative paneling. The planetree is familiar in Europe and America, along urban streets.

Tanoak (Lithocarpus densiflorus). Southwestern Oregon and south to southern California, mostly near coast but also in Sierra Nevada. Sapwood is light reddish-brown, turns darker with age to become almost indistinguishable from heartwood, which also ages to dark reddish-brown. Wood is heavy and hard and in strength properties roughly like Eastern white oak. *Use.* Because it is hard and abrasion-resistant, used for flooring. Commercial importance of wood is recent, but tannin has long been obtained from the bark.

Tupelo, water tupelo, tupelo gum, swamp tupelo, gum (Nyssa aquatica), black tupelo, black gum, sour gum (N. sylvatica), Ogeechee tupelo, sour tupelo, gopher plum, Ogeechee plum (N. ogeche). All but black tupelo grow principally in southeastern U.S. Black tupelo grows in the eastern U.S. from Maine to Texas and Missouri. Heartwood of most tupelos is light brownish-gray, merging gradually into lighter-colored sapwood. Wood has fine, uniform texture, is moderately heavy, strong, hard and stiff; also moderately shock-resistant. Water tupelo, which grows in swamps, has a buttressed (enlarged) base, wood from which is much lighter in weight than that above. *Use.* Lumber for boxes, pallets, crates, baskets, furniture; tupelo is also rotary-peeled for veneer and plywood.

Walnut, black (Juglans nigra). Natural range from Vermont to Great Plains and southward into Louisiana and Texas. Most production from Central states. Heartwood, light to dark brown. Sapwood, nearly white. Wood is normally straight-grained, easily worked, and stable in use. Heavy, hard, strong, stiff and shock-resistant. Well-suited to natural finishes. *Use.* As solid wood or plywood, used for architectural woodwork, paneling, cabinets. A longtime decorative wood. Also used for bowls, other turned items, gunstocks.

Willow, black (Salix nigra). Mostly produced in Mississippi Valley from Louisiana to southern Missouri and Illinois. Heartwood is grayish brown or light reddish brown. Sapwood whitish to creamy yellow. It is light in weight, not particularly strong. *Use.* Wood is not of great commercial importance. Small amounts used for slack cooperage, veneer, excelsior, charcoal, pulpwood, artificial limbs (because it combines light weight with toughness), fenceposts. But principal use is lumber for construction.

Yellow-poplar: poplar, tulip poplar, tulipwood, hickory poplar (Liriodendron tulipifera). From Connecticut and New York southward to Florida and westward to Missouri. Sapwood is white, heartwood yellowish-brown often streaked with green, black, blue or red. Wood generally straight-grained, uniform in texture. Much second-growth wood is heavier, harder and stronger than old-growth. *Use.* Lumber for furniture, interior finish, siding; core stock and cross-banding for plywood; pulpwood, excelsior, slack cooperage staves.

DOMESTIC SOFTWOODS

Alaska-cedar: yellow cypress, yellow cedar (Chamaecyparis nootkatensis). Pacific Coast of North America from southeastern Alaska to southern Oregon. Heartwood is bright, clear yellow; sapwood white to yellowish, hardly distinguishable from heartwood. Wood is fine-textured, straight-grained, moderately heavy, strong and stiff, also moderately hard and high in shock resistance. Shrinks little in drying and is stable after seasoning. Heartwood very resistant to decay. Distinctive resinous odor when freshly cut. *Use.* Not abundant. Commercial uses include boat-building, joinery, furniture. One of the best woods for battery separators.

Baldcypress: cypress, Southern cypress, red cypress, yellow cypress, white cypress (Taxodium distichum). Mostly from southeastern U.S. Less available than formerly. Sapwood is narrow and nearly white. Heartwood color varies from light yellowish-brown to dark brownish red, brown, or chocolate. Wood is moderately heavy, moderately strong and hard, and heartwood of old-growth wood is very decay-resistant. Pecky cypress is marked by pockets of fungus-caused decay which is arrested when wood is cut and dried; it is a durable and useful wood for interior paneling, with a unique appearance. *Use.* A valuable structural wood where resistance to decay is required, as in docks, warehouses, factories, bridges and heavy construction, roofing shingles. Other uses where its special durability is valuable include tanks, vats, cooperage, boatbuilding, railroad ties, poles and piling.

Douglas fir: red fir, Douglas spruce, yellow fir (Pseudotsuga menziesii). From Rockies to Pacific Coast and from Mexico to central British Columbia. Has been introduced and grown commercially in many other temperate countries. Wood is pale to medium red-brown, varies widely in weight and strength. Has a conspicuous growth ring figure, particularly on flat-sawn or rotary-cut surfaces. Dries quickly and well, is noted for strength and workability. Moderately resistant to decay. *Use.* One of the world's most valuable woods and the leading structural wood from western North America. Lumber, timbers, piling and plywood are major structural uses. Also, railroad ties, cooperage, poles, mine timbers, fencing. Douglas fir plywood, as noted elsewhere in this book, has numerous structural, industrial, agricultural and woodworking applications. Douglas fir Christmas trees are the dominant species in the West.

Firs, true (Eastern species): balsam (Abies balsamea), Fraser (A. fraseri). Balsam fir grows principally in New England, New York, Pennsylvania and the Lake states. Fraser fir, in the Appalachians of Virginia, N. Carolina and Tennessee. Wood is creamy white to pale brown, and heartwood and sapwood are indistinguishable. Lightweight, usually straight-grained. *Use.* Mainly pulpwood; some lumber in New England and Lake states.

Firs, true (Western species): subalpine (Abies lasiocarpa), California red (A. magnifica), grand (A. grandis), noble (A. procera), Pacific silver (A.

amabilis), white (A. concolor). Most production from Washington, Oregon, California, western Montana, northern Idaho. Wood is light in weight but somewhat stronger than eastern true firs. *Use.* Lumber for building construction, boxes, crates, sash, doors, millwork. Noble fir lumber is used for interior finish, moldings, siding, aircraft construction. Several of these firs are used for veneers in softwood plywood.

Hemlock, Eastern (Tsuga canadensis). From New England to northern Alabama and Georgia, and in Lake states. Heartwood is pale brown with reddish hue; sapwood not distinctly separated but may be lighter. Wood is coarse and uneven in texture. *Use.* Not an important wood commercially. Used principally for lumber and pulpwood.

Hemlock, Western: West coast hemlock, hemlock spruce, Prince Albert fir, gray fir, other names (Tsuga heterophylla). Along Pacific Coast of Oregon and Washington and British Columbia and in northern Rockies, north to Canada and Alaska. Heartwood and sapwood are almost white, with a purplish tinge. Small, sound black knots in wood are usually tight and stay in place. *Use.* Lumber, pulpwood and plywood. Lumber is used for sheathing, siding, subflooring, framing, and wherever Douglas fir is habitually used. Also in pallets, crates, boxes, flooring.

Incense-cedar (Libocedrus decurrens). California, southwestern Oregon, a little in Nevada. Sapwood is white or cream, heartwood light brown, often tinged with red. Wood has a fine, uniform texture and a spicy odor. Lightweight, moderately low in strength, soft, low in shock resistance and stiffness. Small shrinkage, easy to season with little warpage. Works well, gives a smooth finish. Decay-resistant. *Use.* Principally for lumber and fenceposts (because of decay resistance). Higher grades for pencils and Venetian blinds, some for chests and toys.

Larch, Western (Larix occidentalis). Western Montana, northern Idaho, northeastern Oregon, eastern Washington Cascades. Heartwood is yellowish-brown, sapwood is yellowish-white. Wood is stiff, moderately strong, hard and shock-resistant. Usually straight-grained, splits easily, has small tight knots. One of the hardest and toughest commercial softwoods. Quite resistant to decay. *Use.* Dimension lumber for building construction; railroad ties, piles, poles and posts. Some use of higher-grade wood for interior finish, flooring.

Pine, Eastern white: white, Northern white, Weymouth, soft (Pinus strobus). Maine to Northern Georgia and in Lake states. Heartwood is light brown, turns darker on exposure. Uniform texture, straight-grained. Easily kiln-dried, small shrinkage, high in stability. Easy to work and glue, takes an excellent finish. *Use.* Mostly used for lumber, which goes into a great variety of finished products, such as patterns for casting, sash, doors, millwork, furniture, trim, paneling, caskets, toys. Lower (knotty) grades for containers, packaging.

Pine, jack: scrub, gray, black (Pinus banksiana). Lake states, and scattered areas in New England, northern New York. Sapwood (wide) is nearly white, heartwood light brown to orange. Rather coarse-textured, resinous wood. Lumber generally knotty. *Use.* In lumber uses, jack pine is not separated from other pines with which it grows, such as red pine and Eastern white pine. Also used for pulpwood, fuel. Some use for railroad ties, mine timbers, slack cooperage, poles and posts.

Pine, lodgepole: knotty, black, spruce, jack (Pinus contorta). Rockies and Pacific Coast, north to Alaska. Lodgepole pine takes over on logged or burnt-over land to form dense, pure stands. Wood is pale brown, light and fairly soft. Easy to work. *Use.* Lumber, mine timbers, railroad ties, poles. Increasing use for framing, siding, finish and flooring lumber.

Pine, pitch (Pinus regida). Maine along the mountains to eastern Tennessee and northern Georgia. A minor species in Southern pine grading rules. *Use.* Lumber, fuel, pulpwood.

Pine, pond (Pinus serotina). Coastal region from New Jersey to Florida. A minor species in Southern pine grading rules. *Use.* General construction, railroad ties, posts, poles.

Pine, ponderosa: pondosa, Western soft, black jack, other names (Pinus ponderosa). Major producing areas: Oregon, Washington, California. Also grows in Idaho, Montana, southern Rockies, Black Hills of S. Dakota and Wyoming. Most important pine of western United States. Wood is reddish-brown, medium hard and fine-grained. Uniform texture, little tendency to warp or twist. *Use.* Mainly for lumber, also for railroad ties, piles, posts, mine timbers, veneer, boxes, crates. Clear grades for sash, doors, moldings, paneling, cabinetry. Also used for pulpwood, particleboard, fuel.

Pine, red: Norway, hard, pitch (Pinus resinosa). New England, New York, Pennsylvania, Lake states. Heartwood varies, pale red to reddish-brown. Sapwood nearly white. Moderately heavy, strong, stiff, soft and shock-resistant. Not difficult to dry and stays in place well when seasoned. *Use.* Principally for lumber, also for piles, poles, cabin logs, posts, pulpwood, fuel. Lumber is used wherever Eastern white pine is used.

Pine, Southern: longleaf (Pinus palustris), shortleaf (P. echinata), loblolly (P. taeda), slash (P. elliottii). These four species are the most important among the many trees in the group marketed as Southern pine. Their growth ranges (not the same for all four) include most of southeastern U.S. and west to Texas and Oklahoma. Most production is from Georgia, Alabama, N. Carolina, Arkansas, Louisiana. All Southern pines have similar wood: sapwood yellowish-white, heartwood reddish-brown. Sapwood is wider in second-growth than old-growth trees. Longleaf and slash are somewhat heavier than shortleaf and loblolly. All have moderately large shrinkage but are stable when properly seasoned. *Use.* The more dense lumber is used extensively for heavy construction, as stringers, joists, beams, posts and piles. Lower-density and less strong lumber is also widely used in building, for interior finish, sheathing, subflooring, joists; also for boxes, pallets and crates. Southern pine is used for tight and slack cooperage and, when treated, for railroad ties, piles, poles and mine timbers. Production of structural plywood from Southern pine is great and growing.

Pine, spruce: cedar, poor, Walter, bottom white (Pinus glabra). Grows on low moist lands of coastal southeastern S. Carolina, Georgia, Alabama, Mississippi, Louisiana; also northern and northwestern Florida. Heartwood is light brown, wide sapwood is nearly white. Not as strong as the major Southern pines. *Use.* Lumber, pulpwood and fuel and, increasingly, in plywood.

Pine, sugar: California sugar (Pinus lambertiana). California and southwestern Oregon. Heartwood buff or light brown, sometimes tinged with red. Sapwood creamy white. Straight-grained, uniform in texture, easy to work with tools. Small shrinkage and is readily seasoned; like Eastern white pine, stays in place well, has good nailing properties. *Use.* Lumber for most of the same uses as Eastern white pine.

Pine, Virginia: Jersey, scrub (Pinus virginiana). From New Jersey and Virginia throughout Appalachian region to Georgia and Ohio Valley. Heartwood orange, sapwood nearly white. Moderately heavy, strong, stiff and hard; high shrinkage and high shock resistance. A minor species in Southern pine grading rules. *Use.* Lumber, railroad ties, pulpwood, fuel.

Pine, Western white: Idaho white (Pinus monticola). Mostly from Idaho, smaller amounts harvested in Washington, Montana and Oregon. Heartwood creamy to light reddish-brown, darkens on exposure. Sapwood yellowish white. Wood is straight-grained, easy to work, easily kiln-dried and stable after seasoning. *Use.* As lumber, has similar uses to Eastern white pine and sugar pine: building construction, matches, boxes, millwork. Lower grade boards used for sheathing, knotty paneling, subfloor. Higher-grade, for siding, trim and finish. This is a desirable wood for carving and woodworking.

Port Orford cedar: Lawson cypress, Oregon cedar, white cedar (Chamaecyparis lawsoniana). From Coos Bay, Oregon, southward on Pacific Coast to California. Wood is pale yellow to pale brown, sapwood hardly distinguishable. Has a pleasant spicy odor. Straight grain, fine texture, moderately strong. Heartwood is highly decay-resistant. Dries well and is stable in use. Works easily and well with hand and machine tools, takes good finish. *Use.* Not an abundant wood. Specialized uses include battery separators, mothproof chests, stadium seats, archery supplies. Highly regarded for boatbuilding. In construction, used for sash and door, flooring, interior finish.

Redcedar, Eastern: pencil cedar (Juniperus virginiana). Throughout most of eastern half of U.S. Most production from southern Appalachian and Cumberland Mountain regions. Heartwood is bright or dull red, thin sapwood nearly white. Not particularly strong but very decay-resistant and cuts easily and cleanly; stable in use. Straight-grained but with numerous knots. *Use.* Fenceposts; lumber for chests, wardrobes, closet lining. It was formerly widely used for pencils.

Redwood: coast, California, sequoia (Sequoia sempervirens). (Note: the related giant sequoia or sequoia gigantea, not a commercial tree, grows in protected stands in the Sierra Nevada.) Along coastal regions of California. Heartwood varies from light cherry to dark mahogany; narrow sapwood is almost white. Wood is straight-grained, non-resinous, light in weight, works easily and takes an excellent finish. Heartwood has high resistance to decay. Dries well and when dry is stable in use. *Use.* A choice wood. Used as lumber for siding, sash, doors, blinds, paneling; in plywood; because of durability, much used for vats, tanks, silos, wood-stave pipe, fencing, outdoor furniture.

Spruce, Eastern: red (Picea rubens), white (P. glauca), black (P. mariana). White and black spruce grow in Lake states and New England; red spruce in New England and Appalachians. No distinction is made among the three in marketing. Wood is light-colored, with little difference between heartwood and sapwood. Dries easily and is stable after drying. Moderately light and strong. *Use.* Mostly for pulpwood. Also, framing lumber, millwork, boxes and crates, piano sounding boards.

Spruce, Engelmann: white, mountain, Arizona (Picea engelmannii). At high elevations in Rockies, Cascades. Most production from southern Rocky Mountain states, some from northern Rockies and Oregon. Heartwood nearly white with slight tinge of red; sapwood not very distinguishable. Generally straight-grained. Not very strong. Numerous small knots. *Use.* Mine timbers, railroad ties, poles. Dimension lumber for flooring, sheathing, studding. Also pulpwood, plywood.

Spruce, Sitka: yellow, tideland (Picea sitchensis). Along northwestern coast of North America from California to Alaska. Most production from Washington and Oregon. Sitka spruce is the largest and fastest-growing spruce. Heartwood is light pinkish-brown, merging gradually into creamy white sapwood. Straight grain, fine uniform texture. Moderately lightweight, with high strength for weight. *Use.* Principally used for lumber, pulpwood and cooperage. Was the best wood for aircraft construction. Because of resonance, in demand for piano sounding boards and violins. Also used for furniture, millwork, boxes, crates. Tideland spruce used for boatbuilding.

Tamarack: Eastern larch (Larix laricina). Grows from Maine to Minnesota, mostly in Lake states. Heartwood is yellowish-brown to russet brown, sapwood narrow and whitish. Coarse-textured, intermediate in weight and strength. *Use.* Pulpwood, lumber, railroad ties, fuel, fenceposts, poles.

White-cedar: Northern, arborvitae (Thuja occidentalis), Atlantic, juniper, Southern, swamp, boat (Chaamaecyparis thyoides). Northern white-cedar grows from Maine along Appalachians and westward through northern parts of Lake states. Atlantic white-cedar, a swamp tree, grows near the Atlantic coast from Maine to northern Florida and westward along Gulf coast to Louisiana. Wood from both is used interchangeably. It is light in weight, rather soft and low in strength. Easily worked, holds paint well, and heartwood is decay-reistant. *Use.* Poles, ties, lumber, posts, fencing. Because of durability, often used in tanks, boats, woodenware.

Yew, Pacific (Taxus brevifolia). Western Canada and U.S., British Columbia to California. Not harvested commercially, because of scattered occurrence and crooked nature, but included here for its interest to craftsmen and amateurs of wood. Yew wood is dark reddish-brown, hard, heavy and strong—almost as hard as oak. *Use.* Still used for archery bows (as it was in the Middle Ages, especially the English longbow). Used locally for fenceposts because of excellent durability in contact with soil. Has been experimented with as a cabinet wood.

IMPORTED WOODS

Andiroba (Carapa guianensis). Also known as cedro macho, carapa, crabwood, tangare. From tropical America. Reddish-brown. Durable vs. decay, insects. Easy to work, paint, glue. *Use.* Flooring, furniture, cabinetwork, decorative veneer and plywood.

Angelique (Dicorynia guianensis). A.k.a. basra locus. From French Guiana and Surinam. "Gris" angelique becomes dull brown, "rouge" is redder. Strong, durable, resistant to decay and marine borers. When dried, can be worked only with carbide-tipped tools. *Use.* Heavy marine construction, boats.

Apamate (Tabebuia rosea). A.k.a. roble, mayflower. From S. Mexico through Central America to Venezuela and Ecuador. Pale to dark brown. Works and finishes well. Comparable to American white oaks in bending and compression strength. Durable vs. fungus. *Use.* Furniture, trim, flooring, boats, general construction, paneling.

Apitong (Dipterocarpus grandiflorus, D. gracilis, D. warburgii). Most common structural timber of Philippines. Reddish-brown, strong, hard, heavy. Machines well. *Use.* Truck floors, chutes, flumes, pallets, boardwalks. (Other species of this genus are marketed as Keruing.)

Avodire (Turraeanthus africanus). African rain forest. Pale yellow, darkens to golden yellow with high luster. Similar to English oak in strength. Works and finishes well. *Use.* Attractive mottled figure when sliced or cut on the quarter; this is imported for decorative veneer.

Bagtikan (Parashorea plicata, P. malagnonan). Southeast Asia. Gray to straw or pale brown. Stronger than lauans, not naturally durable, resists preservatives. *Use.* Veneer for plywood.

Balsa (Ochroma pyramidale). From a fast-growing tree of tropical America, mostly comes from Ecuador. Lightest and softest of all commercial woods. White to pale gray, has "velvety" feel. Buoyant, good insulator and sound absorber. Well known to model builders and raft travelers (Thor Heyerdahl's Kon-Tiki was balsa logs). *Use.* Life-saving equipment, for sound absorption, in cold storage.

Banak (Virola koschnyi, V. surinamensis, V. sebifera). From tropical America. Pinkish- or grayish-brown. Non-resistant to decay and insects, but can be preservative-treated. Strength properties like yellow-poplar. A first-class veneer species. *Use.* Lumber and plywood.

Benge (Guibourtia arnoldiana, G. ehie). Similar except in color. Former is yellow-brown to medium brown, with darker striping. Ehie is more golden brown, also striped, considered more attractive. Not well known in U.S. *Use.* Veneer, lumber, furniture.

Capirona includes several species, best known being degame (Calycophyllum candidissimum), which was imported from Cuba for archery equipment. It is a strong, straight-grained wood but is not naturally durable vs. stain, decay, insects. *Use.* Textile industry applications where resilience and strength are desired.

Cativo (Prioria copaifera). Abundant in tropical America. Texture like mahogany. Seasons rapidly and well. Tendency to bleed resinous material has been combatted by improved drying and finishing techniques and uses are increasing. *Use.* Interior trim, veneer for patterns, furniture, cabinets, plywood, picture frames.

Courbaril (Hymenaea courbaril is most important of this 30-species genus). From Amazon Basin. Wide gray-white sapwood, brown to purplish heartwood. Strong, durable. Finishes, turns and glues well. Comparable to white oak in steambending. Not much in U.S. yet. *Use.* Sporting equipment (because it is shock-resistant) or for handles where ash is used. Attractive as veneer and for furniture. Sapwood would be comparable in color to birch.

Ebony (Diospyrus species). Very scarce; some still comes from Africa. Very heavy, hard, brittle. *Use.* A prominent wood for courtly furniture in ancient Egypt, Persia, India.

Gola (Tetraberlinia tubmaniana). A.k.a. African pine and Liberian pine, but it is a hardwood so these are misleading. A promising newcomer to the timber market. *Use.* Workable and decorative products.

Goncalo alves (Astronium graveolens, A. fraxinifolium). From southern Mexico through Central America into Amazon Basin. Turns readily, finishes smoothly, heartwood resists moisture absorption and fungus attack. High density and strength. *Use.* Specialty items as archery bows, billiard cue butts, and for products of turning and carving.

Greenheart (Ocotea rodiaei). The outstanding commercial wood of Guyana; some from Surinam. Heartwood is very resistant to decay and termites and to marine borers (in temperate waters). Exceptionally strong (twice as strong as oak). Will not float. Very valuable where resistance to wear, water and time are required. *Use.* Marine jetties, wharves, docks, ships, lock gates, bridges, trestles.

Ilomba (Pycnanthus angolensis). African rain forest. Similar to banak (q.v.). *Use.* In plywood.

Jarrah (Eucalyptus marginata). Western Australia coast south of Perth. A principal export it is stronger and more durable than oak and resists termites and marine borers. Heartwood resists preservative treatment. Rather hard to work. *Use.* Decking and underframing of piers, jetties and bridges; for piling; shipbuilding.

Kapur (genus Dryobalanops has nine species). Malaya, Sumatra, Borneo. Resembles apitong and keruing but is straighter-grained, finer-textured. Very strong. Like keruing, abrasive to cutting tools because it contains silica. *Use.* Exterior joinery, fenceposts and as construction timbers for piers, piles, marine installations.

Karri (Eucalyptus diversicolor). A huge tree of western Australia. A heavy hardwood resembling jarrah, even harder to work. Comes in large sizes. *Use.* Structural timbers for bridges, piers and wharves; in plywood.

Keruing (see Apitong).

Khaya (Khaya ivorensis or "African mahogany"). West central Africa. It resembles true (American) mahogany, which it is replacing as the latter becomes more scarce. Easy to season, machines and finishes well, not as decay-resistant as American mahogany. *Use.* Furniture, interior paneling, boat construction, veneer, plywood.

Kokradua (Pericopsis elata). A.k.a. afrormosia. A large West African tree that resembles teak, exceeding it in some strength properties. Durable, resists fungi and termites. Will probably increase in use as substitute for teak. *Use.* Boat construction, furniture, veneer, cabinets.

Lapacho (genus Tabebuia has about 20 species). Throughout Latin America except Chile. Very heavy and strong. Air-dried, comparable to greenheart. Resists decay and insects but not marine borers. Heartwood cannot, but sapwood can be treated with preservatives. *Use.* Heavy-duty, durable construction wood.

Lauans or "Philippine mahogany" (genera Shorea, Parashorea, Pentacme). Philippine woods grouped for marketing purposes as "Dark red Philippine mahogany" and "Light red Philippine mahogany." Coarser-textured and less decay-resistant than true (American) mahogany, or "African mahogany." *Use.* Interior trim, paneling, plywood, flush doors, cabinets, furniture, siding, boat construction.

Laurel (Cordia alliodora or laurel, C. goeldiana or freijo, C. trichotoma or peterebi). West Indies, Central and South America. Wood saws and machines easily, in strength is comparable with mahogany and cedro. Attractive woods, not much export. *Use.* Cabinetwork, furniture, boat construction.

Lignum vitae (Guaiacum officinale, G. sanctum). West Indies, coastal Venezuela and Columbia, Central America. As G. officinale of commercial quality became exhausted, G. sanctum became principal export species. Name lignum vitae (tree of life) derives from 16th-century belief that its resin would cure many diseases. Heaviest timber in commercial use. Unique green color, waxy feel, high resin content. Turns well. *Use.* Bearing surfaces for ships' propeller shafts; underwater use.

Limba (Terminalia superba). Abundant in West Central Africa and Congo. Some limba is light-colored, valued for production of blond furniture. Nonresistant to decay, insects, termites. Easy to work, veneers well. Darker, figured limba looks like walnut. *Use.* Paneling, plywood, furniture.

Lupuna (Ceiba samauma). Amazon Basin. Very soft and light, white to pale reddish, nondurable in respect to decay and insects. *Use.* Veneer for plywood.

Mahogany (Swietenia macrophylla). Southern Mexico, through Central America and into South America to Bolivia. Heartwood pale to dark reddish-brown. Wide variety of grain patterns. The original commercial mahogany, brought by Spaniards to Europe in late 16th century. Chippendale, Sheraton and Hepplewhite used it in their 18th-century furniture. It is dimensionally stable, finishes well, is easy to work. *Use.* Furniture, models, patterns, boat construction, radio and TV cabinets, caskets, interior trim, paneling, precision instruments.

Meranti (Genus Shorea, several species). A rather complex group of trees from Malaysia and Indonesia. Timber is marketed as light-red meranti (a lightweight utility hard wood) and dark-red meranti (heavier, used for more exacting purposes). Both are important commercially. *Use.* Lumber, in furniture, and especially in plywood, with many of the same applications as lauans.

Mersawa (genus Anisoptera has about 15 species). From Philippines and Malaysia to Bangladesh. Marketed as krabak (Thailand), mersawa (Malaysia) and palosapis (Philippines). A plain wood and not decorative, it is hard on cutting tools because of silica content. But it can be rotary-peeled. *Use.* Veneer in plywood.

Nogal or Tropical walnut (Juglans neotropica, J. olanchana). Former grows on eastern slope of Andes, latter in northern Central America. Not yet an important commercial import. Darker and coarser than American black walnut.

Oak (About 150 species of Quercus). Mexico and Central America know them as encino and roble. Usually heavier than U.S. oaks. Hard to dry. *Use.* Charcoal.

Obeche (Triplochiton scleroxylon). Also known as samba and wawa.West central Africa. Not decay-resistant, and sapwood stains blue unless precautions are taken. Easy to work and machine. *Use.* Veneer and core stock.

Okoume (Aucoumea klaineana). A.k.a. gaboon. West central Africa, the Congo and Gabon. Leading African wood export, but heretofore mostly to Europe. Now increasing rapidly in U.S. Wood is pale-pink with uniform texture and high luster. Rarely sawn because of silica content, but peeled for veneer. *Use.* Decorative plywood paneling, doors, furniture.

Parana pine (Araucaria angustifolia). A.k.a. pinheiro do Parana or pinho do Parana. A softwood from southeastern Brazil, Paraguay and Argentina, and not a true pine. Available in large-sized clear boards with uniform texture, attractive pattern. Quite strong, comparable with similar softwood species in U.S. *Use.* Framing lumber, interior trim, veneer, furniture.

Pau marfim (Balfourodendron riedelianum). A.k.a. moroti. Southern Brazil, Paraguay, northern Argentina. A relatively recent import to the U.S. Tough, impact-resistant, it looks like birch or hard maple, and may be used where they are. *Use.* Turned items.

Peroba de Campos (Paratecoma peroba). Eastern Brazil. Fine-textured, like birch; yellowish gray sapwood, brown heartwood. Machines easily. Heavier and stronger than teak or white oak.

Pine, Caribbean (Pinus caribaea). Along Caribbean side of Central America, from Belize to northeastern Nicaragua. Wood has strong resinous odor and greasy feel, is easy to machine but requires frequent cleaning of equipment because of high resin content. Similar to slash pine in mechanical properties, used for same purposes as Southern pines.

Pine, ocote (Pinus oocarpa). From higher elevations, north-western Mexico through Guatemala into Nicaragua. Strength properties similar to longleaf pine. Comparable to Southern pines in workability and machining, used for same purposes.

Primavera (Cybistax donnell-smithii). A desirable wood because of machinability, attractive figure patterns, dimensional stability, durability. Now that natural stands are being supplemented by plantations, it is more available. *Use.* Furniture, paneling, trim.

Ramin (Gonystylus bancanus). Native to southeast Asia from Malay Peninsula to Sumatra and Borneo. One of the few moderately heavy woods classified as "blond," it has been in demand for staining or finishing to match other decorative woods. Extensive harvesting since export began in the 1950's has reduced the supply. *Use.* Furniture, plywood for doors, interior trim.

Rosewood, Brazilian (Dalbergia nigra). A.k.a. jacaranda. Eastern Brazil. Long exploited and in short supply. A hard, heavy, variably colored wood (brown, red, and violet shades, some black-streaked). *Use.* Veneer for decorative plywood, also cutlery handles, turned items.

Rosewood, Indian (Dalbergia latifolia). India, except northwest. Dark purplish-brown heartwood with blackish streaks and an attractive figure on flat-sawn surfaces. Similar in appearance to Brazilian rosewood. Hard to work with hand tools and may blunt tools because of calcareous deposits. Turns well. Essentially a decorative wood. *Use.* High-class furniture and cabinets; veneer.

Sande (Genus Brosimum). A.k.a. cocal. Pacific Ecuador and Columbia. Yellowish-white to light brown, non-resistant to decay, insects, stain. *Use.* Lumber, plywood, moldings.

Santa Maria (Calophyllum brasiliense). West Indies, southern Mexico, south through Central America into northern South America. Heartwood pinkish to red, sapwood lighter. Easy to work, compares with hard maple in density and strength. *Use.* Veneer for plywood for boat construction.

Sapele (Entandrophragma cylindricum). Large African rain forest tree, from Sierra Leone to Angola and east through the Congo to Uganda. A mahogany-like wood but finer-textured. Works fairly easily with machine tools, finishes and glues well. Heartwood is moderately durable and resists preservative treatment. *Use.* Where attractive appearance and strength and durability are required, as in window frames, stairways, doors, pianos. Rotary-peeled for veneer for decorative plywood.

Spanish-cedar (Cedrela has about seven species). Tropical America from southern Mexico to northern Argentina. With mahogany, one of the classic timbers of South America. Heartwood, light to dark reddish brown, has a distinctive cedarlike odor. Not high-strength, but is decay-resistant and glues well. *Use.* Locally for construction, furniture, joinery, with little available for export.

Teak (Tectona grandis). One of the world's greatest and most valuable woods. Native to southeast Asia, India and East Indies and has been introduced in plantations elsewhere, as in Latin America and Africa. Wood is uniform golden-brown, occasionally deep brown with black marking. It has a greasy feel and leathery smell. Heavier than mahogany and lighter than oak, has high degree of natural durability. Moderately easy to work, but silica content causes dulling of tools. Does not cause rust or corrosion when in contact with metal, so is in demand in shipbuilding. *Use.* Boats, furniture, flooring, decorative objects, plywood.

Walnut, European (Juglans regia). Native to mountainous regions of southwest Asia but has been transplanted to Europe. A highly-figured veneer is obtained from stumps, burls and crotches of some trees. Wide variation in color, figure and texture of woods from various regions. Easy to machine and finish, in veneer form as well as solid. *Use.* Furniture, paneling, decorative objects. With American black walnut, the classic wood for gunstocks.

Appendix 2: Glossary

Air-dried. See Seasoning.

Annual growth ring. Layer of wood growth put on a tree in a single growing season.

Baseboard. Molding that covers joint between wall and floor.

Base shoe. See Shoe molding.

Battens. Narrow strips of wood to cover joints.

Beam. Load-carrying member, supported at both ends and on which joists or rafters rest.

Beveled siding. Horizontal strip siding with bottom edge of board lapping over top of board below.

Blocking. Lumber pieces that brace framing members.

Bolt. A short section of a tree trunk. In veneer production, a short length of log suitable for peeling in a lathe.

Cambium. Thin layer of tissue between the bark and wood that repeatedly subdivides to form new wood and bark cells.

Casing. Molding that conceals joint between window or door edge and wall.

Cell. A general term for the structural units of the tree tissue, which include wood fibers, vessel members and other elements of diverse structure and function. Differences in cell characteristics account for differences in properties and performance and appearance of the various woods.

Cellulose. Carbohydrate that is the principal constituent of wood and forms the framework of the wood cells.

Check. A lengthwise separation of the wood that usually extends across the rings of annual growth and commonly results from stresses set up in wood during seasoning.

Clapboard. Narrow horizontal siding board.

Cleave. To split a log by a cutting blow, especially along the grain.

Compreg. Material created when veneers impregnated with phenolic resin (but not cured, as with Impreg, q.v.) are then bonded, cured and compressed. It is dimensionally stable, dense, brittle and when pressed in a smooth mold, produces an attractive glossy finish. It is useful for furniture; scratches can be removed by buffing.

Compression wood. Wood formed on the lower side of branches and inclined trunks of softwood trees. Identified by relatively wide annual rings, usually eccentric, relatively large amount of latewood and lack of demarcation between earlywood and latewood, in the same annual rings. Compression wood shrinks excessively lengthwise, as compared with normal wood.

Cooperage. Containers consisting of two round heads and a body composed of staves held together with hoops, such as barrels and kegs. Slack cooperage is used for dry, semidry or solid products. Staves are usually not closely fitted and are held together with beaded steel, wire or wood hoops. Tight cooperage is used for liquids, semisolids, and heavy solids. Staves are well fitted and held tightly with cooperage grade steel hoops.

Course. Horizontal row of shingles, siding boards or bricks.

Density. The mass of wood substance enclosed within boundaries of a given volume unit. Variously expressed as pounds per cubic foot, kilograms per cubic meter, or grams per cubic centimeter at a given moisture content.

Earlywood. The portion of the annual growth ring that is formed during the early part of the growing season. Usually less dense and weaker mechanically than latewood. Also called springwood.

Dowel. A round wooden pin, often inserted in matching holes of two pieces of wood to strengthen the joint.

Edge grain. See Grain.

End grain. See Grain.

Exterior plywood. See Plywood.

Fascia. Roof edge facing board nailed to rafter tails.

Fiberboard. Sheet materials of varying densities manufactured of refined or partly refined wood (or other vegetable) fibers. Bonding agents may be added to increase strength, resistance to moisture, fire or decay.

Figure. The pattern produced in a wood surface by annual growth rings, rays, knots, deviations from regular grain such as interlocked and wavy grain, and irregular colorations.

Filler. In woodworking, any substance used to fill the holes and irregularities in planed or sanded surfaces to decrease the porosity of the surface before applying finish coatings.

Finish. Wood products such as doors, stairs, other fine work required to complete interior construction. Also, coatings of paint, varnish, lacquer, wax, etc., applied to wood surfaces to protect and enhance their durability and appearance.

Flitch. A portion of a log sawn on two or more faces, commonly on opposite faces. For lumber, it is resawn parallel to its original wide faces. Or it may be sliced or sawn into veneer, in which case the resulting sheets of veneer laid together in the sequence of cutting are called a flitch.

Framing. Lumber used for the structural members of a building, such as studs and joists.

Furring strips. Wood strips applied to walls or ceiling as nailing base.

Grade. Designation of quality of a manufactured piece of wood or of logs.

Grademarks, gradestamps. Designation of a material's quality, characteristics, species, etc., usually applied by an association of manufacturers in accordance with Federal standards.

Grain. The direction, size, arrangement, appearance, or quality of the fibers in wood or lumber.

Close-grained wood has narrow, inconspicuous annual rings. Sometimes used to designate wood having small and closely spaced pores, but in this sense the term fine-textured is more often used.

Edge-grained lumber has been sawed so that the wide surfaces extend approximately at right angles to the annual growth rings.

End-grained wood refers to the grain as seen on a cut made at a right angle to the direction of the fibers, as on a cross section of a tree.

Flat-grained wood is lumber that has been sawed parallel to the pith and approximately tangent to the growth rings.

Interlocked-grained wood is characterized by grain in which the fibers put on for several years may slope in a right-handed direction, then for a number of years the slope reverses to a left-handed direction, later changes back to a right-hand pitch, and so on. Such wood is exceedingly difficult to split radially, though it may split more easily tangentially.

Open-grained woods have large pores, such as oak, ash, chestnut, walnut. Also known as coarse textured.

Plainsawed lumber is another term for flat-grained.

Quartersawed lumber is another term for edge-grained.

Straight-grained wood has fibers running parallel to the axis of the piece.

Vertical-grained lumber is another term for edge-grained.

Green. Freshly sawed or undried wood.

Hardboard. Panel manufactured primarily from interfelted ligno-cellulose fibers (usually wood), consolidated under heat and pressure in a hot press to a density of 31 lbs. per cu. ft. or greater, and to which other materials may have been added during manufacture to improve certain properties.

Hardness. A property of wood that enables it to resist indentation.

Heartwood. Wood extending from the pith to the sapwood, the cells of which no longer participate in the life processes of the tree. Heartwood may contain phenolic compounds, gums, resins and other materials that usually make it darker and more decay-resistant than sapwood.

Hollow-core door. Lightweight door with interior air space, for interior use.

Impreg. A modified wood, wherein thin veneers are saturated with phenolic resin, dried, cured and laid up in a thick laminate. The process greatly reduces changes in moisture content and hence in dimension.

Interlocked. See Grain.

Jambs. Members at sides of door or window opening.

Joint. Junction of two pieces of wood or veneer.

Butt joint: an end joint formed by abutting the squared ends of two pieces.

Edge joint: The place where two pieces of wood are joined together edge to edge, commonly by gluing. The joints may be made by gluing two squared edges as in a plain edge joint or by using machined joints of various kinds, such as tongue-and-groove joints.

End joint: The place where two pieces of wood are joined together end to end, commonly by scarf or finger jointing.

Finger joint: An end joint made up of several meshing wedges or fingers of wood bonded together with an adhesive. Fingers are sloped and may be cut parallel to either the wide or edge faces of the piece.

Lap joint: A joint made by placing one member partly over another and bonding the overlapped portions.

Scarf joint: An end joint formed by joining with glue the ends of two pieces that have been tapered or beveled to form sloping plane surfaces, usually to a feather edge, and with the same slope of the plane with respect to the length in both pieces.

Starved joint: A glue joint that is poorly bonded because an insufficient quantity of glue remained in the joint.

Joist. One of a series of parallel beams used to support floors or ceilings and supported in turn by larger beams, girders or bearing walls.

Kiln-dried. See Seasoning.

Knot. The portion of a branch or limb which has been surrounded by subsequent growth of the stem. The shape of the knot as it appears on a cut surface depends on the angle of the cut relative to the long axis of the knot.

Loose knot: One that is not held firmly in place by growth or position and cannot be relied on to remain in place.

Pin knot is not more than ½ in. in diameter.

Sound knot is solid across its face, at least as hard as the surrounding wood, and shows no indication of decay.

Laminated wood. An assembly made by bonding layers of veneer or lumber with an adhesive so that the grain of all laminations is essentially parallel, as in laminated decking, laminated beams (glulams).

Latewood. The portion of the annual growth ring that is formed after the earlywood formation has ceased. Usually denser and stronger mechanically than earlywood. Also called summerwood.

Lignin. The second most abundant constituent of wood, located principally in the secondary wall and the middle lamella, which is the thin cementing layer between wood cells.

Louvers. Slanting overlapping slats fitted into framing, vertically or horizontally.

Lumber. Products of the saw and planing mill not further manufactured than by sawing, resawing, passing lengthwise through a standard planing machine, crosscutting to length, and matching.

Manufacturing defects. In lumber includes all defects or blemishes that are produced in manufacturing, such as chipped grain, loosened grain, raised grain, torn grain, skips in dressing, hit-and-miss (series of surfaced areas with skips between them), variation in sawing, miscut lumber, machine burn, machine gouge, mismatching, and insufficient tongue or groove.

Millwork. Planed and patterned lumber for finish work, including sash, doors, cornices, panelwork, other items or interior or exterior trim. Does not include flooring, ceiling or siding.

Miter. Cutting on an angle, as with molding or for picture frames.

Molding. A wood strip having a curved or projecting surface, used for decorative purposes. Also *moulding* (Brit.).

Mortise. A slot cut into a board, plank or timber, usually edgewise, to receive the tenon of another board, plank or timber to form a joint.

Mullions. Vertical moldings between window units.

Naval stores. Term applied to resins, oils, tars and pitches derived from oleoresin from certain trees, chiefly pines. Historically, these were important items in the stores of wood sailing vessels.

O.C. On center: spacing between centers of framing members.

Old growth. Timber in or from a mature, naturally established forest. When the trees have grown during most if not all of their individual lives in active competition with their companions for sunlight and moisture, this timber is usually straight and relatively free of knots.

Overlay. A thin layer of paper, plastic, film, metal foil, or other material bonded to one or both faces of panel products or to lumber to provide a protective or decorative face or a base for painting.

Pallet. A low wood platform on which material can be stacked to facilitate mechanical handling, moving or storage.

Paneling. Rectangular flat pieces for interior surfacing of walls: may be boards or sheet materials like plywood.

Paperboard. The distinction between paper and paperboard is not sharp, but broadly speaking, the thicker (over 0.012 in.), heavier and more rigid grades of paper are called paperboard.

Parquetry. Hardwood flooring in small wood blocks rather than strips.

Particleboard. Panel manufactured from lignocellulose materials—commonly wood—essentially in the form of particles (as distinct from fibers). Materials are bonded together with synthetic resin or other suitable binder, under heat and pressure, by a process wherein the interparticle bonds are created wholly by the added binder.

Patina. The mellow, soft appearance of wood which has had years of use and has been affected by light, air and tiny dents and scratches.

Peck. Pockets or areas of disintegrated wood caused by advanced stages of localized decay in the living tree. It is usually associated with cypress and incense cedar. There is no further development of peck once lumber is seasoned.

Peel. To convert a log into veneer by rotary cutting. (See Veneer.)

Penny. Old measure of nail length and weight, now a measure of length. Abbreviated d.

Phloem. Tissues of the tree's inner bark, characterized by the presence of sieve tubes and serving for the transport of elaborate foodstuffs.

Pile. A long, heavy timber, round or square, that is driven deep into the ground to provide a secure foundation for structures built on soft, wet or submerged sites, such as landing stages, bridge abutments, piers.

Pith. The small soft core occurring near the center of a tree trunk, branch, twig or log.

Planning mill products. Products worked to pattern, such as flooring, ceiling and siding.

Plank. A broad board, usually more than 1 in. thick, laid with its wide dimension horizontal and used as a bearing surface.

Plumb. Straight up and down.

Plumb bob. The metal part (the weight) on a plumb line.

Plumb line. Cord to which plumb bob is attached.

Plywood. A composite panel or board made up of crossbanded layers of veneer only, or veneer in combination with a core of lumber or of particleboard, bonded with an adhesive. Generally the grain of one or more plies is roughly at right angles to the other plies, and almost always an odd number of plies is used.
Exterior plywood: general term for plywood manufactured of veneers of Grade C and better, and bonded with adhesive that is highly resistant to weather, microorganisms, cold or hot or boiling water, steam and dry heat.

Porous woods. Hardwood having vessels or pores large enough to be seen readily without magnification.

Preservative. Any substance that, for a reasonable length of time, is effective in preventing the development and action of wood-rotting fungi, borers of various kinds, and harmful insects that cause wood to deteriorate.

Quartersawed. See Grain.

Rafter. One of a series of structural members of a roof designed to support roof loads. The rafters of a flat roof are sometimes called roof joists.

Raised grain. A roughened condition of the surface of dressed lumber in which the hard summerwood is raised above the softer springwood but not torn loose from it.

Rays, wood. Strips of cells extending radially within a tree and varying in height from a few cells in some species to 4 in. or more in oak. Rays serve primarily to store food and transport it horizontally in the tree. On quartersawed oak, the rays form a conspicuous figure, sometimes referred to as flecks.

Reaction wood. Wood with more or less distinctive anatomical characters, formed typically in parts of leaning or crooked stems and in branches. In hardwoods this consists of tension wood and in softwoods of compression wood (q.v.).

Resawn. Unmilled or rough surface showing saw marks, on rustic sidings or panelings or shingles. Also rough-sawn.

Rip. To cut lengthwise, parallel to the grain.

Rotary-cut veneer. See Veneer.

Sapwood. The wood of pale color near the outside of the log. Under most conditions sapwood is more susceptible to decay than heartwood.

Sash. A frame structure, normally glazed (i.e., a window) that is hung or fixed in a frame set in an opening.

Saw kerf. Groove or notch made in cutting with a saw. Also, that portion of a log, timber or other piece of wood removed by the saw in parting the material into two pieces.

Scarf joint. See Joint.

Scribe. To make a line by cutting or scratching with a pointed instrument.

Seasoning. Removing moisture from green wood to improve its serviceability.

Air-dried: Dried by exposure to air in a yard or shed, without artificial heat.

Kiln-dried: Dried in a kiln with the use of artificial heat.

Second growth. Timber that has grown after the removal, whether by fire, cutting, wind or other agency, of all or a large part of the previous stand.

Shake. A separation along the wood's grain, the greater part of which occurs between the rings of annual growth. Usually considered to have occurred in the standing tree or during felling.

Shakes. A type of shingle usually hand cleft from a bolt and used for roofing or siding.

Sheathing. The structural covering, usually of plywood, boards or fiberboard, placed over exterior studding or rafters of a structure.

Shiplap. Board joint where long edges are milled to overlap adjacent board.

Shoe molding. Molding used at bottom of baseboard.

Siding. The finish covering of the outside wall of a frame building, whether made of horizontal boards, vertical boards, shingles, plywood or other material.

Sliced veneer. See Veneer.

Soffit. Underside of a roof overhang.

Springwood. See Earlywood.

Stain. A finish coat for wood that changes its color but preserves its distinguishing wood characteristics (as opposed to paint, which totally masks the material).
Penetrating oil stain (semi-transparent) adds color but does not obscure grain pattern or natural wood characteristics.
Opaque (pigmented) oil stain covers wood's natural color, obscures the grain pattern but allows texture to show.

Stool. Shelf-like trim or molding at bottom of a window.

Straight-grained. See Grain.

Stringer. A timber or other support for cross members in floors or ceilings. In stairs, the support on which the stair treads rest.

Stripping. Removal of old finishes, such as paint, varnish, shellac, etc., as well as wax, polish and accumulated dirt, to reveal the bare wood; the first step in refinishing furniture.

Stud. One of a series of slender wood structural members used as supporting elements in walls and partitions.

Subfloor. Rough floor deck of boards or panel material over which finish flooring is laid.

Summerwood. See Latewood.

Tenon. A projecting member left by cutting away the wood around it for insertion into a mortise to make a joint.

Tension wood. A form of wood found in leaning trees of some hardwood species and characterized by the presence of gelatinous fibers and excessive longitudinal shrinkage. Tension wood fibers hold together tenaciously, so that sawed surfaces usually have projecting fibers and planed surfaces often are torn or have raised grain. Tension wood may cause warping.

Toe-nail. To nail through one member at an angle and into another.

Trim. The finish materials in a building, such as moldings, applied around openings (windows, doors) or at the floor and ceiling of some rooms (baseboard, cornice and other moldings).

True. Level or square.

Truss. An assembly of members, such as beams, bars, rods and the like, so combined as to form a rigid framework. Used to support roof or floor loads.

Underlayment. Smooth panel material applied directly under the finish floor covering.

Veneer. A thin layer or sheet of wood.
Rotary-cut veneer: Veneer cut in a lathe, which rotates a log or bolt, chucked in the center, against a knife.
Sawed veneer: Veneer produced by sawing.
Sliced veneer: Veneer that is sliced off a log or bolt or flitch with a knife.

Vertical-grain. See Grain.

Wainscot. Surfacing for lower portion of wall.

Warp. Any variation from a true or plane surface.

Weathering. Mechanical or chemical disintegration and discoloration of surface of wood caused by exposure to light, the action of sand and dust carried by winds, and the alternate shrinking and swelling of surface fibers with the continual variation in moisture content brought by changes in the weather. Weathering does not include decay.

Workability. The degree of ease and smoothness of cut obtainable with hand or machine tools.

Appendix 3:

Other Sources of Information

BOOKS

Brown, Harry Philip. *Textbook of Wood Technology.* McGraw-Hill, 1949.

Capotosto, Robert. *Complete Book of Wood Working.* Harper, 1975.

Champion, F.J. *Products of American Forests.* Forest Products Laboratory, 1973.

Coleman, Donald G. *Woodworking Factbook.* Speller, 1975.

Constantine, Albert. *Know Your Woods.* Scribner, 1975.

Evans, Harry Thomas. *The Woodworker's Book of Facts.* Technical Press (London), 1970.

Feirer, John L. *Wood: Materials and Processes.* Bennett, 1975.

Franklin, Wm. E. *Paper Recycling: The Art of the Possible, 1970-1985.* Midwest Research Institute, 1973.

Gould, Mary Earle. *The Early American House.* Tuttle, 1965.

Gould, Mary Earle. *Early American Woodenware and Other Kitchen Utensils.* Tuttle, 1962.

Grotz, George. *Staining and Finishing Unfinished Furniture and Other Naked Woods.* Doubleday, 1973.

Harlow, William Morehouse. *Inside Wood; Masterpiece of Nature.* American Forestry Association, 1970.

International Paper Co. *International Book of Wood.* Simon & Schuster, 1976.

Johnson, Hugh. *International Book of Trees.* Simon & Schuster, 1973.

Lytle, R.J. *Book of Successful Fireplaces.,* 20th ed. Structures, 1977.

Morgan, Alfred P. *How To Use Tools.* Arco, 1955.

Panshin, A.J. and Carl de Zeeuw. *Textbook of Wood Technology.* McGraw-Hill, 1970.

Panshin, A.J., E.S. Harrar and J.S. Bethel. *Forest Products: Their Sources, Production, and Utilization.* McGraw-Hill, 1962.

Reschke, Robert C. *How to Build Your Own Home.* Structures, 1976.

Reschke, Robert C. *Successful Roofing & Siding.* Structures, 1977.

Savage, Jessie D. *Professional Furniture Refinishing for the Amateur.* Harper, 1975.

Sloane, Eric. *A Museum of Early American Tools.* Funk, 1964.

Sloane, Eric. *A Reverence for Wood.* Funk, 1965.

U.S. Department of Agriculture. *Wood Handbook. Wood as an Engineering Material.* Forest Products Laboratory, 1974.

U.S. Forest Service. *100 Years of Federal Forestry.* Agriculture Information Bulletin 402, 1977.

Wagner, Willis H. *Modern Carpentry.* Goodheart-Willcox, 1977.

Youngquist, W.G. and H.D. Fleischer. *Wood in American Life.* Forest Products Research Society, 1976.

ASSOCIATIONS AND GOVERNMENTAL AGENCIES

American Forest Institute
1619 Massachusetts Ave. N.W.
Washington, D.C. 20036

American Plywood Association
Tacoma, Washington 98401

American Wood Council
1619 Massachusetts Ave. N.W.
Washington, D.C. 20036

American Wood Preservers Institute
1651 Old Meadow Road
McLean, Virginia 22101

California Redwood Association
One Lombard St.
San Francisco, California 94111

Fine Hardwoods—American Walnut Association
666 North Lake Shore Drive
Chicago, Illinois 60611

Forest Products Laboratory
Madison, Wisconsin

National Forest Products Association
1619 Massachusetts Ave. N.W.
Washington, D.C. 20036

National Hardwood Lumber Association
352 South Michigan
Chicago, Illinois

National Particleboard Association
2306 Perkins Place
Silver Spring, Maryland 20910

Northeastern Lumber Manufacturers Association
4 Fundy Road
Falmouth, Maine 04105

Red Cedar Shingle & Handsplit Shake Bureau
515—116th Ave. N.E., Suite 275
Bellevue, Washington 98004

Southern Forest Products Association
P.O. Box 52468
New Orleans, Louisiana 70152

Southern Hardwood Lumber
Manufacturers Association
805 Sterick Building
Memphis, Tennessee 38103

U.S. Forest Service
Department of Agriculture
Washington, D.C.

West Coast Lumber Inspection Bureau
6980 S.W. Varnes Road
Portland, Oregon 97223

Western Wood Products Association
1500 Yeon Building
Portland, Oregon 97024

Wood Moulding & Millwork Producers
P.O. Box 2578
Portland, Oregon 97225

Index

Other SUCCESSFUL Books

SUCCESSFUL PLANTERS, Orcutt. "Definitive book on container gardening." *Philadelphia Inquirer.* Build a planter, and use it for a room divider, a living wall, a kitchen herb garden, a centerpiece, a table, an aquarium—and don't settle for anything that looks homemade! Along with construction steps, there is advice on the best types of planters for individual plants, how to locate them for best sun and shade, and how to provide the best care to keep plants healthy and beautiful, inside or outside the home. 8½"x11"; 136 pp; over 200 photos and illustrations. Cloth $12.00. Paper $4.95.

BOOK OF SUCCESSFUL FIREPLACES, 20th ed., Lytle. The expanded, updated edition of the book that has been a standard of the trade for over 50 years—over a million copies sold! Advice is given on selecting from the many types of fireplaces available, on planning and adding fireplaces, on building fires, on constructing and using barbecues. Also includes new material on wood as a fuel, woodburning stoves, and energy savings. 8½"x11"; 128 pp; over 250 photos and illustrations. $5.95 Paper.

SUCCESSFUL ROOFING & SIDING, Reschke. "This well-illustrated and well-organized book offers many practical ideas for improving a home's exterior." *Library Journal.* Here is full information about dealing with contractors, plus instructions specific enough for the do-it-yourselfer. All topics, from carrying out a structural checkup to supplemental exterior work like dormers, insulation, and gutters, fully covered. Materials to suit all budgets and home styles are reviewed and evaluated. 8½"x11"; 160 pp; over 300 photos and illustrations. $5.95 Paper. (Main selection Popular Science and McGraw-Hill Book Clubs)

PRACTICAL & DECORATIVE CONCRETE, Wilde. "Spells it all out for you...is good for beginner or talented amateur..." *Detroit Sunday News.* Complete information for the layman on the use of concrete inside or outside the home. The author—Executive Director of the American Concrete Institute—gives instructions for the installation, maintenance, and repair of foundations, walkways, driveways, steps, embankments, fences, tree wells, patios, and also suggests "fun" projects. 8½"x11"; 144 pp; over 150 photos and illustrations. $12.00 Cloth. $4.95 Paper. (Featured alternate, Popular Science and McGraw-Hill Book Clubs)

SUCCESSFUL HOME ADDITIONS, Schram. For homeowners who want more room but would like to avoid the inconvenience and distress of moving, three types of home additions are discussed: garage conversion with carport added; bedroom, bathroom, sauna addition; major home renovation which includes the addition of a second-story master suite and family room. All these remodeling projects have been successfully completed and, from them, step-by-step coverage has been reported of almost all potential operations in adding on to a home. The straightforward presentation of information on materials, methods, and costs, as well as a glossary of terms, enables the homeowner to plan, arrange contracting, or take on some of the work personally in order to cut expenses. 8½"x11"; 144 pp; over 300 photos and illustrations. Cloth $12.00. Paper $5.95.

FINISHING OFF, Galvin. A book for both the new-home owner buying a "bonus space" house, and those who want to make use of previously unused areas of their homes. The author advises which jobs can be handled by the homeowner, and which should be contracted out. Projects include: putting in partitions and doors to create rooms; finishing off floors and walls and ceilings; converting attics and basements; designing kitchens and bathrooms, and installing fixtures and cabinets. Information is given for materials that best suit each job, with specifics on tools, costs, and building procedures. 8½"x11"; 144 pp; over 250 photos and illustrations. Cloth $12.00. Paper $5.95.

SUCCESSFUL FAMILY AND RECREATION ROOMS, Cornell. How to best use already finished rooms or convert spaces such as garage, basement, or attic into family/recreation rooms. Along with basics like lighting, ventilation, plumbing, and traffic patterns, the author discusses "mood setters" (color schemes, fireplaces, bars, etc.) and finishing details (flooring, wall covering, ceilings, built-ins, etc.) A special chapter gives quick ideas for problem areas. 8½"x11"; 144 pp; over 250 photos and diagrams. (Featured alternate for McGraw-Hill Book Clubs.) $12.00 Cloth. $4.95 Paper.

SUCCESSFUL HOME GREENHOUSES, Scheller. Instructions, complete with diagrams, for building all types of greenhouses. Among topics covered are: site location, climate control, drainage, ventilation, use of sun, auxiliary equipment, and maintenance. Charts provide characteristics and requirements of plants and greenhouse layouts are included in appendices. "One of the most completely detailed volumes of advice for those contemplating an investment in a greenhouse." *Publishers Weekly.* 8½"x11"; 136 pp; over 200 photos and diagrams. (Featured alternates of the Popular Science and McGraw-Hill Book Clubs). $12.00 Cloth. $4.95 Paper.

SUCCESSFUL SPACE SAVING AT HOME, Galvin. The conquest of inner space in apartments, whether tiny or ample, and homes, inside and out. Storage and built-in possibilities for all living areas, with a special section of illustrated tips from the professional space planners. 8½"x11"; 128 pp; over 150 B-W and color photographs and illustrations. $12.00 Cloth. $4.95 Paper.